MIAMI &
THE KEYS
...LIKE A LOCAL

Aerial view of Seven Mile Bridge at Pigeon Key. Photo: © Kool.com/age fotostock

MICHELIN

MIAMI & THE KEYS...LIKE A LOCAL

Chief Contributing Editor	Peter Greenberg
General Manager	Cynthia Clayton Ochterbeck
Editorial Manager	Jonathan P. Gilbert
Editor	Clive Hebard
Principal Writers	Eric Lucas, Paul Murphy
Production Manager	Natasha G. George
Cartography	John Dear
Photo Editor	Yoshimi Kanazawa
Photo Researcher	Chris Bell
Proofreader	Hannah Witchell
Interior Design	Chris Bell
Layout	Michelin Travel and Lifestyle North America, Natasha G. George
Cover Design	Chris Bell
Cover Layout	Michelin Travel and Lifestyle North America
Peter Greenberg Editorial Team	Sarika Chawla, Lily J. Kosner, Alyssa Caverley, Adriana Padilla
Contact Us	Michelin Travel and Lifestyle North America One Parkway South Greenville, SC 29615 USA travel.lifestyle@us.michelin.com www.michelintravel.com
	Michelin Travel Partner Hannay House 39 Clarendon Road Watford, Herts WD17 1JA, UK ✆01923 205240 travelpubsales@uk.michelin.com www.ViaMichelin.com
Special Sales	For information regarding bulk sales, customized editions and premium sales, please contact us at: Travel.Lifestyle@us.michelin.com www.michelintravel.com

Note to the reader Addresses, phone numbers, opening hours and prices published in this guide are accurate at the time of press. We welcome corrections and suggestions that may assist us in preparing the next edition. While every effort is made to ensure that all information printed in this guide is correct and up-to-date, Michelin North America, Inc. accepts no liability for any direct, indirect or consequential losses howsoever caused so far as such can be excluded by law.

HOW TO USE THIS GUIDE

PLANNING YOUR TRIP
The Planning Your Trip section at the front of the guide gives you ideas for your trip and practical information to help you organise it. You'll find tours, practical information, a host of outdoor activities, a calendar of events, information on shopping, sightseeing, kids' activities and more.

INTRODUCTION
The Introduction section explores the region's nature and geology, history, art and architecture, literature and the region today.

DISCOVERING
The Discovering section features Principal Sights by region, featuring the most interesting local Sights, Walking Tours, nearby Excursions, and detailed Driving Tours. Admission prices shown are normally for a single adult.

ADDRESSES
We've selected the best hotels, restaurants, cafés shops, nightlife and entertainment to fit all budgets. See the Legend on the cover flap for an explanation of the price categories.

STAR RATINGS★★★
Michelin has given star ratings for more than 100 years. If you're pressed for time, we recommend you visit the ★★★, or ★★ sights first:

★★★ Highly recommended
★★ Recommended
★ Interesting

MAPS
😊 Principal Sights map.
😊 Region maps.
😊 Town Maps.
All maps in this guide are oriented north, unless otherwise indicated by a directional arrow. A complete list of included maps appears at the back of this book.

LIKE A LOCAL... FEATURES
Full page features give you the low-down on the best little things that make each region of the Miami and the Keys area special.

ASK PETER...
One-to-one Q&A sessions with Peter answer your worries so that you can enjoy your visit.

Travel Tips: Peter's Travel Tips give you the inside track on local deals, tricks and techniques that you might otherwise miss.

SIDEBARS
Throughout this guide you will find short sidebars with lively anecdotes, detailed history and background information.

CONTENTS

MIAMI & THE KEYS IN PICTURES

WELCOME TO MIAMI & THE KEYS

PLANNING YOUR TRIP

DISCOVERING MIAMI & THE KEYS

MIAMI & THE KEYS...
IN PICTURES

OUTDOOR FUN

Water and warmth are the keystones of outdoor recreation in South Florida, reflecting the climatic balm that has made the region a year-round tourist magnet. The region's waters invite visitors and residents to swim, ski, snorkel, dive, sail, boat, fish or simply stroll along its edge. Warmth, in the form of the peninsula-hugging Gulf Stream, is another gift of the region's waters; but the delights to be found in South Florida's thousands of freshwater lagoons, lakes, streams, springs and swamps are also a highlight of the area. Lake Okeechobee, second largest in the US, and numerous inland waterways draw water-skiers, while the windy Atlantic shores attract kite-boarders who gleefully "catch air" on the coast's waves. The calmer green waters of the Gulf side are favorites for swimming, while the offshore Gulf is a famed game-fish destination. In-shore anglers, particularly in the Everglades backwaters pursue hard-to-catch bonefish, permit and snook; while kayakers in the Everglades islands watch for crocodiles, eagles and dozens of types of waterfowl. Inland, the warmth and gentle terrain please golfers, bikers, hikers and sunbathers.

1 **Everglades City, Everglades National Park, Wootens Air Boat Ride.** The Everglades offers one of the country's premier locales for birdwatching, with herons, eagles and many more. *See p169.*

2 **Reel Lucky Charter Boat, Key West, Florida.** Permit, snook, bonefish and other prize gamefish draw anglers from around the world to the Keys and the nearby islets of the south Everglades. *See p188.*

3 Underwater statue and snorkeler, Key Largo. With continental America's only coral reefs, the Keys are a big draw for snorkelers and divers who cherish the colorful undersea panorama. *See p180.*

4 Southern Duval Street, Key West, Florida. The only place in the continental United States never to record a freezing temperature, Key West exemplifies why South Florida is a haven for bicyclists. *See p195.*

5 Ocean Golf Course. With almost 1,500 courses, Florida has more golf links than any other state. Naples, Fort Myers, Sarasota, Bradenton, Boca Raton and West Palm Beach and are among the top 10 golf destinations in the state. *See p131 and p146.*

1 **Everglades City, Everglades National Park.** A UNESCO World Heritage Site, the Everglades offers paddlers the chance to see wild creatures —such as alligators— and to enjoy the wilderness in serenity. *See p166.*

2 **Colourful parrots, Jungle Gardens, Sarasota.** Though parrots are not native to Florida, many introduced species have established themselves, and these colorful and person- able birds are hugely popular. *See p222.*

3 **'Canopy Walk' in the trees of Myakka River State Park.** The subtropical forests of South Florida are alive with colorful birds, blooms, insects and other wild delights, and a quiet stroll through the treetops reveals this little-seen universe. *See p227.*

FAMILY FUN

With almost limitless sunshine, warmth, water and recreational opportunities — and a wealth of parkland and wilderness— South Florida is a year-round playground for multi-generation families, residents and visitors alike. The balmy climate (more than 300 sunny days each year) means swimming, golfing, beachcombing, sailing and boating, bike riding and hiking are possible almost every day. Beyond those outdoor pursuits lies a vast array of family-oriented attractions that blend enjoyment and education. While world-famous commercial theme parks are found farther north near Orlando, a different sort of park — natural wilderness — offers kids and adults alike the chance to learn about subtropical flora and fauna, and to appreciate the rich marine environments of the Gulf of Mexico and Atlantic Ocean. Whether they are actively propelling themselves through the area's wonders, or simply watching wild creatures in their lush surroundings, visitors to South Florida will be both entertained and enriched.

4 Signpost with directions to Key West tourist attractions. Continental America's southernmost city offers a wealth of attractions that illustrate the area's colorful history and environment — all of them smaller, family friendly places to visit. *See p188.*

5 Lolita the killer whale Miami Seaquarium. The world's largest dolphin is one of the most popular "performers" at outdoor aquariums; Lolita has been entertaining Miami visitors for almost four decades. *See p119.*

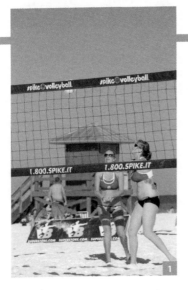

Florida's 1,197-mile coastline includes 663 miles of beaches, more than half the coast. But the beaches vary vastly from place to place and coast to coast—much to the surprise of many, the Keys, whose shores are blocked from accumulating sand by numerous islets, have very few beaches. South Florida's beaches include bustling urban strands, such as that along Ocean Drive in Miami Beach's South Beach district, and the glistening white sands of Marco Island's condominium strips. Families flock to Fort Lauderdale's picturesque palm-shaded golden sand. Back across the peninsula, beachcombers stroll the sands of Sanibel Island seeking colorful shells. Northward, at Sarasota, vacationers relish the crystalline, nearly pure quartz sands at award-winning Siesta Beach. Aside from the traditional swimming, sunbathing and sand-castle construction—all treasured pastimes at Florida beaches—visitors kite-surf, board-surf, snorkel, kayak, sail, play volleyball, jog, beachcomb, ply the waves and, of course, watch the passing parade of people doing all the above.

1   Beach volleyball tournament, Siesta Key, Sarasota. International beach authority Stephen Leatherman chose Sarasota's Siesta Beach the best in the US for 2011, admiring its white sands, shallow safe waters and excellent public facilities. *See p226.*

2   Bal Harbour beach, Miami. Shop then flop: Bal Harbour is famous for its shopping but it also boasts beautiful sands, mostly private, but with public access. *See p139.*

BEACH LIFE

3 Seashells from Sanibel Island. Sanibel Island, on the Gulf Coast near Fort Myers, is considered the finest shell collecting beach in the United States. Beachcombers stroll the sand after storms to gather rare whelks, cones, olives, murexes and others. *See p211.*

4 Coconut cocktail. Mix rum and coconut cream, maybe pineapple juice or banana, add Florida sunshine and enjoy! Lip-smacking refreshment at "America's Best Beach", Siesta Key. *See p226.*

5 Key West beach. Sandy beaches are at a premium in the Keys, where the majority of the coastline is rocky and clad with dense clusters of mangoves. *See p188.*

6 Parasailing on Miami's South Beach. First offered as a tourist activity in the Miami area, boat-drawn parasailing has spread to beaches around the world. Dozens of parasailers can be seen at almost any time along Dade County's Atlantic coast beaches. *See p132.*

SHOPPING

The same buzz of South Florida's entertainment, lodging and culinary scenes energizes its retail commerce. From traditional Seminole garb and crafts—multi-colored handmade jackets or dolls—to designer shoes and clothes, the region's atmosphere and location infuse any shopping trip with its own sultry style. Miami Beach International Fashion Week each March honors Miami's status as a Latin culture hub. Famous shopping districts include the Miracle Mile in Coral Gables, Coconut Grove in Miami, the Shops in Bal Harbour Village, and St. Armand's Circle in Sarasota. Tourists seeking mementoes of their visit will treasure the myriad curios made of Gulf Coast seashells. Note that conch shells are almost certainly not from Florida, where the animal is endangered and harvest is illegal.

1 Collins Avenue Gap store.
Shoppers head to chic boutiques and designer outlets on South Beach's Collins Avenue, behind waterfront Ocean Drive. *See p130.*

2 Coconut Grove organic grocery store. In Coconut Grove, Commodore Plaza is packed with trendy boutiques, Mayfair with niche shops, while Coco-Walk is the place for the big chain stores. *See p115.*

3 Bayside Marketplace, Miami, evening. Florida malls are havens out of the humid warmth. It's the only state to hold two of the ten largest US malls: Sawgrass Mills near Fort Lauderdale, and Aventura Mall near Miami. *See p106.*

4 Seashells for sale, Florida Keys.
In the Keys you will find all sorts of shells for sale right at the roadside; ask the store to confirm that the items on sale have been collected responsibly without damaging the reef. *See p178.*

5 Boutiques and village shops, Key West.
If you can't find that special gift in Key West's charming one-of-a-kind boutiques you're not trying hard enough. *See p188.*

2 Seminole palmetto fiber dolls, Crafts Festival Collier-Seminole State Park.
The famous hand-made jackets crafted by Seminole Indian workers are vivid expressions of a unique art, available at several tribal stores as well as other retail outlets in the region. *See p202 and p216.*

1 A Florida panther resting but very alert in a Florida zoo. There are only 160 or so of these critters left in the wild, so the best chance of a sighting is in captivity. *See p122 and p158.*

2 Adult manatee. This gentle marine mammal can grow up to 12 ft long and is a relative of the elephant. *See p145 and p227.*

3 Roseate Spoonbill, Florida. Often mistaken for flamingos, roseate spoonbills are colorful denizens of the Everglades islands. *See p169.*

The impenetrable thickets and lush swamp forests of the Everglades and Okeechobee wetlands are a huge wilderness in which exotic wild creatures abound. Here, in the continental US' third largest park, just miles from the Miami metropolis, are not only alligators but crocodiles; bald eagles, great blue herons, osprey, flamingos and reoseate spoonbills. The extremely rare Florida panther prowls the woods, while the gentle manatee cruises the back bays and brackish waterways of the coastline. Dolphins soar above the waves, and turtles bask on warm sands—all in a region with more than 7 million residents, one of the most populous in the United States. Aside from urban development and agricultural resource consumption, threats to the area's wild creatures include invasive species such as the thousands of pythons that have proved to be highly successful predators in the Everglades subtropical ecosystem. Vigorous control campaigns are under way.

4 Alligator in the swamp. Also once endangered, the American alligator has made a huge comeback and is now a common sight along South Florida's waterways. *See p169.*

5 Endangered Key Deer found only in the Florida Keys. A distinct subspecies of American whitetail deer, the Key deer is the smallest of all, standing barely 3 ft at the shoulder and weighing less than 75 pounds. They are found only in the Keys, and with fewer than 1,000 left, they are endangered. *See p187.*

FOOD & DRINK

Born in the lush warmth of its subtropical climate, seaside proximity and Hispanic flavor, South Florida's food and drink celebrate tropical fruit, seafood and Latin spice. The quintessential Cuban dish, ropa vieja is a savory pulled pork and rice combo, often served with fried plantains, the semi-sweet cousins of bananas. Oysters arrive at table fried, baked, grilled or raw, with a dash of lemon juice. Conch fritters, breaded and fried, still appear on many menus, though conch meat now comes from Caribbean waters. Mahi-mahi, red snapper, flounder and game fish such as dorado join corn dishes such as hush puppies and grits at the table. The vast variety of tropical fruits grown in South Florida, some available nowhere else in the continental US, sweetens the menu with papaya, bananas, jackfruit, passion fruit, coconut and citrus ranging from kumquats to oranges.

1 **Mojito.** Cuban in origin, the mojito is composed of rum, sugar cane juice, lime juice, mint and sparkling water—a perfect accompaniment to sultry summer nights in Little Havana. *See p107.*

2 **Grouper at the Conch Republic Seafood Company in Key West.** This large, firm-fleshed predator fish is the quintessential Florida dinner seafood filet, its darker color and savory taste lending itself well to breading, nut-crusting and other gourmet preparations. It's best either grilled or braised. *See p201.*

3 **Key Lime Pie.** More than a century after it first appeared in Key West, controversy persists over who originated this tart delight—and what the proper recipe is: Must the crust be made of graham crackers or not? But fanciers all agree it doesn't taste right unless you use real Key lime juice, squeezed from local limes. *See p35.*

4 Half Shell Raw Bar, Old Port, Key West. This place shucks! Tuck into a plate of fresh oysters right by the dock in Key West. *See p201.*

4 Bongos Cuban Cafe, Miami. Cuban cuisine and culture has made great inroads into Floridian sensibilities. *See p107.*

5 Conch Fritters Sign Key West FL, Florida Keys. This seafood snack is the "national" dish of the Conch Republic (a.k.a. Key West). *See p188.*

4 © Richard Nowitz / Apa Publications 5 © Wendell Metzen/age fotostock 6 © Bob Pardue – Florida /Alamy

1 Adrienne Arsht Center, Miami. Roll up, roll up to Florida's largest performing arts center to see the likes of Oprah, The Lion King, Jersey Boys, Avenue Q… *See p104 and p131.*

2 Voodoo market stall, Little Haiti Caribbean Marketplace, Miami. They'll put a spell on you, but only to buy the bewitching wares; candles, statues, herbs, but no goat's head! *See p120.*

3 Jai-alai stadium, Dania, Florida. The quintessential spectator sport of South Florida is a Latin import (Basque in origin), a high-speed racquet-and-ball game played on an indoor court. Balls sometimes move at more than 120 mph. *See p34 and p141.*

CULTURE

The cultural flavor of South Florida derives from its climate, relative remoteness, and proximity to Latin America. The easygoing lifestyle of Key West drew writers such as Ernest Hemingway, Tennessee Williams and Truman Capote, where the conservative strains of American life were hundreds of miles distant. The area's Spanish heritage is reflected in the huge popularity of Latin lifestyle pursuits such as jai-alai and flamenco. Meanwhile, warm winter weather brings horse racing to the Miami area. Caribbean and Latin links make voodoo culture part of life in many neighborhoods, and the Catholic Church enjoys one of its strongest remaining US bastions. South and Central American influences abound on the restaurant scene, local radio and television; and in much-sought-after clothing.

4 Hialeah Park racetrack, Miami. Florida's balmy climate brings more than retirees and snowbirds south— horse racing takes place at the historic Hialeah Park track December through February. *See p131.*

5 Hemingway House and Gardens. The brawny later works of Florida's most famous writer reflect his embrace of the outdoor life in Key West, where he lived 1929–1939. He moved on to Cuba, then Idaho, but still visited often until his death in 1961. His house is a museum today. *See p196.*

CITY LIFE

Often envisioned as a long stretch of palm-shaded suburban retirement communities, Miami is also a dynamic urban hub whose key industries include banking, high-tech, insurance, retail and foreign trade. Though Cuban refugees are the major cultural force, immigrants from many other countries also play a significant role: Miami has not only Little Havana but also Little Haiti, and many residents of Salvadoran, Brazilian, Puerto Rican and West Indian heritage. This means Spanish is heard daily, and the Mexican restaurants so common elsewhere are here often replaced by Caribbean, Cuban and Brazilian bistros. While Miami bustles, the cities northward and along the Gulf Coast are less hectic, less Hispanic and more dominated by the tourism and retirement industries. A day for a Little Havana resident likely includes mass at a local church, with Caribbean food for dinner; in Sarasota, it might be beachcombing, an afternoon of golf, then pan-fried oysters. And in South Beach... the music, dance and people-watching are just starting at 9pm.

1 Máximo Gómez Park, Domino Park, Calle Ocho, Little Havana. The epicenter of Cuban refugee culture in the United States is this vibrant Miami neighborhood of 76,000 residents—often depicted with its famous "domino park" public square. *See p107.*

2 Night time on Ocean Drive. When darkness descends, Miami's beautiful people turn South Beach's Ocean Drive into a Miami Vice-like film set. *See p135.*

3

4

3 Miami skyline – view from Key Biscayne. The business center of the Caribbean region, downtown Miami's skyline has more than 295 high-rise buildings—and, with 200,000 residents, is the city's fastest-growing "neighborhood." *See p119.*

5

4 Ringling Museum of Art built by John Ringling in Sarasota. The annual Sarasota Chalk Festival, each year in October, brings European-style street painting to the US. *See p218.*

5 Cuban cafe on 8th Street, Little Havana. Grab a Café Cubano at the landmark Cafeteria Guardabarranco, perhaps while listening to the music of Celia Cruz and Tito Puente. *See p107.*

1 Marlin Hotel, Art Deco District, Miami. This classic building is known as "The Rock n' Roll Hotel of South Beach" as it is also home to South Beach (recording) Studios, *See p134.*

2 New World Center Performance Hall, scene from Pictures at an Exhibition. Frank Gehry's fantastical New World Center concert hall in Miami, opened in 2011, is as exotic inside as out—and represents South Florida's whole-hearted embrace of 21C style. *See p52.*

ARCHITECTURE

The architecture of South Florida has until recently been almost entirely set by its subtropical climate. The area's indigenous inhabitants lived in simple wood-and-reed structures; the first settlers built housing that aimed for cooling, a desire that culminated in the 19C housing style still commonly seen in South Florida: The Key West Conch House, built on piers to allow air flow underneath. The Gilded Age brought a brief epoch of gargantuan hotels to the Gulf and Atlantic coasts newly served by railroads; but these massive structures proved impractical in the climate. The temperature-moderating stucco-and-tile construction of the early 20C's Mediterranean Revival boom thrives today in many restored hotels; the 1920s and 30s brought Art Deco and Streamline Moderne to Miami Beach. Air conditioning changed everything after WW II, suburban bungalows proliferated, and the metal-and-glass high-rises AC made possible still dominate Miami's skyline.

3 Cà d'Zan, a waterfront mansion restored in 2002. The glory years of the tourism industry in South Florida began with Gilded Age palaces, but these unwieldy monoliths were too big and too costly to operate, so almost all were replaced by more modest Mediterranean Revival, stucco-and-tile resorts that survive today. *See p220.*

4 Traditional wooden houses at Key West. Unique to South Florida, the Conch House originated in Key West and was widely copied in Miami. The open space beneath helps cool the house, and the unornamented clapboard exterior is distinctive. *See p180.*

ENTERTAINMENT

As with so much else in South Florida, the area's status as a Caribbean and Latin American hub wields a huge influence on its entertainment life. Latin music stars Gloria Estefan, Julio and Enrique Iglesias, and Marc Anthony all have ties to South Florida. In addition to baseball, American football is strong here, with the Miami Dolphins and Miami Hurricanes championship winners. Theater, symphony, and other performance arts shine in Miami's 2011 New World Center concert hall. And the discos and clubs of Miami Beach's Ocean Drive keep the music thumping and the dance floor heated up until daybreak. Salsa, tango and rumba and practiced in clubs throughout the region.

1 SET Miami nightclub, Miami Beach. Frequently voted best dance club and with the hottest DJs in town, this is the place to live SoBe nightlife to the max! *See p135.*

2 Cinco De Mayo dancers performing in the town square of The Villages in Florida. Miami's Latin flavor also spurs the popularity of flamenco, which is celebrated in a March festival that brings global stars of this dynamic dance to the area. *See p82.*

5 Margaritaville Cafe, Duval Street, Key West. A temple to Jimmy Buffett, the island life singer-songwriter, perfect for "wastin' away" a few hours while in Key West. *See p192.*

4 Latin dancers at Mango's Tropical Cafe on Ocean Drive. Miami's sultry night-time glamour first reached global audiences in the seminal 1984–1989 *Miami Vice* TV show. Miami nightlife still wows the crowds today. *See p135.*

5 New World Symphony Wallcast concert. Enjoy one of America's finest classical ensembles for free on a 7,000-square-foot "screen" at Miami Beach Soundscape Park. *See p52.*

6 CanesFest, Orange Bowl preseason scrimmage, University of Miami Hurricanes. Though no longer as significant as it once was, Miami's annual Orange Bowl college football game remains a mainstay of the sport, drawing thousands of fans and millions of TV viewers. *See p72 and p82.*

WELCOME TO
MIAMI AND THE KEYS

The Region Today

One of the most popular travel destinations in the world, South Florida is a bustling modern metropolis; a land of legend—both modern and historic; and a lush, subtropical landscape in which wild panthers, crocodiles and alligators prowl the wilderness. World-famous nightclubs throb all night in South Beach, Caribbean culture reaches its greatest US heights in Miami, families relax on palm-shaded beaches in Fort Lauderdale, and the ghosts of famous writers such as Hemingway and Capote haunt Key West. Miami's port and airport are hubs of international commerce and travel; while the peaceful Gulf Coast shores of Marco Island, Sanibel Island and Sarasota reflect a quiet past. Cattle ranches dot the northern interior of this area, towering high-rise condominiums and famed resort hotel line the shores.

By the time Florida became part of the US in 1821, it already had a thriving plantation economy in the northern part of the state, where most of the people lived. After the Civil War, new and diverse industries sprang up: timber, citrus, shipping, cattle

A HAVEN FOR REFUGEES

Florida's long history of ethnic diversity was boosted hugely in the second half of the 20C. Ever since Cubans fleeing the Castro regime began arriving in 1959, Little Havana has remained a magnet for refugees from a variety of Latin nations. Eastern Europeans were the first arrivals into the quarter, reaching their peak population in the early 1950s. By the late 1950s, Hispanics occupied the quarter, paving the way for the subsequent Cuban influx that reached unprecedented proportions during the "Freedom Flights" in 1965.

The large concentration of Cubans in the quarter prompted its nickname, "Little Havana." Densely populated Little Havana is largely an immigrant community with a preponderance of young Latin American families and elderly residents. Although Nicaraguans count among the thousands of Hispanics who call Little Havana home, the sector remains the political nerve center of the influential Cuban exile colony, many of whose members have become voting US citizens, widely considered the reason the US has not achieved any rapprochement with Cuba.

Key West also has a long history as a haven for refugees of a different sort—artists, writers and other creative individuals, many of them gay, such as Truman Capote.

and cigar-making, helped establish Florida's importance in the national marketplace.

Once the railroads linked the state with the rest of the country in the late 19C, Florida's economy began to blossom. Speculative land sales rocketed in the 1920s, but ended just as suddenly several years later. The subsequent downturn in real estate activity, followed by the Depression, slowed the state's growth until after World War II. Since then Florida's population has expanded rapidly: the area is one of America's most-desirable retirement destinations, where a reliably warm climate means visitors and residents alike need almost never don coats to ward off cold, nor clear snow from their sidewalks. With the lilting tones of Spanish plying the air, the sunshine that bathes the land more than 310 days a year, and the intriguing natural environment of the country's most subtropical region, South Florida is truly a land apart from the rest of the USA.

Economy

Tourism, retail and international trade dominate the economy of South Florida; government services and health care are the key drivers in public and semi-public enterprise. Florida's gross domestic product of $673 billion (2010) was impacted by a struggling real estate market in the wake of the global economic downturn. Southern Florida's distance from major US cities has meant **manufacturing** has traditionally taken a back seat to tourism and other service industries; it is, however, likely to be at the forefront of the state's recovery.

With tourism and health care leading the way, Florida's **service** industries are expected to account for about 90 percent of new jobs created in the next decade. Economists forecast that with Florida's ageing population, **health care** will continue to be one of the fastest growing industries. Enlisting about 14 percent of all workers, **government** extends its reach across schools, hospitals, the military and state and local jurisdictions. Also big are **finance and real estate**. Real estate mushroomed with the state's population growth, and once employed more than double the national average. But the national real estate slump hit the region hard, with Miami area property values declining more than half from a 2007 average of $360,000 to $140,000 in 2010. Transportation and foreign trade round out the local economy, with almost $100 billion in international trade in the Miami district per year. Forty percent of all US **exports** to Latin and South America pass through Florida, especially Miami. In South Florida, the Miami and Fort Lauderdale airports are the main gateways, with the former serving almost 36 million passengers a year, 17 million of those international.

ASK PETER...

Q: With resort fees and a market geared to tourism, can I find value when traveling to Florida?
A: You bet you can. According to a recent study, three cities in the state have some of the lowest discriminatory travel taxes. These are taxes that go above and beyond sales tax on hotels and other travel-related services. To avoid those, choose West Palm Beach, Fort Lauderdale and Fort Myers.

Miami's airport is the major North American hub for Latin America and the Caribbean; ranks second in the US for international cargo; and has direct service to 150 cities worldwide.

The **tourism** industry remains strong—visitor numbers slipped only mildly in 2008, rebounding to 85 million in 2010. Visitors spend a total of $65 billion a year and generate work for 981,300 Floridians—about 12 percent of the state's jobs. Miami draws 12 million visitors a year, half of those international.

Florida's waters hold more than 700 species of fish. The **commercial fishing** industry is led by catches of shrimp, lobster, crab and snapper. Ten percent of the US shrimp harvest comes from Florida (particularly the coast around Fort Myers).

Florida grows a variety of fruits, vegetables and nursery plants that are transported fresh to northern markets in the winter and spring. **Citrus fruits**, first introduced around 1570, outpace all other agricultural products, with oranges most prominent. Florida supplies 40 percent of the world's orange juice supply. Florida is the nation's top producer of **sugar cane**, producing nearly half the US' sugar, primarily just south of Lake Okeechobee.

The **movie** business is a major industry in the US, with Florida ranking third for film production (after California and New York respectively) based on revenue generated. In the last few years, however, some of the leading players moved out of Florida, but in 2010 State government were looking at ways (such as legislation on tax credits) to lure back lapsed movie makers and to attract even more film-making talent to the Sunshine State.

Florida also boasts extensive amounts of limestone (its most prevalent **mineral**). Phosphate was discovered in the southwest part of the state in 1881. Florida now produces 80 percent of the country's phosphate—an essential ingredient in fertilizer. Florida also leads the nation in production of rutile and zircon, heavy minerals found in ancient beach deposits and used in ceramics, metals and chemicals. Found in greater quantities here than in any other state, peat is prized as a soil conditioner.

ALIEN INVADERS IN FLORIDA!

South Florida has proven especially prone to invasive non-native species. Perhaps best known are the pythons and other constrictors that have invaded the swamps and forests of the region; descended from abandoned "pets," these predator snakes have devastated local bird and small mammal populations. Biologists estimate there are up to 100,000 pythons and boas in the area. Other problem animals include the Asian walking catfish, scourge of fish farms; and the lantana, an ornamental plant.

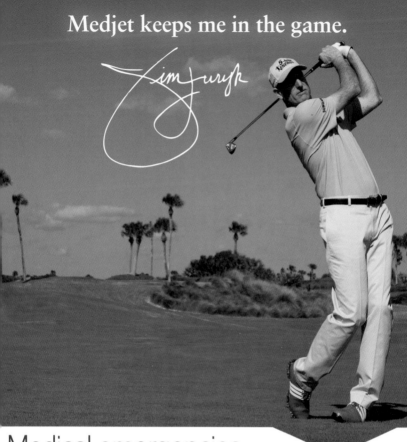

Travel, Dine and Explore with Confidence

TRAVEL ADVICE

mustsees MICHELIN
Bahamas

☐ Must Read Information
☐ Must See Sites
☐ Must Do Activities
☐ Must Know Practicalities

MICHELIN
FLORIDA

Green Guide

NORTH AMERICA

MICHELIN
Road Atlas
USA · CANADA · MEXICO

Michelin, experts in travel guides and maps for more than 100 years. Available wherever books are sold.

www.michelintravel.com

MICHELIN
A better way forward

People

Four out of five Floridians are not native to the state: residents of Florida share the identity of "newcomer" more than anything else, a distinction that holds true in South Florida. Some come seeking job opportunities, others political freedom, others just warm weather—a place in the sun, literally and figuratively.

Florida's phenomenal growth has outstripped most of the rest of the country: in 1900 the state ranked 33rd in population; by 1960 it had risen to 10th. With more than 18.5 million people, it now ranks fourth-largest in the nation. The population has redistributed itself as the South Florida wilderness yielded to pioneers and developers. In 1900 North Florida held 66 percent of the population, compared to five percent in South Florida. Today the north is 20 percent, while the south 37 percent—with one-third of the state's people living along the 65mi strip from Miami to West Palm Beach known as the Gold Coast.

One of the smallest ethnic groups, the **Seminoles** are themselves relatively new to Florida. They coalesced from various southeastern tribes and moved into Florida in the 18C to escape white incursion. Though most were relocated to Oklahoma in the mid-19C, about 2,000 Seminoles still live and maintain their culture in and around the Everglades. The percentage of **African-Americans** decreased from 44 percent of the population in 1900 to some 2.3 million today, about 14 percent.

The centuries-old **North vs. South** dynamic that plays out in the US as a whole is uniquely mirrored—in reverse—in Florida. North Florida, with its large concentration of military retirees and its proximity to Georgia and Alabama, skews conservative politically, while the South, claiming a high number of Jews and Northeasterners, tends toward a more liberal outlook. President Barack Obama won Florida in 2008, largely on the strength of his support in Miami-Dade County.

Since the end of World War II, the elderly have pushed in from less hospitable climes, until Florida now claims a higher percentage of **seniors** than any other state. This group has made southwest Florida one of the fastest-growing areas in the country. Another large number of retirees, known as "snowbirds," migrate to Florida for the winter, then return home in the spring.

The most influential group of arrivals to Florida in recent times, **Hispanics**, have swirled up from Cuba and other Latin regions for the past half-century. More than 750,000 people from the Caribbean and Latin America have moved to Florida, giving the state one of the largest populations of Hispanics in the country: almost 3 million, or nearly 20 percent of the state's population. About 72 percent live on the Gold Coast, imparting their lively language, food, music and customs to the Miami region.

Recreation

Florida's glorious **beaches** top the heap of the state's recreational venues. With fine sand, rolling dunes and gentle surf, these beaches attract sun-worshippers and swimmers. Several Gulf Coast beaches offer **sea shelling** unparalleled anywhere in the country. Over the past few years, 15 Florida beaches have ranked among the top 20 in the nation in independent surveys. Rated for their beauty, water and air temperatures, sand softness, water clarity and solitude, beaches with the highest marks include those at Sanibel Island, Marco Island and Siesta Key.

Water sports of all types abound along both coasts, with **surfing** concentrated on the Atlantic side and **sailing** and **windsurfing** on the calmer Gulf. Florida manufactures more pleasure boats than any other state in the country; many of them are used for **water-skiing** or for taking fishing parties out to cast for mackerel, marlin, bonefish, sailfish and tarpon. Inland, the state's numerous rivers, lakes and springs provide ample opportunity for freshwater **fishing** as well as **canoeing** through primeval swamplands. The Florida Canoe Trail system boasts more than 1000mi of designated routes along 36 rivers and waterways.

Snorkelers don fins and masks along both coasts to explore ancient wrecks and exotic fish. For sheer underwater beauty, **scuba divers** head to the coral reef that stretches off the shores of the Florida Keys. Florida has 1,400 **golf courses**, more than any state in the union; most are open to the public. Another year-round sport, **tennis** is played throughout the state; many hotels and resorts offer vacation packages that include tennis lessons with resident pros. The Everglades and nearby preserves attract **campers** to vast acreages of national and state land, mere miles from the Miami metropolitan area. Hiking is becoming a more and more popular activity, with over 2,300mi of developed trails in the state. In the years ahead, state officials hope to link the **Florida National Scenic Trail** with the Appalachian Trail, thus extending the latter from Alabama and Georgia to the Everglades. The Florida trail currently crosses some 1,400mi through swampland, scrub and hardwood forest.

Among the many spectator sports in the state, **jai alai** is perhaps the most uniquely Floridian. Originating in the Basque region of Spain and imported from Cuba, the game is played on *frontons* (176ft courts) throughout Florida, including America's oldest, the 1926 Miami Jai-Alai Fronton. Players hurl *pelotas* (balls) against curved walls at speeds of 120mph or more and catch them in *cestas* (baskets) attached to their arms.

Racing fans can also watch greyhound or horse track action throughout the state. Miami's Hialeah Park (est. 1925) remains one of the most popular venues for horse racing in the US.

Food and Drink

Taking advantage of the bounty of its offshore waters, its year-round growing season, its Southern heritage and the influence of its Latin and Caribbean immigrants, the Sunshine State offers a wide array of cuisines that have traditionally varied from north to south, though all styles are found statewide. Salt pork, cornmeal, molasses and winter greens were staples for Florida's early settlers. Known as "Crackers", these pioneers hunted squirrel, deer and raccoon to add to their tables. Freshwater fish, caught in local rivers and springs, was pan-fried. The ubiquitous Sabal palm was harvested for its edible bud, said to taste like raw cabbage. Called "swamp cabbage" by the settlers, this same delicacy is known today as "hearts of palm."

Many menus, especially at "soul food" restaurants, still echo these early styles. Steamed Apalachicola Bay oysters, broiled amberjack (a mild, flaky white fish), fried catfish or Gulf shrimp, boiled crawfish, hush puppies (small balls of deep-fried cornmeal dough) and grits (an oatmeal-style gruel made from ground white corn) constitute typical traditional fare. One might also find fried alligator and frog legs, as well as spicy Cajun creations such as the thick stew called gumbo.

South Florida cooking favors the fresh vegetables, exotic fruits and bountiful commercial fish harvested in the state. Here you can sample smoked mullet and freshly caught grouper (try it grilled or encrusted with macadamia nuts), pompano, snapper and mahi mahi—all often paired with tropical fruit salsas. Succulent stone crab claws, chewy conch fritters (made from the mollusk found inside Florida's once abundant state shell, though now imported from the Bahamas) and clawless spiny lobster constitute some of the state's unique shellfish dishes.

Although renowned for its citrus fruit—over 20 varieties are grown here—Florida growers have added exotics such as passion fruit, papaya, mango and carambola to the expanding list of tropical produce. In addition Florida claims the small, yellowish, bracingly tart Key limes used in making **Key lime pie**. A mixture of egg yolks, sweetened condensed milk and key lime juice in a graham-cracker crust, the state's famed dessert is traditionally topped with fluffy meringue.

Florida's ever-evolving cuisine is generously peppered with foreign flavors. Cubans have introduced plantains (cooking bananas), yuca (a mild-tasting root vegetable) and boniato (a nutty Cuban sweet potato) to grocery stores. Entrées on many restaurant menus include black beans and rice; *arroz con pollo* (chicken with yellow rice); and *ropa vieja* (Spanish for "old clothes"), shredded beef or pork dressed with tomatoes, peppers, onions, garlic and white wine.

FLORIDA'S PRODUCE
...LIKE A LOCAL

Want to travel like a local? Then eat like a local. There's more to the state than just oranges. Here's my pick of the fruits that taste freshest in Florida.

Carambola – Each slice of the yellow-green, ridged carambola forms a star, thus its more popular moniker, star fruit. Hailing from East India, the crunchy carambola has a fresh, slightly acidic flavor that enhances desserts and salads.

Kumquat – Eaten raw, this Chinese quail-egg-size citrus fruit tastes tart and its rind bitter. Chefs recommend poaching kumquats in sugar syrup to render them more palatable.

Lychee – Another China native, resembling a small red ball with knobby skin, the lychee grew in Florida as early as 1886. Its honeyed, fragrant white flesh is often served for dessert in Chinese restaurants.

Mango – The dark oval fruit has been cultivated in tropical East Asia for over 6,000 years. Florida growers stagger ripening times so mango-lovers can enjoy this peachy treat for as long as five months a year.

Passionfruit – Encased in a hard, bitter-tasting yellow or purple shell, the juicy, edible pulp of the passion fruit is studded with tiny black seeds. This South American native caught on as a commercial fruit in the 1980s.

Plantain – This jumbo cousin of the banana originated in Africa. Rarely eaten raw, plantains—an essential ingredient in Cuban cuisine—are usually served fried until caramalized (plátanos maduros), boiled or baked.

Sapodilla – Fans of the egg-shaped, brown-skinned sapodilla claim it tastes like a pear infused with maple syrup. This fruit grows wild in parts of Mexico and Central America.

Ugli Fruit – A cross between a tangerine and a grapefruit, the ugli is named for its unappealing thick yellow-green skin. Despite its appearance, this pear-shaped native of Jamaica boasts a sought-after, tart-sweet flavor.

Jackfruit – This large (some reach 5 pounds), knobby, light green fruit is hugely popular in Asia. Sections are cut open and the exposed flesh, eaten with a spoon, is lightly acidic and fragrant. When unripe, the texture is similar to chicken, hence its use as a meat substitute in vegetarian dishes.

Papaya – South Florida growers have adapted one of the tropics' favorite breakfast fruits to Florida growing conditions. Papaya flesh is bright orange, sweet and softer than cantaloupe, usually served as slices in breakfast buffets.

Atemoya – This un-usual cross between a cherimoya and sweetsop is a scaled green fruit, like a large pear, with delightfully fragrant, custard-like flesh beneath the skin; eat it like an avocado.

Pummelo – The progenitor of grapefruit, this citrus giant (sometimes reaching a pound) has a very thick rind and tangy, juicy sections inside.

History

Prehistoric and Native Floridians

Prehistoric peoples probably inhabited the area of North America that now includes Florida as early as 10,000 BC. While it has long been thought that Ice Age nomads filtered southeast after crossing the Bering land bridge from Siberia into Alaska between 20,000 and 15,000 BC, there is now speculation that those who reached the Florida peninsula may have come instead from Central and South America through the Antilles. The earliest Indians here were hunter-gatherers whose diet included the meat of saber-toothed tigers, mastodons, bison and other Pleistocene animals. Divers in Florida rivers often discover fluted stone spearheads, known as Clovis or Suwannee points, used by prehistoric hunters.

The first semi-permanent settlements began to spring up along Florida's waterways around 5,000 BC. Evidence can be found in ancient **midden mounds** (trash heaps) of the shellfish that had become increasingly important to the Indians' diet. Agriculture, including the cultivation of squash, beans and corn introduced from South America or Mexico, began when the population became more sedentary around 1,000 BC.

Archaeologists have found some 14,000 **burial** mounds throughout the state (many lost to modern development). These mysterious mounds are thought to reflect the influence of the Hopewell cultures of Illinois and Ohio. By the Christian era, some of the ceremonial sites had developed into large complexes comprising several individual mounds connected by an intricate system of canals and roadways.

By the time European explorers visited the Florida peninsula in the 16C, the native population numbered an estimated 100,000. There were six main groups: the **Timucua** (occupying northeast Florida as far south as present-day Cape Canaveral), the **Apalachee** (Panhandle), the **Ais** (central and southeast coast), the **Tequesta** (southeast coast), the **Tocobaga** (Tampa Bay area) and the **Calusa** (southwest region). Developing independently, each group maintained a separate culture with specific social orders and sophisticated religious and political institutions. The northern Indians subsisted by farming, while those south of the Everglades generally hunted game and fished for seafood. Within 250 years of European colonization, intertribal wars, Spanish slave raids and European-imported diseases such as smallpox, influenza and measles, had decimated most of the Indian population. Today the only remaining traces of Florida's earliest native cultures are archaeological.

First Spanish Period 1513–1763

European explorers and fortune hunters began making forays into the Caribbean and Florida Straits in the 15C. Soon after Christopher Columbus discovered Hispaniola in 1492, Italian-born cartographer **Giovanni Caboto** (also known as John Cabot), commissioned by England's King Henry VIII, ventured into the New World to chart his findings. Although there is no specific record of it, Cabot and his son Sebastian probably sighted the Florida peninsula in 1497 or 1498. In 1513 explorer **Juan Ponce de León**, armed with a Spanish patent to colonize any lands he found, made the first recorded—and officially sanctioned—landfall. De León, who was looking for the island of Bimini, went ashore somewhere between present-day St. Augustine and the St. Johns River in early April. He gave the name La Florida to an area that covers most of the present-day southeast, west to the Mississippi River and north into the Carolinas. When de León returned to the southwest coast in 1521, he was gravely wounded in a Native American attack; he then sailed to Cuba where he died within a few weeks.

Subsequent Spanish colonization attempts also failed miserably. Accomplished conquistador **Hernando de Soto**'s legendary three-year search (1539–41) for riches in the New World also proved disastrous. After trekking several thousand miles with his 600 men—throughout central and northern Florida and as far west as present-day Oklahoma—de Soto died from fever. Finding plenty of trouble but none of the anticipated riches, Spain (already importing gold and silver from Mexico and Peru) temporarily lost interest in colonizing La Florida. The peninsula's strategic location on the Florida Straits, however, was vital to protecting the country's Caribbean trade routes from pirates. In 1562, a French expedition led by the ardent Calvinist **Jean Ribault** entered the St. Johns River in search of a site for a Huguenot colony. When Ribault's fledgling settlement completed building Fort Caroline near the river's mouth in 1565, an alarmed Spain moved to reclaim her hold. Later that year **Pedro Menéndez de Avilés** sailed into the Florida Straits and founded St. Augustine (to be the first permanent European settlement in Florida). He then massacred the French at Fort Caroline.

British Period 1763–1783

The 1763 **Treaty of Paris** ending the Seven Years War between England and France marked a decisive turning point in Florida history. Under the treaty's provisions, the Spanish colony was ceded to Britain in exchange for Havana, Cuba, which England had captured the previous year. Florida was then split into two parts. East Florida, with a capital at St. Augustine, included the peninsula and the Panhandle as far as the Apalachicola River. West Florida, with Pensacola as its capital, was bounded on the north by the present state line, and on the west by the Mississippi River. By British charter in 1764, Florida gained a section between the Mississippi and Chattahoochee rivers extending north to the present-day cities of Jackson, Mississippi, and Montgomery, Alabama.

In contrast to Spain, Britain attempted a self-supporting colony. Sugar, rice, indigo and cotton plantations were established along the St. Johns River. Export subsidies and generous land grants drew Protestant settlers from Great Britain as well as Tory sympathizers who left Georgia and South Carolina after the American Revolution. The new population also included a 1768 colony of some 2,000 Greeks, Italians and Minorcans at New Smyrna, about 75mi south of St. Augustine. By the 1720s, a number of different loosely organized Indian groups (later known as the Creek Confederacy), pushed by settlers out of Georgia, Alabama and South Carolina, had also begun to filter into northern Florida. From the Creeks, two main nations, the Hitchiti-speaking **Miccosukee** and the Muskogee-speaking **Seminoles**, emerged.

Second Spanish Period 1784–1821

British occupation of Florida was to last only 20 years. With Britain's forces engaged in Revolutionary War battles farther north, Spain (participating in the war indirectly as a French ally) took advantage of Florida's weakened defenses and recaptured Pensacola in 1781. Under the **Second Treaty of Paris** (1783) ending the Revolution, the remainder of Florida reverted to Spanish control—excluding the northern section added above the Panhandle in 1764. By about 1800, Seminole villages were scattered from Apalachicola east to the St. Johns River and from South Georgia down to the Caloosahatchee River. During the War of 1812, violence erupted repeatedly between white settlers and Indians, who were resented for harboring runaway slaves. In 1814, a battle with the Upper Creeks at Horseshoe Bend ended in Indian defeat and a treaty opening 20 million acres of Creek land to US settlement. From 1817 to 1818, Gen. Andrew Jackson led a special US command against the Seminoles, initiating a series of raids later known as the **First Seminole War** and attacking several Spanish settlements.

By this time it was clear that Spain could neither govern nor police its increasingly turbulent territory effectively. Its power thus diminished, Spain negotiated the **Adams-Onís Treaty** in 1819. This agreement transferred the land east of the Mississippi to the US and formalized the boundaries of present-day Florida.

Early Settlement and the Seminole Wars

In 1822 President James Monroe unified the two Floridas into a single territory with two counties: Escambia and St. Johns. Two years later, the first Territorial governor, William P. DuVal, named Tallahassee as the capital. In the new US Territory, the government recognized all land grants made before 1818, pending fulfillment of the original terms. Congress also granted the right of pre-emption to settlers, allowing squatters to remain if they purchased 80 acres of land at $1.25 an acre. With the area now open to settlers, tensions mounted over the Indian presence.

In the 1820s the US government attempted to contain the native population on a single tract of land in central Florida. When this effort failed, Jackson, now president, signed the **Indian Removal Act** in 1830, in hope of resolving Indian conflicts once and for all by relocating eastern tribes to a designated area west of the Mississippi River. This law specified that the Indians must consent to moving, that they would be paid for their land and they would hold perpetual title to their new territories in the west. The Seminoles demonstrated the greatest resistance to this infamous forced exodus, known as the **Trail of Tears**. In 1832 a small group of Seminoles (unauthorized by their leaders) signed the **Treaty of Payne's Landing**, requiring the Indians to relinquish their land and relocate to a reservation in Arkansas (now Oklahoma). At the end of a three-year grace period, however, not a single Seminole had left.

US troops arrived in 1835 to enforce the treaty. In December Seminoles ambushed the command of Maj. Francis Dade near Bushnell, precipitating the **Second Seminole War**. The leader of the Seminole resistance was **Osceola**. Still remembered for his cunning and courage, this great man met a bitter end. In late 1837, he was tricked into entering a US army camp near St. Augustine. There under a flag of truce, he was imprisoned and transferred to Fort Moultrie in Charleston, South Carolina, where he died in 1838. The Seminole Wars ended in 1842, when at least 3,000 Indians and blacks were sent to Oklahoma, where their descendants live today. Eluding capture, several hundred Seminoles melted into the Everglades.

In 1845 Florida was admitted to the Union as the 27th state. Indian rights remained unresolved, as Floridians kept pressing the US government for total removal of the Seminoles from the state. Increasing incursions of the white man into Indian reservation land eventually led to the **Third Seminole War** of 1855–58, an inconclusive series of swamp skirmishes that ended with the surrender of Seminole chief Billy Bowlegs and never resulted in a formal treaty with the US government.

The Plantation Belt

During early statehood, settlement remained primarily between the Suwannee and Apalachicola rivers in an area called Middle Florida, where pioneers and cattle drivers established small farms. The dark, sandy loam there also proved excellent for **cotton** cultivation and hundreds of plantations flourished by 1850, building a cotton economy comparable to that of antebellum Georgia. In 1834 the first railroad incorporated in Florida connected the cotton market of Tallahassee to the port of St. Marks. Aside from cotton, timber, turpentine and sugar cane were common plantation products. Sugar cane plantations were concentrated along the St. Johns and Manatee rivers. While plantation size varied from 1,000 to 5,000 acres, wealth was measured by the number of slaves one owned. "Planters" were those with 20 or more slaves. The number of planters who owned 30 or more slaves doubled between 1850 and 1860.

The Steamboat Age

The riverboat industry was critical to Florida's economic development and settlement. The first steamboat service was offered in 1827 on the Apalachicola River. This water body, along with the Chattahoochee and Flint rivers, formed an important cotton outlet. Lumber, then a major export, was also ferried via steamer. During the Second Seminole War, the government chartered 40 steamboats to transport troops and supplies. By 1848 service from Jacksonville connected Palatka and Enterprise on the St. Johns River. With the steamers came Florida's first winter tourists, a major portion of whom were northerners whose doctors had recommended a sunny clime to cure ailments such as consumption. Sick and healthy passengers alike slept in elegantly furnished staterooms and dined on fine food.

Civil War and Reconstruction

A steady flow of settlers and the sound plantation economy increased Florida's population of 34,700 in 1830 to 140,400 in 1860. Almost half of them were "non-white." To protect its one-sided economy, which relied heavily on slave labor, the state seceded from the Union in 1861 and became an important supplier of beef, cotton and salt to the Confederacy.

The war almost bankrupted the state, but Reconstruction brought new investors from the north, ready to finance business, land speculation, transportation and tourism. Sharecroppers and tenant farmers, including freed blacks, took over the plantations. Cotton, timber and cattle sales helped boost the economy. In the late 1860s, some 6,000 Cubans immigrated to Florida at the start of Cuba's Ten Years War of Independence

(1868–78), establishing Key West as a major cigar-making center and starting an exodus that has continued off and on since. Soon thereafter, the commercial sponge market, established in Key West in 1849, moved its hub north after new beds were discovered off Tarpon Springs in the 1870s.

The Railroad Boom

Florida's late 19C growth was closely linked to its rapid railroad development, spurred by the state's 1881 sale of four million acres of swamp and overflow land in central Florida to Philadelphia entrepreneur **Hamilton Disston**. Most importantly, this sale provided funds to clear the titles of state-owned land from earlier railroad promotions and opened the way for subsidies and land grants to new railroad builders, much as similar government activity brought railroads to the Western US. The undisputed leaders in the field—and in Florida development—remain two of the most colorful figures in the state's history: railroad tycoons **Henry Bradley Plant** and **Henry Morrison Flagler**. Plant consolidated and expanded numerous existing short lines and extended track to Tampa in 1884 to create an important link to northern markets. The Plant system merged with the Atlantic Coast Line in 1902 to complete a network of about 2,250mi of track originating in Richmond, Virginia. Flagler concentrated on the **Florida East Coast Railway** (FEC), extending it from Jacksonville to St. Augustine in 1886 and subsequently to Palm Beach (1894), Miami (1896) and Key West (1912). As the railway system expanded to link Florida to the rail lines crossing the US, it also spurred the state's winter production of fruit and vegetables.

Extravagant hotels strategically placed at each new railhead, such as the Royal Poinciana in Palm Beach (the dining room seated 1,600), and Miami's Royal Palm (with its circular six-hole golf course) became fashionable resort destinations for the northern social set in the late 19C.

20C Development

The early 20C was Florida's gilded age, a brief period of glamor, extravagance and no income or inheritance tax. Millionaire industrialists luxuriated in fabulous villas. The economy had benefited from the 1898 **Spanish-American War**, when embarkation camps for American troops were located in Tampa, Miami and Jacksonville. After the US won its bid to gain Cuba independence from Spain, many soldiers returned to Florida with their families. For the first time, good roads—the Florida Road Department was established in 1915—and the affordable Model T automobile, made vacations accessible to people who

could not afford luxury hotels. Modest, family-operated motels and tourist courts sprouted on the Florida roadside. By the 1920s "tin-can tourist camps," filled with Tin Lizzies outfitted as campers, had appeared in every major Florida city.

Dozens of land speculators, including Carl Fisher in Miami Beach and George Merrick in Coral Gables, not only peddled Spanish bungalows, but also a new lifestyle and a rosy future. From 1920–25, the state grew four times faster than any other. Unfortunately, the subsequent bust was just as rapid as the boom. The real-estate crash in 1926 came on the heels of overspeculation and a destructive hurricane that beheaded palm trees, leveled cheaper construction and stopped new building in its tracks. A ruinous Mediterranean fruit fly invasion in 1929 devastated the citrus industry. The onset of the national Depression that same year only confirmed what Floridians already knew.

Effects of World War II

Despite the lean years, Florida's population had grown to around 2 million by 1940. This number was supplemented by another 3 million tourists annually. World War II stimulated the economy with defense-related industry, road-building, and new and revitalized naval bases. After the war, servicemen who trained on the beaches of Daytona, Miami and St. Petersburg returned to find jobs or enroll in Florida colleges under the GI bill. The economy diversified. Frozen citrus juice concentrates became a major industry. In 1950, the US inaugurated a long-range, missile-testing program at Cape Canaveral, followed by a new space satellite program eight years later.

After World War II, a strong Florida government made efforts to bring corporate industry to the state. Millions of people began to vacation here as the two-week paid vacation became standard. To accommodate them, more new hotels appeared in Greater Miami between 1945 and 1954 than in all the other US states combined. In 1958 the first US domestic jet service, from New York to Miami, opened the way for more tourists. Highway travel increased, too, and with it small attractions—featuring everything from alligators to mermaids—mushroomed along the Florida roadside. These private businesses were the forerunners of corporate theme parks, including the Disney empire. Today, some 85 million visitors come to Florida each year.

During the same period, Florida hosted another growing population: foreign refugees. Most notably, the 1959 Cuban Revolution sent waves of exiles into Dade County in that year and again in 1961. Between 1965 and 1973, a series of Cuban government-controlled airlifts—"Freedom Flights"—carried thousands more refugees to Florida. In 1980 the Cuban government again allowed emigration. This time, more than 125,000 residents of the port of Mariel, among them criminals released from Cuban prisons, landed on Miami's shores.

Florida Today

Only a few decades ago, Florida was seen as a region of infinite potential. "So many of Florida's resources are as yet undeveloped, so much wealth lies hidden in her soil, so great an area of wilderness beauty is yet to be discovered and appreciated," boasted a 1930 promotional booklet. Many would argue that during the next half-century, those same resources were not only overdeveloped, but exhausted. The boom cycles, transportation advancements and population influxes that define Florida history also brought the inevitable housing complexes, strip malls, high-rise beach developments and traffic jams—making it difficult to believe that the peninsula was a beckoning frontier as recently as the early 20C. The state's proximity to South America means that much of the US illegal drug trade filters through Florida. The influx of Cuban exiles, Haitians, Nicaraguans, Jamaicans, Hondurans and many other groups continues. Another type of immigrant—northern retirees—has also made an indelible mark on the Florida landscape, boosting the economy yet crowding roads and towns.

Florida's aesthetic resources still abound—its sunshine remains reliable, its palm trees still wave in ocean breezes—and in recent decades a trend toward preserving them has emerged. An effort to restore natural water flow to the Everglades by removing man-made locks and spillways is reviving habitat for more than 60 threatened and endangered species, as well as providing flood control and a reliable water supply to Southern Florida. In 2008 the state bought 187,000 acres of land abutting the 'Glades from the US Sugar Corporation, one of the biggest such state-led enviromental conservation projects ever. The good news is that phosphorous concentrations in Everglades waters have been reduced to 12 parts per billion, compared to 170 parts per billion a decade ago, but much remains to be done to restore America's River of Grass.

Unchecked urban sprawl has long been a Florida problem, affecting quality of life and the environment. A 2005 study by urban planners ranked Miami among the worst sprawling communities nationwide. Strip malls and condo complexes continue to sprout like weeds on undeveloped tracts of land, diminishing the appeal of areas such as the Keys and other pockets of Old Florida. Maintaining a balance between tourism, growth, and preserving the character and environment of the state will continue to challenge the leaders of the Sunshine State.

Time Line

10,000–8,000 BC First migration of prehistoric Indians to the Florida peninsula.

5000 BC First semi-permanent Native American settlements in Florida.

1492 Christopher Columbus lands in the region of the present-day Bahamas.

1513 Spanish explorer **Juan Ponce de León** lands in the area of present-day St. Augustine and names the land *"La Florida."*

1521 Ponce de León returns to the southwestern coast of the Florida peninsula and attempts to establish a colony.

1528 Explorer **Pánfilo de Narváez** goes ashore at Tampa Bay and marches to Apalachee in search of gold.

1539–1541 Conquistador **Hernando de Soto** explores the Florida interior, trekking north and west into the continent.

1559 Spanish nobleman **Tristán de Luna** attempts to establish a settlement at Pensacola Bay.

1562 French Protestant **Jean Ribault** explores the banks of the St. Johns River as a possible site for a Huguenot colony; led by René de Laudonnière, the colony is established in 1564.

1565 **Pedro Menéndez de Avilés** founds San Augustine, the first permanent European settlement in America.

1672 Work begins on the **Castillo de San Marcos** at St. Augustine, the first stone fort built by the Spanish in Florida.

1702 British colonel James Moore destroys St. Augustine but fails to capture the Castillo de San Marcos. Britain begins attacks on Spanish missions two years later.

1719 French soldiers capture Pensacola but soon return the colony to Spain. France occupies the Gulf Coast west of Pensacola.

1720s First migration of Creek groups— later called the Seminoles and **Miccosukee**—from Georgia into Florida.

1740 The British military invades Florida from Georgia.

1763 **Treaty of Paris** ends the Seven Years War (1756–63) between Britain and France. Britain gains Florida from Spain and splits the region into two provinces divided by the Apalachicola River.

1768 Minorcan, Italian and Greek colonists establish a colony at New Smyrna.

1781 Spanish recapture Pensacola from the British.

1783 The **Second Treaty of Paris** ends the American Revolution. Florida returns to Spanish control.

1814 Driven from their land in Alabama, homeless Creeks migrate to Florida, doubling the territory's Indian population.

1817–1818 Gen. Andrew Jackson initiates raids against the Seminoles, later known as the **First Seminole War**.

1821 Spain gains the Texas territory and relinquishes Florida to the US under the terms of the **Adams-Onís Treaty**. Jackson is elected the first governor of the two Florida colonies.

1822 President James Monroe unifies East and West Florida into one territory and settlement begins. Jacksonville is founded.

1824 Tallahassee is chosen as the state capital. Key West becomes a US naval station.

1827 The first steamboat service is established on the Apalachicola River.

1830 President Andrew Jackson signs the **Indian Removal Act** authorizing the relocation of eastern tribes to an area west of the Mississippi River.

1831 First cigar factory built in Key West.

1832 US claims Seminole lands in Florida under the **Treaty of Payne's Landing**.

1834 Florida's first railroad, the mule-drawn Tallahassee-St. Mark's line, is incorporated.

1835–1842 US military forces and Florida Indians clash in the **Second Seminole War**. At least 3,000 Indians and blacks are relocated to Arkansas; the Kissimmee area is opened to white settlement.

1837 Seminole leader **Osceola** is imprisoned under a flag of truce at a St. Augustine army base.

1838 Osceola dies at age 34 in a South Carolina dungeon. First Constitutional Convention held in St. Joseph (Port St. Joe).

1845 Florida becomes the 27th US state under President John Tyler. William D. Moseley is elected the first governor.

1849 The first commercial sponge market opens in Key West.

1855 Under Florida's **Internal Improvement Act**, undeveloped Florida land is made available to investors.

1855–1858 Billy Bowlegs—the last chief under whom all Seminoles were united—leads the Indian resistance in the **Third Seminole War**.

1860 The first east-west Florida railroad, linking Cedar Key with Fernandina Beach, is completed.

1861 Florida secedes from the Union.

1864 Confederate troops win the **Battle of Olustee** near Lake City, Florida, preserving interior supply lines to Georgia.

1865 Florida militia repulse Union forces at **Natural Bridge**, saving Tallahassee from capture.

1868 New Florida constitution is adopted.

1875 The city of Orlando is incorporated.

1881 Philadelphia industrialist **Hamilton Disston** buys four million acres of land in central Florida and begins the first private land development in the state.

1885 **Henry Flagler** begins building a rail line between Jacksonville and St. Augustine and establishes the Florida East Coast Railway.

1886 Fire destroys the entire commercial district of Key West. Labor disputes cause the cigar industry to relocate from Key West to Tampa.

1894–1895 Winter freezes destroy citrus crops in central and north Florida and force the citrus industry to move south.

1896 In April, Flagler extends railroad to Miami; three months later, the City of Miami is incorporated.

1898 Embarkation camps for American troops are established in Tampa, Miami and Jacksonville during the **Spanish-American War**.

1906 Drainage of the Everglades begins, spearheaded by Florida governor Napoleon Bonaparte Broward.

1912 Flagler's **Overseas Railroad** from Homestead (near Miami) to Key West is completed.

1917–1918 World War I soldiers and aviators train in Florida.

1926 Miami takes a direct hit from a deadly September hurricane.

1927 Pan American Airways inaugurates commercial service with a flight from Key West to Havana, Cuba.

1928 The Tamiami Trail (US-41) across the Everglades is opened.

1929 A Mediterranean fruit-fly infestation destroys citrus crops in 20 central Florida counties.

1935 A devastating Labor Day hurricane batters Key West, destroying the Overseas Railroad.

1941–1945 Defense-related industry boosts the Florida economy during **World War II**.

1947 President Harry S. Truman dedicates **Everglades National Park**.

1950 Frozen citrus concentrates become a major Florida business. US inaugurates long-range missile-testing program at Cape Canaveral.

1954 The Sunshine Skyway bridge connects St. Petersburg with Manatee County to the south.

1955 Florida legislature authorizes the construction of a turnpike to run the length of the state.

1958 Newly formed National Aeronautics and Space Administration (NASA) begins operations at Cape Canaveral and launches first US satellite.

1959 The first regularly scheduled domestic jet flights begin between New York and Miami.

1959–1962 Thousands of refugees flee Cuba for Florida to escape Fidel Castro's communist regime.

1962 The first black students are admitted to undergraduate schools at Florida State University and the University of Florida.

1969 On July 16, the first manned moon launch lifts off from Cape Kennedy.

1972 Miami Beach hosts both the Democratic and Republican national conventions.

1972 The Miami Dolphins football team wins all its games—still the only undefeated team in NFL history.

1973 Freedom flights from Cuba to Miami end after bringing over 250,000 refugees to the US.

1979 The Miami Beach Art Deco district is designated a National Register Historic District.

1980 Some 125,000 Cuban refugees land in Miami. Riots erupt in Miami after four white policemen are acquitted in the beating to death of a black man.

1981 On April 12, the Kennedy Space Center launches the first space shuttle, Columbia.

1983 A Christmas freeze strikes central Florida citrus groves; losses exceed $1 billion.

1989 Serial killer Theodore Bundy—who confessed to 31 murders in nine states—is executed in Florida's electric chair.

1990 Senator Gwen Margolis, a Democrat from Miami Beach, is elected first woman president of the Florida Senate.

1992 **Hurricane Andrew** smashes into Dade County on August 24, sending 80,000 citizens into shelters.

1993 President Clinton names Janet Reno, State Attorney of Dade County, as US Attorney General. Nine foreign tourists are murdered in Florida within 12 months.

1994 Florida Legislature passes the **Everglades Forever Act**, authorizing removal of agricultural pollutants from the area's waters.

1995 Hurricane Opal wreaks havoc along the Panhandle coast in October.

1996 Vice President Al Gore announces a comprehensive seven-year plan to restore the Everglades ecosystem in south Florida.

1998 Environmental advocate **Marjory Stoneman Douglas**, champion of the Everglades, dies at the age of 108. Major grass fires ravage northeast Florida, forcing 70,000 residents to evacuate their homes.

2000 The state holds the outcome of US presidential elections in the balance for six weeks as its ballots are painstakingly recounted. Florida's secretary of state reads the final tally, with George W. Bush receiving the majority of votes. The Supreme Court declares Bush the next president.

2001 By summer's end, 24 of the 42 shark attacks worldwide occur off Florida's coast, several at New Smyrna Beach.

2004 Hurricane Charlie makes landfall, with wind gusts topping 180mph in Punta Gorda, during one of Florida's deadliest hurricane seasons, causing $13 billion worth of damage.

2008–2009 After the the onset of the US banking and investment financial crisis, Florida leads the nation in foreclosure rates, with deep and long-lasting effects on real estate. Housing prices in South Florida plummet more than 50 percent.

2011 Naples businessman Rick Scott is inaugurated as Florida's 45th governor.

Art and Architecture

Visual Arts

A number of 19C painters visited Florida and captured its sun-drenched landscapes on canvas. Among them were Boston artist **William Morris Hunt** (1824–1879), who sought Florida's subtropical climate in 1873 as a balm for his jangled nerves; and British painter **Thomas Moran** (1837–1926), who chose Fort George Island to illustrate an issue of *Scribner's Monthly*.

Honoring those who have made significant contributions in the state, the Florida **Artists Hall of Fame** recognizes several nationally and internationally famous artists, including **Robert Rauschenberg**, a modern experimental painter who lived off and on in Florida for many years. The abstract expressionist creations of **Hiram Williams**, a former University of Florida faculty member, earned him a national reputation. Also at the University of Florida, surrealist photographer **Jerry Uelsmann** has exerted a widespread influence on his field.

West Palm Beach's **Norton Museum of Art** and the **Key West Museum of Art & History** are among museums with fine collections of art by Floridians.

Performing Arts

Florida's performing arts have also blossomed in the last few decades. Since the founding of the **Greater Miami Opera** in 1941, six more companies have sprung up around the state. Florida now offers nearly 80 theater companies as well as more than 30 dance groups, including the **Miami City Ballet**

Most of Florida's major cities have professional symphony orchestras, and numerous regional and university music ensembles present frequent concerts. The **Florida West Coast Symphony** performs for audiences in Bradenton and Sarasota. Florida's official teaching festival, the **Sarasota Music Festival** takes place every June, attracting talented young professionals from around the world. Young musicians (aged 21–30) also fill the ranks of the Miami Beach-based **New World Symphony.** Moving up the coast, the **Florida Philharmonic Orchestra** plays in Fort Lauderdale and southeast Florida.

Fueled by the success of singer **Gloria Estefan** and her producer-husband Emilio, Miami Beach has become the national capital for the Latin music boom. The Estefans' Sony Building in the Art Deco Historic District has full music- and video-production facilities. Another longtime Florida resident is singer-songwriter **Jimmy Buffett**, whose vagabond-sailor persona has beguiled an international following.

Film and Television

Famous for its theme parks that celebrate film and TV, Florida has carved out a solid niche for itself in the **movie industry**. After years of providing the jungle backdrop for such early films (1940s and 50s) as the Tarzan series and the *Creature from the Black Lagoon*, Florida welcomed Universal and Disney-MGM studios in the late 1980s. Recent big-budget pictures filmed in Florida include *There's Something About Mary*, *Ocean's 11*, *The Truman Show* and *Miami Vice*. Over the years, the state has also hosted a number of television series, including *Flipper*, *Miami Vice*, *SeaQuest*, *CSI: Miami* and several Latin soap operas.

Folk Arts

Ethnic and regional **folk arts** are kept alive through numerous festivals, apprenticeships and grants. The annual Florida Folk Festival, held each May at the **Stephen Foster State Folk Culture Center** in White Springs, illustrates regional folklife through music, dancing and farm crafts. Namesake of the Folk Culture Center, Pennsylvania-born composer **Stephen Collins Foster** (1826–1864) immortalized Florida's Suwannee River in his 1851 song *Old Folks At Home*. In 1935 this folk tune was officially designated as the state song.

Florida hands out $32 million every year in grants to artists, many of whom preserve ethnic folklife traditions. **Cubans** in Key West, Miami and Tampa's Ybor City make woodcarvings and *guayaberas*—shirts decorated with pleating and embroidery. Caribbean transplants continue a rich maritime craft tradition with handmade boats, sails and fishing gear. **Greeks**, who have maintained a presence in Tarpon Springs since the early 20C, bring their own nautical arts to modern Florida, along with sponge diving, Greek dance, colorful embroidery and music.

South Florida is home to tribes of **Seminole** and **Miccosukee** Indians, who still craft bracelets, bead necklaces, palmetto-fiber dolls, pine-needle and sweet-grass baskets, and dazzling calico clothing. The latter features colorful patchwork designs suggesting lightning, arrows, diamonds and other symbols. These wares are available in reservation gift shops in the Everglades' Miccosukee Indian Village and Ah-Tha-Thi-Ki Museum.

Architecture

Florida claims a remarkably rich and diverse heritage of building traditions incorporating the practical, the outrageous, the witty and the bizarre in equal measure. A strong Mediterranean current has run through the architectural landscape here ever since 17C Spanish colonization. The tropical terrain and climate also influenced early design and continue to do so today.

Historic Structures

The traditional dwelling of the Miccosukee and Seminole tribes was the **chickee**, an open-air shelter framed with rot-resistant cypress poles and thatched with palmetto fronds. Well-adapted to the swampy glades where the tribes hid their camps, the practical structures featured a platform floor of split logs or sawn boards elevated about 3ft off the ground to provide protection from snakes, alligators and flood tides.

Shotgun houses served as cheap housing for laborers along the Gulf Coast in South Florida's early Bahamian settlements. This narrow one-room-wide structure with a long row of back-to-back rooms is thought to be an African form that evolved on Haitian sugar plantations. It was said that if a shotgun were fired through the front door, the load would pass straight through the line of rooms and out the back door. Built from the 1830s to 1920s, the **Conch house** of Key West is named for the Bahamian islanders—colloquially known as "Conchs"—who settled in the Keys in the 19C. The one- or two-story clapboard Conch house is usually raised on stone or brick piers and topped by a peaked roof (shingled or tin) with the gable end facing front; louvered blinds at the doors and windows block the heat of the fierce tropical sun. The first **plantation houses** built after Florida became a US Territory in 1821 were unpretentious two-story, wood-frame structures. In the antebellum years these were replaced by imposing **Greek Revival** mansions fronted by columned two-story porches. Dating from the late 19C, when many citrus and railroad fortunes were made, elaborate **Queen Anne** houses—featuring asymmetrical facades, turrets, ample verandas, recessed balconies, gingerbread trim, spindles, turned railings and decorated gables—are common.

20th Century

The building boom of the early 20C coincided with the rise of the **Mediterranean Revival** style, which borrowed loosely from medieval Moorish and Spanish architecture. Pastel-colored stucco walls, red-clay roof tiles, arcaded loggias, towers, arched windows and ornate wrought-iron detailing not only suited Florida's tropical landscape, but also "…express[ed] the spirit of a land dedicated to long, carefree vacations," as a 1925 issue of *House Beautiful* described it. The style became the unifying design theme for dozens of Florida's boom-era developments, including Carl Fisher's Miami Beach, George Merrick's model suburb Coral Gables, and Addison Mizner's 1,600-acre architectural playground, Boca Raton. Perhaps the most distinctive symbols of Florida's heyday are the great resort hotels of the pre-Depression era. The tradition of extravagant hospitality

catering to affluent northerners started in the late 19C. The friendly rivalry of railroad magnates Henry Bradley Plant and Henry Morrison Flagler extended to gigantic (and often unprofitable) hotels located at each major railhead. Flagler's massive Royal Poinciana, in Palm Beach, at its greatest extent at the turn of the 20C, its 1,800-foot length and accommodations for 2,000 guests made it the world's largest wood structure. Victorian hotels declined in popularity in the Great Depression, however, and the Royal Poinciana met an ignominious end when it was bulldozed in 1935. A second wave of expensive resorts reached its peak in the 1920s. By this time, the **Mediterranean Revival** style was considered the apex of architectural design, and most of these enormous structures were built of masonry, adorned with decorative tiles, stone carvings, frescoes and woodwork. While many of the hotels fell into disrepair after the economic crash of 1926, a recent restoration movement has returned a few choice examples to their original luster. Examples include the majestic Coral Gables **Biltmore Hotel**, the Palm Beach Breakers Hotel, the Brazilian Court Hotel, also in Palm Beach, and Mizner's **Cloister Inn** in Boca Raton. The first widely popular style in the US to purposely break with traditional historical revivals, and a light-filled reaction to the dark ambience of Victorian design, **Art Deco** transformed hundreds of gas stations, diners, theaters, houses, hotels, motel courts and storefronts across the US into eye-catching streamlined designs between the late 1920s and the 1940s. An offshoot of the **International Style** with its simple forms and austere surfaces, Deco adopted the sleek lines, cubic massing and new materials of the technology-oriented modernist aesthetic that was emerging in Europe after World War I. Rather than reject ornament, as pure modernists did, Florida's Art Deco designers, like their California counterparts, embraced fanciful decoration wholeheartedly—in particular exotic motifs (palmettos, chevrons and ziggurats) inspired by ancient Egyptian, Aztec and Mayan design. A later phase of Art Deco, called **Streamline Moderne**, took on an even more futuristic look incorporating new materials. Beginning in the 1930s, buildings were stripped of surface decoration and angular elevations were smoothed with rounded vers, horizontal bands ("speed lines") and porthole windows inspired by contemporary streamlined trains, planes and ocean liners. New mass-produced materials—steel, chrome, glass block and concrete block—made it possible to build quickly and cheaply, but stylishly. These benefits proved a plus for developers of post-war boom towns like Miami Beach. "America's Riviera" now possesses the largest and best-preserved concentration of Art Deco and Streamline Moderne buildings in the world,

more than 800 in all. The city's oceanfront South Beach area is now a National Historic Landmark district, with a stupendous collection of Mediterranean Revival, Art Deco and Streamline Moderne buildings all jumbled together. The area's designation as a historic landmark in 1979 is credited with spurring its revitalization into perhaps the best-known nightclub, dining and people-watching district in the US. A stroll along Ocean Drive and Collins Street will take the visitor past a dazzling array of pink, sunflower, vermilion and glass-block buildings.

By the 1950s Florida was better known for its glitzy resort architecture, most notably **Morris Lapidus**' stupendous movie-set Miami Beach hotels, such as the Fontainebleau and the Eden Roc. More recently renowned modern architects such as Frank Gehry have helped make Florida's metropolitan skylines as sophisticated as any in the US. Downtown Miami boasts landmarks by I.M. Pei (International Place, 1985), Skidmore, Owings & Merrill (First Union Financial Center, 1984) and John Burgee and Philip Johnson (Miami-Dade Cultural Center, 1982). Florida's best-known architectural firm, Miami's **Arquitectonica**, features witty, brash designs incorporating both high-tech and historical references rendered in bold geometry and bright colors. Their work—described by critics as "beach blanket Bauhaus"— includes the exuberant Miracle Center Mall in Coral Gables as well as three extravagant luxury apartment towers erected during Miami's "Mondo-Condo" building boom of the early 1980s: the Palace, the 21-story Atlantis, and the Imperial.

Florida is also the original home of the **New Urbanist** movement, which emphasizes human scale, historical references and the relationship of a building to its neighbors. The nostalgic pastel wood-frame buildings intentionally recall Florida's 19C pioneer houses. More than 100 Florida areas labeled New Urbanist can be found from Port Richey to Fort Lauderdale, including Mirabella, CODA and Hammon Park on the Atlantic Coast.

DESIGNED TO LIVE

Miami might be forever associated with Art Deco architecture, but don't expect the city to look dated. In fact, in the last decade, the city has been almost overrun by new construction from celebrity architects such as Frank Gehry, Enrique Norten and Jacques Herzog and Pierre de Meuron. There is designer architecture in cultural hubs like Gehry's New World Center, which is home to symphony. But the modern architectural influence is everywhere. Case in point: you can even park your car in a designer parking structure; both Erique Norten and Herzog & de Meuron have recently put their names to buildings at Park 420 and 1111 Lincoln, respectively.

WHAT TO WATCH

Los Angeles and New York may dominate the movie landscape these days, but Miami has been the location of some of the most famous and memorable movies in cinematic history.

Comedy lovers will know Miami as a common backdrop from their favorite films. When Tony Curtis and Jack Lemmon were running from the mob in *Some Like It Hot*, it was Miami where the two men—dressed in drag—found sanctuary and a sultry Monroe. More recently, another blonde, this time played by Cameron Diaz, was the object of Ben Stiller's desire in the Miami-based comedy, *There's Something about Mary*. Other South Florida comedies include, *Marley and Me* (West Palm Beach and Fort Lauderdale), *The Birdcage* (South Beach), and *Ace Ventura: Pet Detective*, (Miami) starring Jim Carrey.

Miami is also the setting for plenty of **mobster** movies, perhaps owing to its Mafia history. Most famously, the city is one of the settings for Francis Ford Coppola's *The Godfather: Part II*, with Miami Beach playing the home of Jewish Gangster Hyman Roth, with whom Michael Corleone (Al Pacino) engages in a deadly battle of wills. Pacino returns to Miami as an entirely different type of gangster in the legendary *Scarface*, playing Tony Montana the Cuban drug kingpin.

Mobsters aren't the only cinematic hardmen drawn to the Magic City. Miami is one of **James Bond**'s favorite cinema haunts. Two of Bond's earliest films, starring Sean Connery, were set in Miami. Bond trails villain Auric Goldfinger on Miami Beach in *Goldfinger*, the movie in which Shirley Eaton is famously killed as she is entombed in liquid gold. In *Thunderball*, Bond tracked down two atomic bombs stolen by SPECTRE, which were aimed at… you guessed it…Miami. When the Bond franchise was rebooted in 2006, a new Bond, Daniel Craig, returned to Miami in *Casino Royale*, stopping a terrorist attack on Miami International Airport. But James Bond isn't the only spy to save Miami. Arnold Schwarzenegger's secret agent in the movie *True Lies* is a Miami-native and in the film's climactic scene he saves his home town from nuclear annihilation.

Maybe it's the humidity, but Miami is also a common location for steamy **neo-noir** film thrillers. Movies like the *Lady in Cement*, *Blood and Wine*, *Body Heat* and *Wild Things* all use Miami as the set for their stories of crime and punishment.

Move over *Miami Vice* and the *Golden Girls*. The city's had quite a presence on the **small screen** in recent years, with TV shows like *Dexter*, *Burn Notice*, and *CSI: Miami*. The sultry weather year-round and access to remote, swampy areas make it a writer's room playground for TV crime dramas. Miami is also a mecca for **Latin** television and film production.

Literature

Early Voices

Naturalists were among the first visitors to chronicle Florida. Appointed "Royal Botanist of the Floridas" by King George III, **John Bartram** (1699–1777) traveled from Philadelphia into the tropical wilderness in 1765–66, documenting unknown species of flora and fauna in *A Description of East Florida* (1769). His son William Bartram followed with *Travels Through North and South Carolina, Georgia, East and West Florida* in 1791.During the 19C, magazine fiction and travel stories constituted a major body of Florida writing. In the 1830s and 40s, the monthlies *Knicker-bocker* and *Graham's* published Florida adventure tales by such popular figures as **Washington Irving** and **James Fenimore Cooper**. In 1897 **Stephen Crane** (1871–1900), author of *The Red Badge of Courage* (1896) and a brief resident of Jacksonville, wrote The Open Boat. This dramatic story was based on a shipwreck he survived off New Smyrna Beach on his way to Cuba to fight in the Spanish-American War. Contemporary travel guides were pivotal in bringing settlers and tourists to Florida. Among the classics now coveted by collectors are *Florida for Tourists, Invalids, and Settlers* (1881) by George Barbour (a phenomenal bestseller in its day) and *Florida: Its Scenery, Climate, and History* (1875) by the acclaimed southern poet **Sydney Lanier** (1842–1881).

Black Voices

Black writers have helped shape the state's literary tradition. Eatonville's master storyteller **Zora Neale Hurston** (1891–1960) is acclaimed for fiction and essays that celebrate black culture and bespeak the honest values of rural southern life: they include the autobiographical *Dust Tracks On A Road* (1942) and *Their Eyes Were Watching God* (1937), considered one of the first 20C black feminist novels.

Remaining unspoiled well into the 20C, the rugged beauty of backwoods Florida captivated many northern writers, including **Marjorie Kinnan Rawlings** (1896–1953). Rawlings settled in the hamlet of Cross Creek in 1928, and shaped many of her novels and stories around characters and settings inspired by her rural surroundings. The 1938 classic *The Yearling*—the story of a young boy and his pet deer in the Big Scrub (now Ocala National Forest)—won a Pulitzer Prize in 1939. Other Florida-inspired Rawlings titles include *South Moon Under* (1933) and *Cross Creek* (1942). A longtime resident of Coconut Grove, **Marjory**

Stoneman Douglas (1890–1998) arrived in Miami in 1915 and became one of the state's first environmentalists. Her 1947 volume, *The Everglades: River of Grass*, remains an eloquent warning against the exploitation of this imperiled natural resource.

During the 1930s and 40s, America's then-Poet Laureate **Robert Frost** (1874–1963) taught at the University of Miami's Winter Institute of Literature.

Call of the Keys

Key West's sultry atmosphere also proved a magnet for writers. **Wallace Stevens** (1879–1955), who frequented the island on his yearly travels south from Connecticut, touted the tropical lushness of South Florida in his poetry anthology, *Harmonium* (1923). **Ernest Hemingway**, Florida's favorite literary son, spent most of the 1930s in Key West (and several local nightclubs still tout his attendance at their bars). Among the many works he wrote there, *To Have and Have Not* (1937) evokes the dignity and despair of the Depression-era life in the then-hard-bitten fishing village. Hemingway's fascination with the physical and intellectual challenge of deep-sea fishing and boating was later reflected in *The Old Man and the Sea* (1952) and his posthumously published novel, *Islands in the Stream* (1970).

Among the plays **Tennessee Williams** (1911–1983) wrote in his Duncan Street studio were *The Rose Tattoo* (1950) and *Night of the Iguana* (1961). Other well-known literary figures attracted to Key West include; Thornton Wilder, who penned *The Matchmaker* there in 1954; poet and playwright Archibald MacLeish; humorist S.J. Perelman; and poet Richard Wilbur. Controversial author and celebrity **Truman Capote**, one of America's first openly gay public figures, is still notorious in Key West for his frequent scuffles with sailors in local bars when he went out drinking dressed in drag. Contemporary Key West writers include Thomas McGuane (whose 1978 novel *Panama* is set in Key West).

... and Beyond

Elsewhere in Florida, mystery writer and former Sarasota resident **John D. MacDonald** (1916–1986), author of *Condominium* (1977) and *The Lonely Silver Rain* (1985), used Florida's Gold Coast for the exploits of his philosophical private eye, Travis McGee. Carl Hiaasen, Gore Vidal and Alison Lurie number among the other writers and essayists attracted to the Sunshine State. Humorist **Dave Barry**, a former columnist for the *Miami Herald*, has enjoyed great popularity nationwide for his chronicling of the foibles of life in South Florida.

WELCOME TO MIAMI AND THE KEYS

Nature and Environment

Florida is surrounded by the sea: 1,197 mi of coastline give the Sunshine State the second largest coastal area in the US after Alaska. To the east lies the Atlantic Ocean, to the south, the Straits of Florida, and to the west, the Gulf of Mexico. On land, to the north and northwest, lie Georgia and Alabama, whose narrow corridor to the Gulf Coast reaches around Florida's extreme northwestern border along the Perdido River. Thanks to the state's peninsular shape, no point is more than 80mi from salt water. Land elevations vary only slightly; the highest point above sea level, found in the Panhandle, is just 345ft. Ranking 22nd in land mass, the state comprises 59,988sq mi, of which 5,991sq mi is water. Florida has more lakes than any US state south of Wisconsin, with an estimated 30,000 lakes, including Lake Okeechobee, the nation's third-largest freshwater lake. Most of the lakes are natural, many the result of sinkholes. Nearly a quarter of the nation's first-magnitude springs (those that discharge 64.6 million gallons or more of water per day) surface in Florida.

Geologic Foundations

Lacking the telltale exposed strata of eroded mountain outcrops, Florida reveals its geology much less readily than other states. Early efforts at peering into the geological past were mainly a side benefit from deep well borings and other commercial explorations below the land surface. The evidence amassed by earth scientists over the years has helped sketch a composite portrait of what is probably the youngest region in the continental US—that is, the last to emerge from a primordial, subtropical sea only ten to 15 million years ago.

Origins

During the late Paleozoic era, Florida was part of the supercontinent Pangea, a C-shaped, crustal conglomerate formed by the earth's colliding major landmasses some 280 million years ago. Straddling the equator, Pangea split along a north-south axis 130 million years later and began to break up into the modern continents of Eurasia, Africa, North and South America, Antarctica and Australia. The Atlantic Ocean was born as the larger continental plates drifted away from the sea's mid-ocean ridge. Precambrian Florida was one of the many terranes, or smaller crustal pieces, set afloat among the larger continents. Tracking northwards, it was grafted onto the much larger North American plate at a time when a chain of volcanic islands erupted off the mainland and arced into what are now the Bahamas.

Over time balmy shallow seas covered this bedrock. While dinosaurs roamed the great landmass to the north, silts and clays washed down from the Appalachian Mountains and fanned out into extensive submarine deltas along Florida's northern shore. To the south, marine shells mixed with micro-scopic carbonate fragments accumulated in a massive layer of limestone and dolomite. In places 13,000ft to 18,000ft thick, these sedimentary rocks cover much of the Florida Plateau from the Gulf escarpment to the Atlantic Ocean.

During the late Oligocene, the plateau broke the surface of the sea. Florida's land area grew to up to twice its present-day size as Ice Age glaciers locked up more and more of the earth's water. During the early Pleistocene, this part of the continent became a haven for mammoths, mastodons, saber-toothed tigers, sloths and other large mammals retreating overland from the frozen north.

The Florida Plateau Today

As the continental ice sheets melted and refroze, the sea level rose and fell several times, etching successive terraces into an-cient shorelines that are still visible today. Though much the same size, the plateau now lies half submerged, its edges defin-ing the continental shelf which surrounds Florida at some 300ft below the sea. Deepwater harbors on the Gulf side result from a pronounced westward dip of the plateau that continues to this day: the plateau's surface rises about 6ft at Miami, and it tilts downward about 30ft at Pensacola.

Regional Landscapes

For the most part a flat terrain with sandy and clay soils, Florida holds within its boundaries an astonishing diversity of land-scapes, each exhibiting its own distinct characteristics. From hardwood forests to freshwater marshes, from coastal dunes and barrier islands to tropical coral reefs, the Sunshine State is home to a stunning collection of natural environments.

Central Highlands

The green spine of Florida runs down the middle of the penin-sula from the southernmost reaches of the Okefenokee Swamp (the swamp dips across the Georgia border into northeast Florida) for 250mi to Lake Okeechobee.

Though the northern section bulges to 60mi in width, the re-gion tapers to a point in the south, where it converges with the Everglades and the Coastal Lowlands. Characterized by longi-

tudinal ridges and upland plains and valleys, this region boasts thousands of lakes.

The world's heaviest concentration of **citrus trees** flourishes along a 100mi-long ridge (1mi to 25mi wide and 240ft high) from Leesburg to Sebring. Acclaimed science writer John McPhee noted that "The Ridge is the Florida Divide, the peninsular watershed, and, to hear Floridians describe it, the world's most stupendous mountain range after the Himalayas and the Andes..." This famous ridge reaches its pinnacle at 302ft Mount Sugarloaf. The thick limestone bedrock peters out south of Lake Okeechobee.

Coastal Lowlands

Harboring nearly all the state's major commercial, industrial and resort areas, the flat, low-lying areas rimming the peninsula spread inland as much as 60mi in some places and include the Florida Keys and the Everglades. Dominated by pastureland and extensive farming, the region's interior contrasts sharply with its glittering margins, where the state's environment-based tourism and recreational activities are focused.

Florida's fine quartz and calcium carbonate (shell fragments) sand makes dazzling white beaches. The oldest, finest—and purest quartz—sand, washed over the eons to a powdery texture, can be found on Florida's west coast near Sarasota and along the Panhandle coast.

Blessed with a gentle climate and warm Gulf and Atlantic waters, the state's coastal areas encompass a variety of natural environments. **Estuaries**, the most productive marine habitat in Florida, line nearly the entire coast where fresh water mingles with salt water. These shallow-water communities are vital for the development of a tremendous number of marine organisms. Another nursery for fish and shellfish, **mangrove swamps** edge the southeast and southwest coasts. More than 200 different types of fish and 180 bird species find habitat here, as do the endangered American crocodile and Florida manatee. Wind-blown **dunes** and their backdrop of **maritime forest** harbor sea oats and 22 other native plant species. Along both the Atlantic and Gulf coasts, strings of narrow, elongated sandy spits form protective **barrier islands** sheltering the mainland's many inlets, bays and estuaries. In addition to the periodic damage caused by hurricanes and violent winter storms, their ecological survival is severely tested by coastal development.

The Everglades

Considered a separate ecosystem, the broad expanse of the Everglades is covered by a shallow, slow-moving river that flows southward from Lake Okeechobee to the Florida Bay. Freshwater marshes, saw grass prairies, swamps and hardwood hammocks cover this depression.

The youngest part of Florida, the area south of Lake Okeechobee emerged from the sea upon built-up layers of live coral clinging to submerged oolitic limestone. With the eventual formation of sand dunes that sealed out the ocean, a new freshwater basin filled with marine plant life and eventually became the peat- and boglands that served as the forerunner to the Everglades—a territory unlike any other in the world.

Tropical Coral Reef

Vital to Florida's economy, **coral reefs** extend in a 150mi-long curve from near Miami to the Dry Tortugas, 69mi west of Key West. Commercial and recreational fishing industries depend on the reef ecosystems, as do diving and snorkeling enthusiasts. Found nowhere else in the continental US, these spectacular underwater worlds are composed of calcified limestone secreted by invertebrate coral polyps: the formations began some 7,000 years ago. Colorful fans, coral branches and plumes on the reef create intricate forests inhabited by diverse communities of tropical fish, sponges, spiny lobsters and other exotic sea creatures, making the Keys one of the world's most popular diving destinations.

Climate

Perhaps its most important natural resource, South Florida's gentle climate remains pleasant year-round. Conditions vary from tropical in the Keys to subtropical in the central region. Positioned at a more southerly latitude than any US state except Hawaii, Florida claims the country's highest average year-round temperatures, with Key West ranking as the hottest city at an average of 77.4°F. The warm Gulf Stream, which flows north up the Atlantic coast from the tropics, tempers the prevailing easterly wind that blows over the peninsula.

More than half the average annual rainfall (52in) falls between the beginning of June and the end of September (the month when most hurricanes occur). These hot, humid summers bring hordes of mosquitoes to the forests and marshes. Winter, the main tourist season, enjoys mild and relatively dry weather—especially in central and South Florida. Snow is very rare.

The combination of moist air and sun-heated land and water surfaces in Florida provides ideal conditions for the formation of **thunderstorms**. In fact, the state experiences more than anywhere in the world except East Africa. On summer days, hot air rises over the peninsula. When it meets with damp air from the

Gulf and the Atlantic, converging airstreams force air upward, where it condenses into towering thunderheads. Parts of South Florida have more than 90 storms a year.

Hurricanes

Florida lies in the path of intense tropical cyclones spawned in the Atlantic, the Caribbean and the Gulf of Mexico. Most common in August and September when weak low-pressure systems develop over warm water, hurricanes can measure upwards of 500mi in diameter and contain winds greater than 200mph (a tropical depression officially becomes a hurricane once its winds reach a speed of 74mph). These doughnut-shaped storms commonly churn across the Atlantic coast between Cape Canaveral and the Keys.

An average of one hurricane a year, usually of low or moderate intensity, strikes Florida. Several devastating storms have hit in this century; most recently, Hurricane Andrew mowed an 8mi swath across south Miami-Dade County in 1992, leaving in its wake 85 dead, 10,000 injured, and $30 billion in damage. An unprecedented four hurricanes—Charley, Frances, Ivan and Jeanne—hit Florida in 2004.

On the positive side, Florida's epic storms invigorate its natural environment. The combination of winds and heavy rains stirs up sediments and nutrients on the bottoms of bays and backwaters. When hurricanes level forests and other protective ground cover, sun-loving plants and small animals quickly exploit the newly available niches, regenerating the cycle of life.

Water Resources

Floridians have one of the highest per capita rates of water use in the country, thanks to the seemingly inexhaustible reserves of the **Floridan Aquifer**, the state's largest aquifer. Called "Florida's rain barrel," the Floridan underlies the entire state and varies in depth up to 2,000ft in the areas surrounding Jacksonville and Orlando. Along with the shallower **Biscayne Aquifer**, which serves southeast Florida, the Floridan provides nearly 90 percent of the state's water for drinking, recreation, irrigation and waste disposal.

One of the largest sources of surface water in the state, **Lake Okeechobee** (Seminole for "big water") supplies south Florida's cities and farms, as well as the Everglades. At 700sq mi it ranks as the state's largest lake. After Okeechobee inundated nearby farming communities as a result of hurricanes in 1926 and 1928, the US Army Corps of Engineers began taming the lake with a new system of canals, dikes, pumping stations and spillways. Now its waters can be manipulated to control flooding of sur-

rounding fields and towns. With an ever-increasing population n South Florida, Lake Okeechobee today lies at the heart of many complex land-use controversies, which pit environmentalists against the area's farmers.

Flora and Fauna

Dubbed by Ponce de León "Isle of Flowers" (for the Spanish *Pascua florida* Eastertime feast), Florida boasts an abundance of lush vegetation. Early botanists catalogued over 3,000 types of indigenous flowering plants, from tiny orchids to showy magnolias. Thousands of tropical and subtropical plants have been added to this total over the years. Symbol of a luxuriant lifestyle, the **palm** proliferates in Florida, which claims several hundred species—more than any other state. The only known trees that can survive in salt water, **mangroves** have received much attention in recent decades, rising in status from developers' nuisance to coastal guardian. Their cagelike root systems can stabilize a shoreline better than a seawall, as well as provide sanctuary for hundreds of species of fish. While the increasing human population continues to reduce available territory for wildlife, a conservation movement has arisen to protect Florida's wildlife habitat, which encompasses 100 species of mammals and more than 400 species and subspecies of birds.

At the coast you are likely to see bottle-nosed **dolphins**—a perennial favorite with visitors and residents—frolicking offshore. These sleek mammals frequent the shallow waters of the Gulf of Mexico as well as the Atlantic.

Perhaps the most easily observed animals, dozens of species of water birds make permanent or part-time homes in Florida. Of the species more likely to be found in Florida than anywhere else, the long-necked **anhinga** is known for its skill in spearing fish with its beak. Bird-watchers may also add **roseate spoonbills** to their must-see lists; sometimes mistaken for flamingos, spoonbills are also pink but much shorter than flamingoes with flat, spoon-shaped beaks. Florida provides haven to more than 67 species of threatened or endangered animals. Prominent on the endangered list are the reclusive **Florida panther**; the West Indian **manatee**; the diminutive **Key deer**; the **wood stork**, a wading bird once prevalent in mangrove and cypress swamps; and the **Florida sandhill crane**, another long-legged wader. The five kinds of **sea turtles** that nest in Florida are all either endangered or threatened; and the **American crocodile**, nearly extinct in the US, lives only in southern Florida.

Once hunted almost to extinction, **alligators** (which help control populations of snakes and small mammals) have enjoyed a renaissance in Florida and now number more than a million.

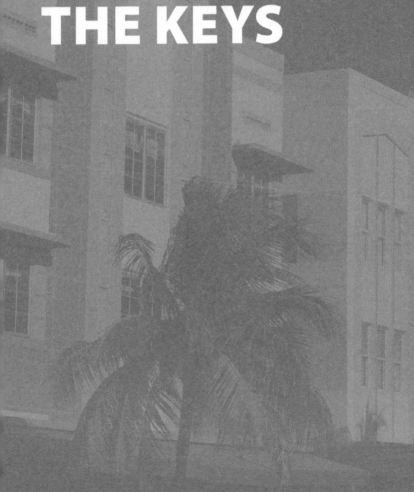

PLANNING
YOUR TRIP TO
MIAMI AND
THE KEYS

When to Go

ASK PETER...

Q: I'm heading to Florida in the winter; I can leave my sweater at home, right?
A: I know most people associate Florida with constant sun, but even in the Sunshine State it can get chilly in the winter months, especially first thing in the morning or at night. Florida is never northeast cold, but do check the forecast in case long sleeves or jackets are advised. Conversely, August is typically uncomfortably hot and humid, so pack accordingly.

In South Florida most sights and attractions are open ye round, although peak seasons vary. High season in Sou Florida is during the **winter** (Oct–Apr) when many visitors cape colder climates. Daytime winter temperatures avera 70°F/21°C, while in the Everglades and Keys daytime tempe tures reach 73°F/23°C. The traditional four seasons are son what evident in the central part of South Florida, as well as the Sarasota area. January is usually the coldest month. Wint when mosquitoes are tolerable and migratory birds are plenti is the best time to view wildlife in parks and reserves. Insect pellent is necessary year-round. Although **summer** months hot and humid throughout the region, sea breezes moder temperatures along the coasts. Daytime temperatures avera 88°F/31°C and daily afternoon showers are common betwe June and September. The **hurricane season** is June to Nove ber, with the greatest activity occurring from August to Octob Water temperatures are typically pleasant year-round, thou Gulf side waters cool a bit from November–March. Beaches crowded during school holidays, spring breaks and sumn vacation periods. Reduced admissions to sights are genera available for senior citizens, students and children under 12. Casual dress is accepted in most facilities, though only pool a beach-side cafes allow diners in beach garb. A few fine dini restaurants may request that men wear jackets, but rarely i tie required. A hat will come in handy while standing in li especially during the summer heat. A good sunscreen, even a cloudy day, and sunglasses are recommended.

Useful Websites

Visit Florida: ℘850-488-5607 or 888-735-2872 www.visitflorida.com. **Miami:** ℘305-539-3000 or 800-933-8448 www.miamiandbeaches.com. **Sarasota:** www.sarasota fl.org. **Naples region:** www.paradisecoast.com.

AVERAGE DAILY TEMPERATURES

	January	April	July	Octobe
Key West	69°F/21°C	78°F/26°C	84°F/29°C	80°F/27°
Miami	68°F/20°C	76°F/24°C	83°F/29°C	78°F/26°
Naples	65°F/19°C	73°F/23°C	82°F/28°C	77°F/25
Sarasota	60°F/16°C	72°F/22°C	83°F/29°C	75°F/24°

Travel, Dine and Explore with Confidence

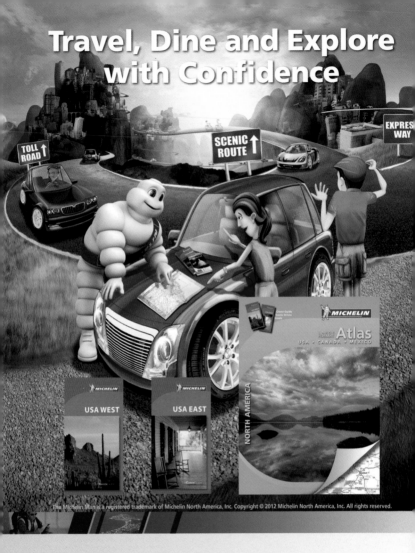

Michelin, experts in travel guides and maps for more than 100 years. Available wherever books are sold.

www.michelintravel.com

A better way forward

Where to Go

South Florida has such a huge choice of visitor attractions, both natural and man-made, plus other active things to do, that it's well worth carefully planning your trip in advance. Here are three popular ideas that most visitors will want to consider, plus our themed vacations tips and suggestions.

Short Breaks
Weekend in Miami
A weekend in the most vibrant city in Florida will just fly by. Take a tour of the Art Deco District in South Beach (SoBe) then spend the rest of the day on the beach and/or shopping on trendy Lincoln Road. Coconut Grove is a must-see neighborhood; don't miss Vizcaya, one of the finest estates in the US. Zoo Miami is a great half- or full-day out while Coral Castle intrigues all its visitors. By night dress to impress and return to glittering SoBe.

A Weekend at the Beach
There are scores to choose from, but why not listen to "Dr. Beach" and visit Sarasota's Siesta Key, nominated best in the USA in 2011 (👁see p12). Lapped by the Gulf of Mexico, in 1987 its sand was scientifically proven to be the world's finest, whitest beach sand! Popular with a youngish, laid-back crowd it has many amenities and can get busy, if it's too busy, adjacent Crescent Beach and Turtle Beach offer extra space and very similar quality. Sarasota is a perfect weekend break destination, with the fabulous Ringling Museum of Art by day and by night, the Van Wezel Performing Arts Hall, and the city's bars and clubs.

Miami to the Keys
It's 160 mi and just over 3hrs drive from Miami to Key West. But if you have time, take it easy and enjoy the sights en route.
First stop is Key Largo, not only the "Diving capital of the world", but great for those who snorkel too. Next in line is Islamorada, "Sportfishing capital of the world", though you don't *have* to catch 'em; swimming with dolphins (or just watching them) at two visitor attractions here is a thrill.
The engineering marvel that is the Seven Mile Bridge transports you to the peaceful Lower Keys where you might spot the tiny Key deer, or perhaps relax on the Keys' best Beach at Bahia Honda. End of the line is lush tropical Key West, a little bit of Cuba, a little bit of the Bahamas, pirates and shipwrecks and Hemingway aplenty, and partying way into the night.

ASK PETER...
Q: Hurricanes and Florida seem to have a long history; how can I protect myself?
A: First off, you can purchase travel insurance, which offers you protection during hurricanes. However, even if your flights are heavily disturbed, don't expect to see a refund if the airport is open and you can eventually get to your destination. Some tropical properties also have a "hurricane guarantee," which will cover you instead of travel insurance. However, in order for those guarantees to kick in, it must be considered a category 1 hurricane by the National Hurricane Center.

Themed Vacations

Budget Travel

In general, South Florida is more expensive than the north of the state. If you want your dollars to work hard for you, then it's probably best to avoid the Palm Beach area altogether and you may need to plan carefully if visiting Naples, the Sarasota area and the trendier parts of Miami. The good news is that there are cheap chain-hotels all over the South; for RV Parks and Camp-grounds visit *http://campflorida.com*.

Senior Travel

With its welcoming year-round climate, South Florida is a natural destination for senior travel; in fact many resorts and communities developed specifically with retirees in mind. Party places you may wish to avoid are Key West (particularly the Old Town) and South Beach, Miami, but even here, only a few blocks separate the trendiest nightclubs from snowbirds' holiday properties.

Solo Travel

Male and female solo travelers should head for Key West where the laid-back no-hassle lifestyle makes it easy to meet new friends. Key West is also a very gay-oriented destination.

Many parts of Miami Beach are also the buzzing kinds of place where you should be able to meet like-minded people quickly. The staid monied resorts of the Palm Beach area are probably unsuitable (unless you are of a certain age and income), as are many of the Gulf Beach resorts, which cater almost exclusively for families and couples.

Romantic Travel

Whether it's watching the famous Sunset Celebrations at Key West, cruising the elegant waterways of Fort Lauderdale or Naples, or walking barefoot along the powder-white sands of the Gulf beaches, you'll find romance pretty much all over South Florida. The Tahitian-like islands of Captiva and Sanibel are top of most lovers' lists.

Culinary Travel

Florida's many ethnic cuisines become more pronounced the further south you travel and Miami is an indispensible stop for Latin gourmets. Here you can taste Cuban, Italian, Colombian Argentine, Peruvian and Kosher cuisine, among many more styles. If you'd like a guided tour Miami Culinary Tours (*www.miamiculinarytours.com*) should satisy your taste buds.

Bahamian influences can be tasted in Key West, most notably in their seafood, and of course this is the home of the ubiquitous Key Lime Pie. Ironically traditional Floridian and "good ol' American comfort food" is not so easy to find; look for diners off the beaten trail.

Family Travel

The wonderful beaches of South Florida mean that most seaside places fall into the family travel category. However it is worth noting that children are probably best seen and not heard in certain enclaves in the Palm Beach area, and that Key West and South Beach are adult-oriented destinations. In terms of our top-ranked family-friendly visitor attractions (that is, with one or more stars) Miami is a good choice with Zoo Miami, Jungle Island, Monkey Jungle, Miami Seaquarium, Miami Science Museum. Fort Lauderdale also boasts a fine Museum of Discovery & Science, and Butterfly World, while West Palm Beach features Lion County Safari. If you do want to visit Walt Disney World, base yourself in or near Sarasota, which is within a two-hour drive. The Sarasota area also boasts arguably Florida's best beaches and some excellent attractions for older children.

Luxury Travel

You can find luxurious hideaways all over South Florida. Palm Beach and West Palm Beach are synonymous with deluxe vacations, but Sarasota, Naples, Fort Lauderdale and Fort Myers also boast their share of well-heeled visitors. In Miami, you can stay on glitzy South Beach alongside music and fashion magnates and execs, or rub shoulders with "old-world money" in elegant Coral Gables and Coconut Grove.

SPRING BREAK

You can't talk about Florida without mentioning spring break. Did you know that Florida was the original spring break destination? The tradition dates back to the 1930s when a college swim coach brought his team down to Fort Lauderdale to train in Casino Pool, the first Olympic-size pool in Florida. Soon the destination became a college swim meet spot and slowly it morphed into one big party. Fort Lauderdale and Daytona Beach may have been the original Florida spring break destinations, but these cities choose to crack down on underage drinking and noise violations. Today, Panama City remains Florida's main college spring break spot.

Sun Tips: Watch out for the sun. It's not just a sunburn you need to worry about, but sun stroke, also known as heat exhaustion or heat stroke. If you're spending a day sightseeing, dress lightly and wear sunscreen and a hat. Drink plenty of water and take frequent breaks in the shade or air conditioning. Signs of heat exhaustion are excessive sweating, dizziness, fainting, and nausea. If you feel any of those symptoms occur, move to a cooler place, sip cold water, and apply a cold compress.

Storm Safety Tips
♦ Take cover.
♦ Stay away from trees, metal objects, doors and windows.
♦ If riding in a vehicle, remain inside until the storm has passed.
♦ Avoid being in or near water.
♦ If in a boat, head for the nearest shore.
♦ Do not use electrical appliances, especially the telephone.

What to See and Do

Florida's sultry air is filled with the sound of music. Year-round outdoor concerts—often free—take place in local bandshells. Although you'll definitely encounter a fair share of Jimmy Buffett wannabes, you can often find good live jazz, folk music, country jazz, and bluegrass, even at the beach bars. If you're looking for international artists, **The Adrienne Arsht Center for the Performing Arts of Miami-Dade County** is a don't-miss venue. It is also home to the Florida Grand Opera, the Miami City Ballet, and the New World Symphony. The sophisticated little city of **Sarasota** is one of Florida's artiest enclaves, with several resident theater companies, the Sarasota Opera, and the Sarasota Film Society (sponsoring daily showings of foreign and art films). Sarasota's Van Wezel Performing Arts Hall hosts 200 or so performances a year, including rock concerts and Broadway shows. Florida's major arts festival is **Art Basel**, Miami Beach, a mammoth extravaganza of modern art featuring famous artists and promising unknowns (early Dec).

Outdoor Fun
National Parks, Seashores and Monuments
Huge areas of Florida are protected and include three national parks, two national seashores, three national forests and more than 100 state parks. **Camping** is permissible *(fees range from $10–$28)* at Everglades, Biscayne and Dry Tortugas national parks and Gulf Islands National Seashore *(www.recreation.gov)*. Most visitor centers offer interpretive exhibits, slide presentations and maps and picnic areas are provided at parks and seashores. In some cases, visitors can explore the surroundings on self-guided nature trails and participate in ranger-led hikes. **Boat rentals** may be available. Most park beaches do not have lifeguards. For detailed information, contact the individual park or visit the National Park Service website *(www.nps.gov)*.

State and Local Parks
Visitors can choose from an ever-expanding state park system, including nature preserves and historic landmarks. **State parks** are generally open year-round daily 8am–dusk. Entrance fees are usually $3.25–$5/vehicle (up to 8 people), $1/person when entering on foot or by bicycle. Camping fees vary according to season and location *(average $8–$19). For details of individual parks visit www.floridastateparks.org)*. **Local parks** are generally open year-round daily 8am–dusk and are free of charge.

Biking

Cycling is popular throughout the state, not least because of the flat terrain. The cooler months (Oct–May) are the best cycling "season" since summer temperatures and high humidity can make long rides a challenge. Bicycles are not allowed on highways, limited-access highways, expressways or some bridges. Beach areas on Captiva and Sanibel Islands, offer pleasant riding paths. For more information, visit *www.florida greenwaysandtrails.com*.

Fishing

Florida's rivers, lakes, ponds and wilderness waterways offer anglers some of the best fishing waters in the US. And you don't have to rent expensive boats to enjoy a day of fishing. Many coastal communities have public fishing piers where equipment can be rented from bait-and-tackle shops for a minimal fee. Fish camps along inland waterways offer boat and houseboat rentals and guided fishing trips for the whole family.

Miles of coastline on the Atlantic Ocean and Gulf of Mexico give the **saltwater** enthusiast the opportunity to catch more than 70 species of fish. Surf casting and bridge and pier fishing are popular, while boat-charter services can accommodate every level of expertise and budget. Many marinas rent boats ranging from canoes to pontoon boats. Most backcountry channels in the Gulf are unmarked, so consider enlisting the services of a local, licensed guide who can lead you to the best fishing spots.

There are some 33 species of **freshwater** fish in Florida. Residents and nonresidents must have a **fishing license**; anglers are not required to have both freshwater and saltwater licenses, unless they are taking both freshwater and saltwater species. Licenses can usually be obtained at sporting-goods stores. For all **fishing regulations**, licenses, limits, seasons, and lots more information, visit *www.myfwc.com*.

Deep-Sea Fishing – Many species can be found along the Florida Keys year-round, offering a great variety of offshore game fishing. Large "party boats" can take up to 20 people and offer half-day and full-day trips; the captain will change locations, according to where the fish are biting. Most boats have a fishing license and knowledgeable crew. Prices range from $80–$300/person and up.

Charter boats specializing in deep-sea sport fishing will appeal to the experienced fisherman who is looking to reel in sailfish, wahoo, tuna, kingfish and blue or white marlin. Charters are costly but include equipment, bait and fishing licenses.

Biking Safety Tips:

When riding a bicycle in an unfamiliar city, bike safety becomes even more important. It's not just about wearing a helmet, which is essential, it's about being comfortable on the bike and on the roads. Whenever possible choose protected bike lanes. Hotels or bike rentals should be able to guide you to the best route. Lastly, remember to stay alert, obey all traffic signs and don't drink and bike.

◆ Obey all traffic laws and ride single file.
◆ The law requires cyclists under 16 to wear a helmet.
◆ Do not travel at night.
◆ Do not use electrical appliances, such as a cell phone, or listen to music through headphones.

Golf Tip: Golfing getaways don't usually go hand-in-hand with budget travel. But there are ways to get more value out of your golf vacation. Like other areas of travel, the trick is to play when everyone else isn't—that is, during off-peak times. Many courses will drop their prices mid-morning, weekdays or late afternoon.

Golf

Ranked one of the nation's top golfing destinations, Florida boasts well over 1,200 golf courses, several designed by such legends as Jack Nicklaus and Arnold Palmer. Florida's balmy climate makes golf accessible year-round. Duffers can practice their driving and putting expertise at numerous public courses or watch professional golfers at one of the numerous tournaments that take place throughout the state.

Many hotels and resorts include golf facilities, and some private courses allow non-members to play. Numerous courses offer golf clinics and private instruction. Make reservations well ahead of time; teeing off during midday means less-crowded fairways and lower humidity. Greens fees average around $80 winter, $50 summer.

Tee Times USA (*www.teetimesusa.com*) will make reservations free of charge for tee times at more than 300 selected golf courses. Discount golf packages are also available. For more general information visit *www.visitflorida.com/golfing*.

Hiking

The best time to hike is from late fall to early spring when temperatures are cooler, humidity is lower, and the insect population is at its lowest ebb. Stay on marked trails; taking shortcuts is dangerous and can cause erosion. Obtain up-to-date weather forecasts; a sudden storm can flood trails in swampy areas. If hiking alone, notify someone of your destination and anticipated return time.

The USDA Forest Service and the Florida Trail Assn. maintain the 1,400mi **Florida National Scenic Trail**, which extends from the Gulf Islands National Seashore in northwestern Florida to the Big Cypress National Preserve in southwestern Florida. All trails are marked; camping is limited. Some segments of the trail may be closed during hunting season. For more information and to download maps and trails visit *www.florida-trail.org*.

Horseback Riding

Many of Florida's state parks and state forests offer miles of unpaved roads and trails for horseback riding. A few provide overnight camping for riders and horses. For more details on trails, visit *www.dep.state.fl.us/gwt/PDF/Equestrian_Trails_Brochure.pdf*. Regulations require proof of a recent negative Coggins test for all horses entering park areas. Riders are required to stay on designated trails. Horseback riding is allowed on several beaches. Check with local authorities before setting out.

Hunting

Many different types of game await the sports hunter in Florida's forests, grasslands and vast swamps. Florida residents and visitors need a Florida hunting license, unless they are exempt. The limited entry permit program offers high quality hunting on wildlife-management areas (WMAs). Hunting is permitted in Big Cypress National Preserve, WMAs and most state and national forests. Whether fishing or hunting, sportsmen should be aware that native species of birds are protected by law, as are all endangered and threatened animals. For all hunting **regulations**, bag limits, seasons and a free copy of the *Florida Hunting Handbook*, visit *www.myfwc.com/hunting*.

Expeditions and Cruises
Outdoor Adventures

Bird-watching tours in the Keys and Dry Tortugas are led by Victor Emanuel Nature Tours *(www.ventbird.com)*. Weekend and three-day **kayaking trips** to beautiful natural areas like the Everglades and The Ten Thousand Islands are offered by Adventure Kayaking *(www.paddleflorida.com)* based in Vero Beach, just north of Fort Pierce. Some trips combine kayaking with camping; others include overnight stays in local lodgings.

A noisier way of exploring the 'glades is aboard an airboat. Wootens *(www.wootensairboats.com)* have been running their tours since 1953. They also offer swamp tours on their swamp buggy, an unusual vehicle with its carriage elevated high above its chassis and outsized tractor wheels, for perfect viewing.

Cruises

A variety of cruises, from those catering to families, to party cruises for singles are available. Choose from a four-day sail to the Bahamas with ample time to explore the islands; a relaxing cruise to Mexico's Yucatan Peninsula or through the Panama Canal to Los Angeles; or a voyage to an island that includes educational lectures and on-shore excursions. Most cruise lines offer air/sea packages and discounts for early bookings.

Two of Florida's largest ports, the Port of Miami and Port Everglades (Fort Lauderdale), are in the South and offer cruises year-round. Major cruise lines departing from these ports include Carnival, Cunard, Holland America, Norwegian, Princess, Royal Caribbean. All ports provide parking facilities. For up-to-date information, check with individual cruise lines or contact the Cruise Lines International Association *(www.cruising.org)* for a listing of travel agents that specialize in cruise vacations.

Boating Safety Tip:
BUI, or boating under the influence, is a huge problem. Florida waters enjoy a 12-month boating season. A combination of the sun and the dehydration that ofeen comes with spending time on the water means boating operators are likely to become impaired more quickly than a car driver, drink for drink. Check out the U.S. Coast Guard website for hands-on courses to operate personal water crafts. A personal floatation device for each passenger is also a must; parents, know that an adult life jacket is not appropriate for children.

Spectator Sports

For an overview of spectator sports available in Florida, see the Recreation section in the Introduction at the front of this guide.

Horses and Greyhounds

Winter brings the best horses and riders to south Florida. You can experience the thrill of **thoroughbred racing** at South Florida's premier horseracing track, Gulfstream Park, Hallandale *(Dec–early Apr; www.gulfstreampark.com)* and also at Calder Race Course *(www.calderracecourse.com)*.

From October through June Pompano Park *(http://pompano-park.isleofcapricasinos.com)*, just north of Fort Lauderdale, is the nation's "Winter Capital" of **harness racing**. West Palm Beach, Boca Raton and Vero Beach stage **polo** matches from November to mid-April.

Greyhound racing takes place at: Flagler Greyhound Track, Miami *(www.flaglerdogs.com)*; Naples-Fort Myers Greyhound Track at Bonita Springs *(www.naplesfortmyersdogs.com)*; Palm Beach Kennel Club, West Palm Beach *(www.pbkennelclub.com)*; Hallandale Mardi Gras Track *(www.playmardigras.com/racing-south-florida.html)*.

Jai-Alai

Jai-alai ("high-a-lie") or *pelota*, as it is also known, is a game that originated in the Basque region of northern Spain. It is played on a three-walled *fronton* (court) with a hard rubber ball *(pelota)* that is caught and thrown with a *cesta*, a long, curved wicker scoop that is strapped to the player's arm. The ball can travel up to 180mph, making this officially the fastest ball-game in the world, Although jai-alai is enjoyed in its own right as a spectator sport it is the element of pari-mutuel gambling that attracts most interest. The professional game in the US originated at the Miami Fronton; there are also frontons in Dania (near Fort Lauderdale) and Fort Pierce. For more details visit *www.jai-alai.info.*

Baseball

In spring many of the country's Major League Baseball (MLB) teams head for training camps in Florida. Warm-up practice starts in late February and "Grapefruit League" exhibition games are played daily through March. Practices are held between 10am–2pm and are free. For the full schedule visit *http://spring trainingonline.com.* The *Spring Training* Yearbook *($7)*, published annually in late January, also gives schedules as well as team histories, ticket details, directions and accommodations. To order the magazine, visit *www.springtrainingmagazine.com.*

The MLB season begins on the first Sunday in April and ends on the first Sunday in October. Florida has two MLB representatives. **Miami Marlins** *(http://marlins.mlb.com)*, formerly the Florida Marlins, are set to move to a new ballpark in Little Havana in 2012. The team has a proud history, winning the World Series in 1997 and 2003. In 2009 they achieved a bitter-sweet best non-playoff season but 2011 was a disappointing fifth place.

Tampa Bay Rays *(http://tampabay.rays.mlb.com)* play at Tropicana Field in Tampa (an hour drive northeast of Sarasota).

American Football

Two South/Central Florida teams play in the top tier of the National Football League (NFL). The regular season runs early September to 1 January, the playoffs take place a week later and the SuperBowl is held late January or early February. **Miami Dolphins** *(www.miamidolphins.com)* play their home games at the Sun Life Stadium, in Miami Gardens, 15 mi north of downtown. Their training facility is in Davie.

Tampa Bay Buccaneers *(www.buccaneers.com)*, play at the Raymond James Stadium, Tampa. From 1997 to 2007 they were consistent playoff contenders, and won the Super Bowl at the end of the 2002 season. They just missed the playoffs in 2010.

Basketball

South Florida's top NBA team is the **Miami Heat** *(www.nba.com/heat)*, who play at the American Airlines Arena. The Heat finished first in the 2005–2006 season but were beaten in the first round of the playoffs. They were top again in the 2010–2011 season, this time reaching the final of the playoffs, losing to Dallas Mavericks.

The season begins in the first week of November and ends around the end of April although there is a break in between.

Ice Hockey

Although not as popular in the Sunshine State as in the colder northern states, South Florida has its own National Hockey League (NHL) team. The **Florida Panthers** *(http://panthers.nhl.com)* are based in Sunrise, a suburb of Fort Lauderdale, and play their home games at the BankAtlantic Center.

They have a record of underachieving and despite finishing the 2008–09 season with their second-best ever season, they have slumped again in the last two seasons.

The season is divided into an exhibition season (September), a regular season (first week October through early/mid-April), and the Stanley Cup playoffs, from April through early June.

NATURE AND SAFETY

Hurricanes: Precautionary Measures

♦ Pay attention to warnings such as high surf advisories from local authorities.

♦ Fill up your car's gas tank.

♦ Make sure you have a battery-operated flashlight, radio and extra batteries.

♦ Familiarise yourself with evacuation routes.

♦ Stay indoors once the hurricane has struck.

♦ Be aware of storm surges in coastal regions.

♦ Most important, never take a hurricane lightly, and follow instructions issued by authorities, especially evacuation orders.

Fauna Great and Small

A multitude of creatures share South Florida's subtropical climate, including the not-so-beloved mosquitoes, chiggers, scorpions, lovebugs, fire ants, sand flies and cockroaches.

Mosquitoes are unavoidable, especially from June to September—the rainy months when humidity is high. In southern coastal areas mosquitoes are active year-round. Insect repellent is widely available; brands with DEET work best. Also consider wearing lightweight long-sleeved shirts and long pants.

You probably won't encounter **alligators** up close; they tend to avoid people unless provoked. However, stay clear of a mother guarding her young and do not swim in remote lakes, especially during gator mating season (April). Florida law prohibits feeding or molesting alligators, and neither is advisable.

Forty-four species of **snakes** inhabit the Florida landscape: the poisonous ones include several species of rattlesnakes and the coral snake. However, like most wildlife, snakes generally do not pose a threat to people unless provoked. Always wear appropriate footwear, look where you are walking and do not attempt to approach or handle snakes.

Visitor Impact

When visiting a national park, wildlife refuge, state park or national forest, remember that while the disturbance of a single person may be small, the cumulative impact of a large number of visitors may be disastrous. "Take nothing but pictures; leave nothing but footprints" is a worthy philosophy that applies to all of South Florida's many landscapes, public and private.

Hurricanes

The hurricane season typically runs from June to November with the greatest activity occuring from August to October. Hurricanes begin as tropical depressions and are classified as hurricanes once winds reach 74mph. The National Hurricane Center in Miami tracks all storms and issues advisories every six hours; stay tuned to radio and television. A hurricane **watch** is announced if hurricane conditions may threaten an area within 36 hours; a hurricane **warning** is issued if sustained winds of at least 74mph are expected within 24 hours.

Thunderstorms and Lightning

Storms occur almost daily in the summer in Florida (Jun–Sept) and can pass quickly. Peak lightning season is May through August. Thunderstorms can be severe, featuring hail and dangerous lightning. When you hear thunder, leave the water if you are swimming or boating; and take shelter in a car or building—not under a tree, which may attract lightning.

Beach and Water Safety

In the strong subtropical sun, visitors run the risk of sunburn, even in winter. Reflections from white sand and water increase the sun's intensity. Use sunglasses, wear a wide-brimmed hat and drink plenty of liquids. Apply sunscreen even on overcast days, since ultraviolet rays penetrate the cloud cover. Avoid strenuous exercise during midday. Never swim alone and heed **red warning flags** that indicate dangerous conditions such as rip tides. Warning flags are posted every mile along public beaches: blue means calm waters; yellow indicates choppy waters. Most public beaches employ lifeguards seasonally. Take care when swimming at an unguarded beach. Children should be supervised at all times. Scuba diving and snorkeling should never be undertaken alone. Attacks by **sharks**, though rare, have been on the increase along Florida shores recently. Be on the alert and heed instructions from lifeguards.

Stinging creatures such as jellyfish and sea urchins inhabit shallow waters. Although most jellyfish stings produce only an itchy skin rash, some can cause painful swelling. Treating the affected area with papain-type meat tenderizer or calamine lotion may give relief. Sting rays and the Portuguese man-of-war jellyfish (though they look like jellyfish, they are in fact siphonophora) can inflict a more serious sting; seek medical treatment immediately. Occasionally, **toxic "tides"** occur along Florida's coast, caused by micro-organisms that release poisons into the water, discoloring it and creating a nauseating odor. The toxins can be irritating to people.

Boating

Check with local authorities about conditions before setting out on the water. If you rent a canoe or charter a small boat, first familiarize yourself with the craft and obtain maps and the latest weather information. Some boating requires a boating safety certificate. Most outfitters will offer some instruction before sending you out on your own. Always advise someone of your itinerary. **Life jackets** must be available for all passengers; they should be worn by adults and *must* be worn by children under six years old.

Visiting Public Lands

♦ Enjoy the native vegetation, but please leave it untouched.

♦ Do not feed animals; they may become too accustomed to people.

♦ Keep your distance from wildlife.

♦ Do not walk on sand dunes when there are boardwalks.

♦ Do not litter.

♦ Remember to pack out everything you pack in.

♦ Learn to recognize and avoid poisonwood, poison sumac, manchineel poison oak and poison ivy. Contact may require medical attention.

Florida's beaches
are home to
endangered sea
turtles. Development
along the beaches
has threatened the
turtles, who often
try to return to the
same beaches every
year. There are many
organizations that
work to preserve
the turtles and
there's even a sea
turtle hospital in
the Keys. Visitors
can learn about sea
turtles with Miami
Eco Adventures. You
can also visit the
Sea Turtle Hospital
in Marathon or the
Seaquarium in Miami.

The Coastline
Beaches
Florida beaches are ranked among the finest in the world. The most authoritative list is that compiled by Stephen Leatherman ("Dr. Beach"), director of Florida International University's Laboratory for Coastal Research. Top of the 2011 list was **Siesta Beach** in Sarasota with **Cape Florida State Park** in Key Biscayne (No. 10). Other highly ranked beaches in recent years are **Fort De Soto** and **Caladesi Island**. Fortunately, for most of Florida, the Deepwater Horizon oil disaster of 2010 only came as far as the Alabama–Northwest Florida state line, with a clean-up effort mandated to eradicate long-term damage.

The waters along Florida beaches are generally warm compared to the rest of the US. Surf tends to be higher on the Atlantic coast, with relatively little surf on the Gulf coast. Water temperature is also warmer on the Gulf coast than on the Atlantic coast. Gulf coast beaches tend to be fine white sand. Beaches along the Atlantic tend to shade towards light beige with a somewhat coarser texture. If you are looking for shells choose **Sanibel Island**.

If you want lively beaches with every amenity to hand, head for the likes of Miami, Fort Lauderdale, Fort Myers and Key West. The most pristine and least commercialized beaches of all are those managed by the Florida State Parks (denoted by the suffix SP) or designated as a State Recreation Area (SRA).

Aside from the beaches mentioned above, the following is a list of selected beaches that are the best of their kind.

Around Miami and the Keys – Bahia Honda SP; Bill Baggs Cape Florida SP; Crandon Park; Fort Lauderdale Beach; Haulover Beach; Hugh Taylor Birch SP; J. D. MacArthur SP, J. U. Lloyd Beach SP; Miami Beach.

Gulf Coast – Coquina Beach, Anna Maria Island, near Sarasota; Delnor-Wiggins SP, near Naples; Gasparilla Island SP, near Fort Myers; Longboat Key and Lovers Key SRA, both near Sarasota; Sanibel Island beaches; Venice Beach, south of Sarasota.

Water Sports
With hundreds of miles of prime coastline bordering the Atlantic and Gulf of Mexico, Florida is Water Sports Central, year-round. Inland lakes, rivers and springs create more opportunities to **swim**, paddle or simply enjoy the sound of the surf. Although Florida's Atlantic coast is not known for its large waves, **surfing** and also **kiteboarding** is popular in Miami. Surfboards and sailboards can be rented locally. Check water conditions with lifeguards or local authorities before setting out to surf or windsurf.

Canoeing and Kayaking

South Florida's vast system of rivers and creeks makes the area a paddlers' paradise. The recently developed **Great Calusa Blue-way** is a 100mi marked paddling trail that meanders the coast-line of Lee County, from Charlotte Harbor to Bonita Springs on the Gulf of Mexico, past pristine islands and lush mangroves. Along the way are inns, camping areas and outfitters. Lee County Convention & Visitors Bureau. Visit *www.greatcalusablueway. com*, or *www.fortmyers-sanibel.com* for more information.

Flat-water wilderness canoeing can be experienced along the Wilderness Waterway in the Everglades. For canoeing in the Ten Thousand Islands area, contact Everglades Rentals & Eco Adventures *(www.evergladesadventures.com)*.

If you plan on doing your own thing remember the law requires that each occupant wear a flotation device. Best carry an extra paddle to be on the safe side. Get a map of canoeing routes and keep abreast of weather conditions; also keep in mind that coastal rivers are affected by tides. Always avoid flooded rivers! In Central and South Florida rivers generally run high in summer and fall. Carry drinking water, and always advise someone of your plans.

Scuba Diving and Snorkeling

Dive shops can be found all over South Florida and the Keys and offer trips and equipment For more information visit *www.southfloridadiving.com* and *www.fla-keys.com/diving*.

A **Certified Diver's Card** is required to scuba dive. Courses are offered by most diving shops. Choose an instructor who is certi-fied by the Professional Association of Dive Instructors (PADI) or the National Association of Underwater Instructors (NAUI).

Snorkelers and scuba divers can enjoy the living coral reef that lies off the Florida Keys. To get close to the reef without an air tank, try **snuba**, which bridges the gap between snorkeling and scuba diving. This lets you explore the reef while taking in air from a 20ft breathing hose that is attached to an air tank secured to a raft on the surface. It is safe and easy and does not require certification. Expeditions are led by Tilden's Scuba Centers *(www.tildensscubacenter.com)*, based in Marathon and Duck Key, who offer snorkelling, scuba and snuba. You can also snuba at Key West *(www.snuba.com)*. Advance reservations are required for all dive and snorkel trips. Note that seas are usually rougher in winter and can produce poor visibility on the reefs.

ASK PETER...

Q: How can I keep my stuff safe on the beach while I'm swimming?
A: Consider a travel or beach safe. These are usually secure lock boxes made of plastic or metal. It's not completely safe unless you can secure it with a cable lock to a fixed object (or in your vehicle), but at the very least, it will keep your electronics and other valuables close by, free from water and sand.

A DAY IN THE LIFE OF PETER GREENBERG

In my experience, there are two types of people who visit Miami—those who think their happiness is dependent on South Beach nightlife, and those who visit SoBe during more reasonable hours. I start my day here by waking up early and walking to breakfast or brunch. For brunch, I head either to David's Cafe or Big Pink. Then keep walking on Lincoln Road. Head into Books & Books, where it doesn't take much convincing to buy a few new art books. Lincoln Road has open-air markets on the weekend so you can do a little more shopping there.

Starting your day in Miami doesn't mean you have to spend your whole day there. A quick trip out of town and you have a number activities at your fingertips. Divers can check out the wrecks outside Fort Lauderdale. Golfers should head to one of Boca Raton's public courses that cater less to country club members and more to locals looking to get in nine holes. I'm always a big fan of seeing native animals, so I may drive another hour into the Everglades.

On my way back into town, I'll probably stop for a late lunch at Captain Charlie's Reef Grill in Juno Beach (12846 US Highway 1). You'll have to wait in line, but spend the time reading the huge menu, whichis changed daily. And while you can get fresh seafood on almost every corner of Florida; this unassuming strip mall restaurant has some of the freshest and most imaginative seafood dishes. Rock shrimp tortizza, anyone?

On my way back into Miami, I'll stop through Wynnwood. If I'm traveling on a Friday or Saturday, there's a chance an art walk is taking place. In which case, I'll get to gallery hop with the crowds. For dinner, I'll stop into El Carajo. Some people think it's a liquor store, but folks go there for the best tapas. Then, I'll end up back in South Beach, where it's time for a nightcap at Bougainvillea's and Keg South.

CUBA LIBRE

Miami is known for its Latin culture, particularly the large Cuban community. Little Havana was established in the early 1960s after a number of Cuban exiles from the Communist Revolution migrated to Miami. There you'll find Cuban restaurants, salsa clubs, cigar vendors, coffee shops, bright buildings and colorful murals. Stop to eat at Havana Harry's and Versailles. Then go salsa dancing at Quiereme Mucho Morena or Yambo Restaurant. Top off your trip with a visit to the El Credito Cigar Factory. Outside of Miami, you'll also find a large Cuban population in Key West. In fact, Key West airport is a charter hub for flights to Cuba.

Shopping

Florida is a shopper's paradise, with a huge range of goods catering for all tastes and budgets, from upscale boutiques to outlet malls and flea markets. Swimsuits, T-shirts, Disney-style merchandise and citrus-hued resort wear can be purchased in every large coastal city in Florida. For more details on shopping in the state have a look at the advice and information at *www. visitflorida.com/shopping.*

Outlet Malls
Sawgrass Mills (*www.sawgrassmills.com*) at Sunrise, near Fort Lauderdale is the biggest mall in Florida with over 400 stores. Next in order of size is the upscale **Aventura Mall**, in Aventura, northern Miami (*www.aventuramall.com*), with around 300 stores, anchored by Bloomingdale's, Nordstrom and Macy's.
Miromar Outlets in Estero, between Naples and Fort Myers boasts 140 outlets and has been voted Southwest Florida's Best Factory Outlet Shopping Center for 13 years in a row; Ellenton Premium Outlets (*www.premiumoutlets.com*) at Ellenton, immediately north of Sarasota, also features around 140 stores.

Crafts and Souvenirs
Handmade dolls, beaded belts and other **Native American crafts** are sold at the Miccosukee and Seminole reservations in the Everglades.
Seashells are offered in countless souvenir shops, especially on Sanibel Island and along the southwest coast. The **Shell Factory** (*www.shellfactory.com*) near Fort Myers boasts the largest commercial assortment of shells in the world and is a visitor attraction in its own right.
In Little Havana, Miami, fine hand-rolled **cigars** make a prized gift for the connoisseur.

Farm Produce
Agriculture is big business in the Sunshine State. Behold the bounty at local **farmers' markets**, held most Saturday mornings, and shop for produce, fresh fish, and flowers grown in nearby nurseries. Take some of Florida's sunshine with you when you buy oranges, grapefruit and other **citrus fruits**. **Mixon Fruit Farms** (*www.mixon.com*) at Bradenton, immediately north of Sarasota, is a popular place, also offering grove tours. Fruit can be shipped anywhere in the continental US, but do inquire about shipping costs as they can run higher than the merchandise.

Shopping Tip:
What better way to soak up the local flavor than in an independent bookstore? Books & Books has both coffee table books and coffee. So you can visit the Lincoln Road store to browse books on art, design, fashion, and architecture, and then peruse your finds over a drink in the center of South Beach.

Antiques & Fleamarkets

If you're in search of antiques, collectibles, crafts, second-hand furniture, jewelry and much much more, the biggest fleamarkets in the South is **Swap Shop** (*www.floridaswapshop.com*) at Fort Lauderdale, with around 2,000 vendors open daily.

It claims to be the state's original fleamarket and is something of a Florida instiution in its own right. The following major markets all have around 500 stalls:

Red Barn (*www.redbarnfleamarket.com*) at Bradenton, near Sarasota; the **B&A Flea Market** (*www.bafleamarket.com*) at Stuart, 30 mi north of Palm Beach; **Festival Flea Market Mall** at Pompano Beach (*www.festival.com*), near Fort Lauderdale; **Ortiz Avenue Flea Market** (*http://ortizavenuefleamarket.com*) at Fort Myers.

Flamingo Island Flea Market (*http://flamingoisland.com*) at Bonita Springs features around 200 dealers. Dr Flea's at West Palm Beach (*www.drfleas.com*) and Lake Worth Flea Market proves it's not all Versace and Gucci shopping in these parts. Miami hosts several fleamarkets; the classiest is the fortnightly **Lincoln Road Antique & Collectible Market** (*www.antiquecollectiblemarket.com*); try also the Opa Locka Hialeah (*http://opalockahialeahfleamarket.net*).

A good site for checking out Florida fleamarkets is *www.keysfleamarket.com*.

The best **vintage clothing** stores are to be found in Sarasota and Miami.

Upscale

Worth Avenue in Palm Beach attracts the monied set with its posh boutiques and trendy art galleries. South Florida's other glitziest shopping zones are Bal Harbour, Streets of Mayfair, Village of Merrick Park (Coral Gables) in Miami; St. Armands Circle in Sarasota; Galleria Mall (*www.galleriamall-fl.com*) and Las Olas Boulevard (*www.lasolasboulevard.com*) at Fort Lauderdale; Waterside Shops at Naples; St. Armands Circle Sarasota.

Specialty

For something sophisticated in Miami try the **Lincoln Road Shopping District** (*www.lincolnroad.org*) and specifically for **Art Deco** gifts, call in at the Art Deco Welcome Center and Gift Shop (*www.mdpl.org*).

The **Dania Beach Marine Flea Market** (*www.daniamarineflea market.com*) is the largest event of its type in the world. Private individuals and corporate vendors sell marine equipment, coral encrusted antiques, used boats, fishing tackle, diving gear, marine artwork and other boating related items.

Activities For Kids

The Sunshine State could be labeled The Playground State on account of its myriad family-friendly visitor attractions. All sights offer reduced admission for children (usually under 12 years of age), as well as combination family tickets. Theme parks are top on the wish lists of many vacationers, and if the lure of **Disney**, **Universal**, **Sea World**, etc., is irresistible, it's only a 2-hour drive from the Sarasota area to Orlando.

"South of the Mouse" we like:

Miami Science Museum (*p116*), Miami Seaquarium (*p119*), Zoo Miami (*p122*), Coral Castle (*p123*), Jungle Island (p*124*), Museum of Discovery & Science Fort Lauderdale (*p142*), Butterfly World (*p145*), Flamingo Gardens (*p145*), Palm Beach Zoo (*p158*), South Florida Science Museum (*p158*), Lion County Safari (*p159*), Loggerhead Marinelife Center, Jupiter (*p165*), Theater of the Sea, Lower Keys (*p183*), Ripley's Believe It or Not! Key West (*p194*), Everglades Wonder Gardens (*p214*), Sarasota Jungle Gardens (*p222*), Myakka River State Park (*p227*), South Florida Museum (*p227*).

If you're on a tight budget and/or prefer the simple joys of the natural world, it's worth noting that most state parks and nature reserves organise activities for families.

By contrast look out for miniature golf courses, which, with special effects like spewing volcanoes, have risen to an art form in Florida! And of course South Florida's many colorful local festivals and fairs (♨*see Calendar of Events*) are often great fun (and free) for youngsters.

Travel Tip: When looking for a kids' program, make sure you have a clear definition of terms. Many resorts offer kids' programs but sometimes they are no more than a cleared-out room with a few toys and games. When evaluating different programs, ask about activities for different age groups, educational or outdoor options, the program's cost, and of course adult supervision. Last but not least, know the ratio of adults to kids.

Travel Tip: In Miami, many museums and art galleries have monthly gallery walks and events which keep them open late. If you're looking for a nightlife alternative, check out the calendar of cultural events that are not on everybody's radar online at Art Circuits http://artcircuits.com.

Calendar of Events

Listed below is a selection of South Florida's most popular annual events; some dates may vary from year to year. For detailed information, contact local tourism offices or Visit Florida *(www. visitflorida.com/events)*.

January
early January: Discover Orange Bowl – *www.orange bowl.org*. College football, Sun Life Stadium Miami.
mid-January: Art Deco Weekend Festival – *www.mdpl.org*. Miami Beach. Around 85 events including guided tours, movies, theatre, dance, classic cars, food, antiques, art and collectibles vendors and a Saturday morning parade.

February–March
February:
Miami International Boat Show – *www.miamiboatshow.com*. Miami Beach.
Coconut Grove Arts Festival – *www.coconutgroveartsfestcom*. Coconut Grove, Miami. One of the nation's premier outdoor fine Arts Festivals, also including fine cuisine and live entertainment.
Kite Day Festival – *www.skywardkites.com*. Haulover Park, Miami Beach.
Miami Beach Antique Show – *www.originalmiamibeach antiqueshow.com*. Miami Beach Convention Centre, Miami Beach. The world's largest indoor antiques show.
March:
Carnaval Miami/Calle Ocho Festival – *www.carnavalmiami.com*. Miami. Two weeks of Cuban culture including the nation's largest street festival.
Miami International Fashion Week – *www.miamibeachconvention.com*. Miami Beach.
Flamenco Festival Miami – *www.arshcenter.org*. Adrienne Arsht Center Performing Arts, Miami.

April–May
April: Seven-Mile Bridge Run – *www.southernmostrunners.com*. Florida Keys
April–May: SunFest – *www.sunfest.com*. West Palm Beach. Florida's largest waterfront music and art festival features 50 bands, on three stages, over five days.

June
Goombay Festival – *www.miamiandbeaches.com*.

Coconut Grove, Miami. One of the largest black heritage festivals in the United States. Caribbean-style entertainment, plus over 300 vendors selling arts, crafts and food.
Sarasota Music Festival – *www.sarasotaorchestra.org*. Sarasota. Classical concert series.

July
Hemingway Days – *www.fla-keys.com*. Key West. This celebration of Ernest Hemingway. includes literary events, a look-alike competition, a zany "Running of the Bulls" and a three-day marlin tournament.
America's Birthday Bash – *www.bayfrontparkmiami.com*. Miami.

September
Hollywood Beach Latin Festival – *www.hollywoodlatinfestival.com*. Hollywood Beach (between Fort Lauderdale and Miami). Latin-themed music and entertainment on and around the beach.

October
Goombay Festival – *www.goombay-keywest.org*. Key West. Bahamian-themed street entertainment (part of Fantasy Fest).
Fantasy Fest – *www.fantasyfest.net*. Key West. Carnival meets Halloween with balls, costume competitions, body painting, drag queen contests, and a grand parade.
Fort Lauderdale International Boat Show – *www.showmanagement.com*. The world's largest boat extravaganza, showcases over 1,600 vessels including super yachts and accessories.

November–December
Pirates in Paradise – *www.piratesinparadise.com*. Key West. Pirate escapades celebrating the town's maritime heritage.

December
Winterfest Boat Parade – *www.winterfestparade.com*; Fort Lauderdale. One of Florida's largest spectator events culminating in a spectacular night-time parade of over 100 boats.
King Mango Strut – *www.kingmangostrut.org*. Coconut Grove, Miami. A spoof satirical parade on New Year's Eve afternoon.
Indian Arts Festival – Miccosukee Indian Village, Everglades.
Art Basel – *www.ArtBasel.com*. Miami Beach. The biggest contemporary art event in the United States, featuring works from over 250 leading galleries.

Time Zone: South Florida is on Eastern Standard Time (EST), 5hrs behind Greenwich Mean Time (GMT). Daylight Saving Time (clocks are advanced 1hr) is in effect for most of the US from the second Sunday in March until the first Sunday in November.

Know Before You Go

Florida Department of Environmental Protection
Division of Recreation & Parks
📞850-245-2157; *www.dep.state.fl.us./parks*
Office of Fisheries Management
📞850-922-4340; *www.myflorida.com*
Office of Greenways and Trails
📞850-245-2052 or 877-822-5208; *www.myflorida.com*

Florida Association of RV Parks & Campgrounds
📞850-562-7151; *www.floridacamping.com*

Florida Department of Transportation
📞850-414-4100 or 866-374-3368; *www.dot.state.fl.us*

Florida Sports Foundation
📞850-488-8347; *www.flasports.com*

US Forest Service
📞850-523-8500; *www.fs.fed.us*

Helpful Websites
www.petergreenberg.com; Travel news you can use, travel videos and even more tips and destination highlights.
www.myflorida.com; State of Florida general information.
www.flheritage.com; State Office of Cultural and Historical Programs; information includes archeology and museum news; arts, and cultural resources.
www.floridastateparks.org; Information on features, fees and reservations at Florida's state parks.
www.see-florida.com; Attractions, lodgings, dining and recreation.
www.accuweather.com; Independent weather-forecasting service; excellent source of hurricane information.

Tourism Offices
To request the *Florida Vacation Guide* (published annually) or a state map, contact **Visit Florida** (*www.visitflorida.com*). You can also download brochures and guides from here.
Local tourist offices (telephone numbers listed under each entry) provide information free of charge on accommodations, shopping, entertainment, festivals and recreation.

International Visitors

Entry Requirements

Citizens of countries participating in the Visa Waiver Pilot Program (VWPP) are not required to obtain a visa to enter the US for visits of fewer than 90 days if they have a machine-readable passport. Residents of visa-waiver countries must apply ahead for travel authorization online through the **ESTA program** *(fee payable; www.cbp.gov/esta)*.

ESTA applications may be submitted at anytime prior to travel, though it is recommended travelers apply when they begin preparing travel plans. Citizens of non-participating countries must have a visitor's visa. Upon entry, non-resident foreign visitors must present a valid passport and round-trip transportation ticket. Canadian citizens need a government-issued photo I.D., such as a driver's license, plus proof of citizenship (such as a birth certificate) to enter the US. Naturalized Canadian citizens should carry their citizenship papers.

Air travelers between the US and Canada, Mexico, Central and South America, the Caribbean and Bermuda are also required to present a passport, Air NEXUS card or comparable documentation. All persons traveling between the US and destinations listed above, by land or by sea (including ferry), may be required to present a valid passport or other documentation, as determined by the US. Department of Homeland Security. Inoculations are generally not required, but check with the US embassy or consulate before departing.

Customs Regulations

All articles brought into the US must be declared at time of entry. **Items exempt** from customs regulations: personal effects; 150 ml (5 fl oz) of alcoholic beverage (providing visitor is at least 21 years old); 150 ml (5 fl oz) of perfume containing alcohol; 50 cigarettes and 10 cigars; and gifts (to persons in the US) that do not exceed $200 in value. **Prohibited items** include plant material, firearms and ammunition (if not intended for sporting purposes), and meat and poultry products. For other prohibited items, exemptions and information, contact the **US Customs Service** *(www.cbp.gov)*.

Embassies and Consulates

In addition to the tourism offices throughout Florida, visitors from outside the US can obtain information in French, German, Japanese, Portuguese and Spanish from the website of **Visit Florida** *(www.flausa.com)*, or from the US embassy or consulate in their country of residence. For a complete list of American consulates and embassies abroad, visit the US State

---

Credit Cards and Travelers Checks

Rental-car agencies and most hotels require credit cards. Most banks will cash brand-name traveler's checks and provide cash advances on major credit cards with proper identification. Traveler's checks are no longer accepted at most businesses.

American Express Co. Travel Service

has offices in Miami, Fort Lauderdale, Sarasota, and affiliated agencies in other cities *(www.americanexpress.com)*.

Lost or stolen cards

Contact your bank or:

American Express
📞 800-528-4800

Diners Club
📞 800-346-3779

MasterCard
📞 800-627-8372

Visa 📞 800-VISA-911

Currency Exchange

For a small fee, main offices of many major banks will exchange foreign currency. Some smaller statewide banks exchange major foreign currencies at main branches. Also try Thomas Cook exchange offices (📞 800-287-7362; thomascook.com).

Telephones:

For emergencies (fire, police, ambulance), dial 911. Some public telephones accept credit cards. For **long-distance calls** in the US and Canada, dial 1 + area code (3 digits) + number (7 digits). To place a **local call**, dial the 7-digit number without 1 or the area code (unless the local calling area includes several area codes). To find a local number (within your area code), check the local telephone directory or dial **411** for information; to find a **long-distance** number, dial 1 + area code + 555-1212 *(there is a charge for both services)*. To place an **international call**, dial **011** + country code + area code + number. To place a collect call (person receiving the call pays charges), dial **0** + area code + number and tell the operator you are calling collect. Most telephone numbers in this guide that start with **800**, **888**, **877** or **866** are toll-free (no charge) in the US and may not be accessible outside North America.

Department Bureau of Consular Affairs listing on the Internet at *http://travel.state.gov*. Many foreign countries have consular offices in Miami.

Health

The US does not have a national health program that covers foreign nationals. Before departing, visitors from abroad should check their healthcare insurance to determine if doctors' visits, medication and hospitalization in the US are covered. Prescription drugs should be properly identified, and accompanied by a copy of the prescription. Hotel staff can often make recommendations for doctors and other medical services.

Companies offering travel insurance within the US include:

Access America (*800-284-8300; www.accessamerica.com*), **Travelex** (*800-228-9792; www.travelex-insurance.com*), and **Travel Insured International** (*800-243-3174; www.travelinsured.com*).

Disabled Travelers

Many of the sights described in this guide are accessible to people with special needs. Sights marked with the symbol ♿ offer access for wheelchair users, but it is advisable to check beforehand by telephone.

Federal law requires that businesses, including hotels and restaurants, provide access for disabled people, devices for people who are hearing impaired, and designated parking spaces. Many public buses are equipped with wheelchair lifts and many hotels have rooms designed for disabled guests.

For further information, contact the **Society for the Advancement of Travel and Hospitality** (SATH; *212-447-7284; www.sath.org*).

All **national parks** have facilities for disabled visitors. Free or discounted passes are available. For more details visit *www.nps.gov/pub_aff/access*). For **state parks**, visit *www.floridastateparks.org/accessforall*.

Passengers who will need assistance with **train** or **bus** travel should give advance notice to Amtrak (*www.amtrak.com) or Greyhound (www.greyhound.com*).

Senior Citizens

Many establishments offer discounts to those over age 62, including to members of the **American Association of Retired Persons** (AARP; *www.aarp.org*).

TRAVEL ...LIKE A LOCAL

Traveling like a local can mean a lot of things in Miami. Maybe it means going beyond South Beach or finding those out-of-the-way hidden gems. No matter what, it means not getting on the tour bus or following the crowds. Here are my top five tips to have the local experience:

Get off the computer
I've said it before and it's worth repeating. Don't do all your research online. You learn so much more by talking to a human being. If you Google map your trip to the Florida Keys, you're probably going to be stuck in traffic on the Overseas Highway. However, locals will clue you into an alternate route to the Keys—Card Sound Road and the Card Sound Bridge may cost $1, but it's worth it to escape the crowds. Similarly, don't rigidly stick to a pre-prepared itinerary: let yourself be spontaneous—take the advice of a local who recommends somewhere for lunch, or a hidden gem of an attraction that hasn't made its way on to the Internet yet.

Eat Like a Local
You probably don't realize that some of the hottest meals in Miami these days are coming from food trucks rather than restaurants. Check out Miami Food Trucks online (http://miamifoodtrucks.com) for the whereabouts of the best churros, grilled cheese, burgers and more gourmet offerings such as the slow food truck, which serves seasonal, locally-sourced fare. You'll undoubtedly bump up against locals who can give you an invaluable tip for what else is hot right now in the neighborhood. Instead of waiting in the crowds at Joe's Stone Crabs, do as the locals do and go straight to the source: the Keys Fisheries' boats supply Joe's, and you can get the freshest catch of the day here.

Visit Residential Neighborhoods
Tourists think that all of Miami centers around South Beach, but visiting residential neighborhoods lets you check out local boutiques and see a different kind of architecture. I stroll through the Spanish Mediterranean buildings in Coral Gables and try to grab a bite at lunchtime in the Biltmore Hotel.

Make your own excursion
Airboat tours are a dime a dozen in the Florida Everglades. Instead of finding yourself locked into a run-of-the-mill experience, check out the Everglades National Park programming or volunteer with a local wildlife and nature organization. Or go way off the beaten path to Cabbage Key, a 100-acre island that is only accessible by water.

Go to local hot spots
The Ritz-Carlton Sarasota caters to guests with restaurants and poolside dining, but if you go just off the property, the Lido Key Tiki Bar is a beachside gem, which has such a loyal following that locals fought to preserve it when the hotel was built.

Getting There

By Plane

Most US airlines offer direct and non-stop flights to Florida. Twelve **international airports**—the largest are Miami, Orlando and Tampa International—offer services between Florida and Europe, Central and South America and the Caribbean. Smaller **regional airports** are usually accessible through commuter carriers.

By Train

The **Amtrak rail network** (*www.amtrak.com*) offers various train travel packages that may combine rail, air and bus. First-class, coach and sleeping cars are available; on some routes, **bi-level Superliner cars** with floor-to-ceiling windows give panoramic views.

The **USA Rail Pass** offers unlimited travel within Amtrak-designated regions at discounted rates: Passes are available in three travel durations and travel segments (15/30/45 days and 8/12/18 segments, throughout the entire US. Daily service is provided on the **Silver Star** or **Silver Meteor** (New York–Miami, stopping at many other Florida stations en route).

The **Auto Train** travels non-stop from Sanford, in central Florida, to Lorton, Virginia (17 miles from Washington, DC). It offers first-class sleeping accommodations, a full-service restaurant, floor-to-ceiling windows in the Sightseer Lounge and a movie presentation, all included in the ticket price *(leaves Lorton daily 4pm; arrives Sanford, Florida 9am)*. Only passengers with automobiles, vans, motorcycles, SUVs, small boats, jet-skis or other recreational vehicles are permitted on the train.

Amtrak has established a **Thruway Motorcoach** service partnerships with Greyhound throughout the country. For schedule and route information visit *www.amtrak.com*.

By Car

Most car travelers enter the Sunshine State via one of two major north-to-south interstate highways: I-95, running along Florida's east coast, from just north of Jacksonville to Miami; and I-75, which enters the state north of Gainesville, and swings toward the west coast, ending in Fort Lauderdale. L-10 runs west to east across the Panhandle.

By Bus

Greyhound offers access to most cities in Florida. The **Discovery Pass** (*www.discoverypass.com*) allows unlimited travel anywhere for 7, 15, 30 or 60 days.

Liquor Laws:

The minimum age for purchase and consumption of alcoholic beverages is 21; proof of age is normally required. Liquor is sold in liquor stores only, while beer and wine are available at grocery stores. Consuming liquor in public places and carrying an open liquor container in a moving vehicle is illegal. Drunk driving is strictly prohibited, and the threshold is .08 percent blood alcohol.

Getting Around

By Car

Distances in South Florida are relatively short; it only takes a couple of hours to travel between the east and west coasts, and around 3 hours 30 mins between Sarasota and Miami. From here it is just over 3 hours to Key West. Many towns are serviced by Amtrak. In some areas links are maintained with bus connections. Some of the more remote communities, especially along beaches, can only be reached by car.

Florida has an extensive system of well-maintained major roads, some of which are designated limited-access highways that require a toll; I-95 travels the length of Florida's east coast, ending at Miami. Welcome Centers on the interstates may greet visitors with samples of free citrus juice and information offices will supply answers to your travel questions. Many rest areas have picnic tables; most are open 24 hours and are patrolled by security officers at night. Beware wildlife on roads in remote areas. Along highways and major urban thoroughfares, many gas stations stay open 24 hours. Most self-service gas stations do not offer car repair, although many sell standard maintenance items. For free maps phone the tourist office for your destination or contact Visit Florida. The **Florida Turnpike** (toll road) branches off I-75 northwest of Orlando and slants southeastward across the state until it ends below Miami in Florida City *(around $25 for the entire distance)*. Toll booths are staffed, but for quick travel motorists should carry correct change. Call boxes placed at mile intervals allow travelers to phone for help.

Rental Cars

Most large rental companies have offices at (or near) major airports and downtown locations. Rentals typically include unlim-

RENTAL CAR COMPANIES

Alamo	800-327-9633	www.alamo.com
Avis	800-331-1212	www.avis.com
Budget	800-527-0700	www.budget.com
Dollar	800-800-4000	www.dollar.com
Enterprise	800-325-8007	www.enterprise.com
Hertz	800-654-3131	www.hertz.com
National	800-227-7368	www.nationalcar.com
Thrifty	800-331-4200	www.thrifty.com

Driving in the US:
Visitors bearing valid driver's licenses issued by their country of residence are not required to obtain an International Driver's Permit to drive in the US (though an IDP is a good idea). Drivers must carry vehicle registration and/or rental contract, and proof of automobile insurance at all times. Rental cars in the US are usually equipped with automatic transmission. Rental rates tend to be less expensive than overseas, and payment is often not required until the car is returned. Most gas stations do not offer car repair, although many sell standard maintenance items.

Road regulations in the US require that vehicles be driven on the right side of the road. Distances are posted in miles (1mi=1.6km). Do not stop if strangers try to flag your car down. Don't stop if your car is bumped from the rear; instead proceed to the nearest well-lit public area and contact the police.

MIAMI

METROMOVER SYSTEM | Transfer Stations to Metrorail

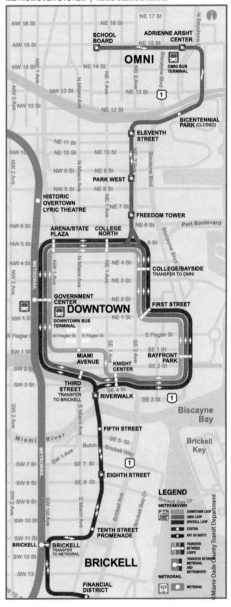

ted mileage. Minimum age for rental is 21. A surcharge may be applied for persons up to age 24.

Be sure to check for proper insurance coverage, offered at extra charge. Liability is not automatically included in the terms of the lease. If you own a car and carry comprehensive car insurance for collision and liability, your personal auto insurance may cover a rental. Check your policy to be sure. Some credit cards offer CDW (collision damage waiver coverage). In addition to the national rental agencies, check out local companies too.

Recreational Vehicle (RV) Rentals

Motor-home rentals are offered from several locations in Florida. Up to eight people can be accommodated; service can include free mileage and airport transfers. Make reservations at least 2–3 weeks in advance, double that during the summer and during holiday seasons. Contact Cruise America RV Rentals (www.cruiseamerica.com).

Road Regulations

The maximum speed limit on interstate highways is 70mph, 60mph on state highways, unless otherwise posted. Speed limits are generally 30mph within city limits and residential areas. Right turns on red are allowed after coming to a complete stop, unless otherwise indicated. Florida law requires headlights to be turned on when driving in fog and rain.

Seat belts must be worn by all front-seat occupants. Children under 6 must ride in child restraint devices (child safety seats are offered by most car-rental agencies). The law requires motorists in both directions to bring their vehicles to a complete stop when warning signals on a **school bus** are activated.

Drivers are required to have personal injury protection and property liability insurance. Carry proof of insurance at all times. Apart from local authorities, the **American Automobile Association** (AAA) (www.aaa.com) offers road assistance.

In Case of an Accident

If you are involved in an accident resulting in personal injury or property damage, you must notify the local police and remain at the scene until dismissed. If blocking traffic, vehicles should be moved as soon as possible. In the case of property damage to an unattended vehicle, the driver must attempt to locate the owner or leave written notice in a conspicuous place of driver's name, address and car registration number.

By Bus

Florida's largest cities all offer decent local bus services.

Motoring Safety Tips: Don't stop if strangers flag your car down. If you carry a cell phone, dial FHP (*347) for the Florida Highway Patrol. Don't stop if your car is bumped from the rear; proceed to the nearest well-lit public area and contact the police. Ask at your hotel what parts of the city to avoid. Ensure you have a battery-operated radio and extra batteries.

Driving Tip: Keep cool and calm when you're driving in Miami. Yes, the traffic during rush hour on the I-95 is pretty much unbearable, and the drivers aren't any better. The city has been voted as having the rudest drivers in the country for two years and counting. And to make matters worse, road signage in Miami has always been nonexistent or misleading. So here's a tip: Just remember, "streets" run east and west and "avenues" go north and south.

Where to Stay and Eat

ASK PETER...

Q: Are there any affordable Miami hotel options?

A: Few people think of staying in bed and breakfasts when heading to a big city like Miami. It's time to think again. Touted as "Miami's only Bed and Breakfast," the Miami River Inn (*see p108 and p.127*) is located a short walk from downtown and has been renting out rooms since 1908, with rates starting as low as $99 per night. The B&B spirit is alive at the Inn every afternoon when guests gather together in the backyard for a glass of wine.

Smoking: Smoking is banned in most enclosed indoor places, including restaurants. Exceptions include stand-alone bars, where food is merely incidental, and tobacco shops. Some hotels offer smoking rooms, but they are becoming rare.

Where to Stay

Although South Florida is a year-round destination, rates are lower **off-season**; May to October. In some hotels children under 18 stay free when sharing a room with their parents. Some small hotel and many motel rooms include efficiency kitchens. All but the most basic accommodations are air-conditioned. Hotel taxes, which vary according to location, range from 6% to 12.5%, and are not included in rates quoted. The Official Florida Vacation Guide lists members of the Florida Hotel & Motel Association and is available from **Visit Florida**. State-wide hotel information service: ✆850-488-5607; *www.visitflorida.com*.

Traditional Lodgings
Hotels/Motels

Accommodations range from luxury hotels (*$250 and up*) and superior hotels (*$150–$250*) to moderate motels (*$80-$150*). Rates vary greatly according to season and location and tend to be higher during holidays and peak seasons. Many properties offer packages which might include meals, passes to local attractions, and organized trips. Some hotels include breakfast in the room rate. Advance reservations are recommended. Always advise the reservations clerk of late arrival; unless confirmed with a credit card, rooms may not be held after 5pm.

Bed and Breakfasts and Country Inns

Most B&Bs are privately owned and many are located in historic dwellings in residential sections of cities, or in small towns and rural areas. Amenities include complimentary breakfast ranging from simple continental fare to full home-cooking; some offer afternoon tea and the use of sitting rooms or garden areas where hosts and guests mingle.

Most establishments are small and offer fewer than ten rooms. Private baths are not always available, and often there is no phone in individual rooms. Make reservations well in advance especially during holiday seasons, and be sure to ask about minimum stay, cancellation and refund policies. Most establishments accept major credit cards. Rates vary seasonally from $100 to $250 for a double room per night, with higher charges for things like ocean views.

Resorts and Spas

Many of the grand and famous South Florida resorts have been lavishly restored in recent years, combining modern amenities

and luxuries with Old World trapping. On-site fine dining restaurants, indoor and outdoor swimming pools, tennis courts, fitness centers, 18-hole golf courses and even marinas have become standard features of large resort hotels. Destination spas offer a variety of programs from fitness, beauty and wellness to weight management, stress relief and outdoor adventure. Guests are pampered with mud baths, daily massages, state-of-the-art fitness and exercise programs, cooking classes and nutritional counseling.

Spas, most of which are fairly informal, offer luxurious facilities in beautiful settings that can include championship golf courses and tennis courts. Most offer packages for stays ranging from two to ten nights, which include health and fitness programs and spa treatments. Prices range from $1,000/week in summer to $4,000/week during the winter season, depending on choice of program. For more information contact Spa Finder. **Reservation service**: ☏ 800-255-7727; *www.spafinder.com*.

Other Accommodations
Condominiums

Furnished apartments or houses are more cost-effective than hotels for families with children. Amenities include separate living quarters, fully equipped kitchen with dining area, several bedrooms and bathrooms, and laundry facilities. Most condos provide televisions, basic linens and maid service. Depending on location, properties might include sports and recreational facilities, patios and beach access.

Most require a minimum stay of three nights or one week, especially during peak season. When making reservations, ask about cancellation penalties and refund policies. Chambers of commerce and tourist offices have listings of local property management agencies that can assist with the selection. For vacation homes in Naples and the Orlando area, contact **Florida Choice** (☏ *800-847-2731; www.floridachoice.com*) and see their Vacation Home Rentals.

Hostels

Simple budget accommodations are offered at hostels in many resorts including Florida City, Key West, Fort Lauderdale, and Miami Beach. Dormitory-style rooms average around $15–$40/night. Private rooms are available at additional charge and amenities may include swimming pools, air-conditioning, common living room, laundry facilities, self-service kitchen and dining room. Blankets and pillows are provided; linens can be rented. Reservations are suggested. All hostels accept credit cards. For information and reservations, visit *www.hostels.com*.

Cash: Most banks are members of the network of Automated Teller Machines (ATM), allowing visitors from around the world to withdraw cash using bank cards and major credit cards. ATMs can usually be found in airports, banks, grocery stores and shopping malls.

Temperature and Measurement: In the US temperatures are measured in degrees Fahrenheit and measurements are expressed in feet and inches, pounds, miles, gallons and other imperial measures. Most Americans are unfamiliar with metric measurements; a mile is slightly less than 2 kilometers; a gallon is approximately 4 liters. Thus the highway speed limit, usually 60-70mph, is analagous to 100kph; and the average car's gas tank holds 14-18 gallons of gas.

Camping

Campsites are located in national parks, state parks, national forests, along beaches and in private campgrounds. Many camp sites are located in central Florida near theme parks: most offer full utility hookups, lodges or cabins and recreational facilities. Florida's many rivers and lakes allow boat camping and usually include mooring facilities and marinas. Advance reservations are recommended for all types of organized camping, especially during holidays and school vacations.

Primitive (wilderness) camping is for the experienced camper only. Because there may be mosquitoes and other creatures present, plan to sleep well-protected in the outdoors. Make sure your tent is waterproof; sudden thunderstorms can soak through quickly.

A variety of camping facilities, from full-facility camping to cabins, resort lodges, boat camping and primitive camping, await the outdoor enthusiast in Florida's national and state parks. Some facilities are available on a first-come, first-served basis while others require advance reservations; permits are required for certain campsites. Reservations for campsites are accepted in advance; cabin rentals may be made up to 11 months in advance. Rates vary according to season and facilities: cabins *($20–$130/day)*, campsites *($8–$31)*. For reservations *(generally only taken Mon–Fri 8am–5pm)* contact the park directly. For a free brochure listing all state park facilities, contact: **Florida Department of Environmental Protection**, Division of Recreation & Parks *(☎ 850-245-2157; www.floridastateparks.org).*

Campgrounds and Recreational Vehicle (RV) Parks

The Florida Association of RV Parks & Campgrounds lists member sites and offers details on hookups, laundry facilities, pools, playgrounds, sporting facilities, freeway access and shopping. You can view their directory *Camp Florida* online at *http://campflorida.com* or order a free copy to be sent to you. Either request it online or call ☎ 850-562-7151. Parks are family-oriented and open year-round. Most campgrounds offer daily, weekly or monthly occupancy for recreational vehicles. Prices range from $10–$60/night for campsites and average $20–$25/night for RVs. Reservations are recommended, especially for longer stays and in popular resort areas, including the Keys.

KOA Kampgrounds are located all across Florida; some resort properties offer pools, hot tubs, air-conditioned cabins, restaurants, boat ramps, deep-sea fishing and snorkeling. For a directory *($6, includes shipping)*, order online or write to KOA Kampgrounds, PO Box 30558, Billings MT 59114 *(☎ 888-562-0000, www.koa.com).*

Emergencies:
In most areas in the US dial **911** to telephone the police, ambulance or fire department. In hotels, another way to report an emergency is to dial **0** for the operator.

Where to Eat

Blessed with hundreds of miles of coastline, South Florida is famous for fresh seafood: whether you opt for mullet, stone crabs or blackened grouper, you'll find a huge variety of fresh fish and shellfish on restaurant menus in many different types of establishment. Salmon won't be local, but grouper, mackerel, red snapper, pompano, dolphin (the fish, *mahi mahi*, not the mammal) and yellowfin tuna were most likely caught in Florida waters. Look for stone crabs in season (mid-May through mid-October), and don't leave the Keys without sampling conch fritters (conch is the "meat" of a sea snail) or ceviche (typically made from fresh raw fish marinated in citrus juices and spiced with chilli peppers). The Keys are of course also famous for the now ubiquitous Key Lime Pie.

Thanks to Florida's melting pot of island cultures and influx of immigrants, "Floribbean" cuisine reigns in many restaurant kitchens, a tantalizing fusion of fresh Floridian fish and citrus, spiked with Caribbean and Latin flavors. Other menu items you're likely to encounter are 'gator tail (yes, it's actually alligator and tastes rather like chicken) and hearts of palm salad.

In Miami, some of the best food can be found in Little Havana, where Cuban classics are the order of the day. Miami is coming on strong as one of the country's top dining destinations, as the long waits for reservations at top tables will attest. Be sure to make advance bookings if there is a restaurant you particularly want to sample.

Many restaurants add a gratuity to the bill, a practice familar to their Latin American and European guests.

TAXES AND TIPS

Prices displayed or quoted in the US do not generally include **sales tax** (6–7.5% in Florida, depending on the county). Sales tax is added at the time of purchase. Hotel occupancy taxes (6%–12.5%) and tax rates for rental cars vary according to location; additional daily surcharges may be added as well.

Taxes and fees are generally higher in major metropolitan areas such as Miami. The US does not collect a value-added tax (VAT). In the US it is customary to give a **tip** for services rendered by waiters/waitresses, porters, hotel maids and taxi drivers. It is customary in restaurants to tip the server 10%–20% of the bill. In popular tourist locations restaurants may automatically add a service charge; check your bill before you tip). At hotels, porters are generally given $1 per suitcase, housekeeping staff $1 per day. Taxi drivers are usually tipped 10% of the fare.

Festivals Tip:
Miami is home to celebrity chefs and some of the country's best restaurants, but you should also consider purchasing tickets to the South Beach Food and Wine Festival. Held at the end of February, you can go to talks and panels with celebrity chefs, eat your way through tasting villages and learn about the latest in food and wine. Not bad for a Miami night out.

Electricity:
Electrical current in the US is 120 volts AC, 60 Hz. Foreign-made appliances may need voltage transformers and North American flat-blade adapter plugs (available at specialty travel and electronics stores), including charge cords for phones, computers and the like.

DISCOVERING

MIAMI AND THE KEYS

Whenever I tell people "I'm headed to Miami" they immediately assume I'm going to Miami Beach, which many refer to interchangeably with South Beach. Step one for any trip to the area may sound cliched, but promise me you'll do it. Look at a map to get a sense of how big the city really is. Miami proper is just west of Miami Beach, and the area encompasses more than just South Beach. Sure, I'll probably end up on Lincoln Road at some point during my trip, but limiting myself to this area is definitely not traveling like a local.

Let's just take a moment to break down everywhere in Miami. There's Coral Gables, Downtown Miami, the Design District, Little Havana, Midtown/Little San Juan, Coconut Grove, Key Biscayne, and Wynwood. And that's just Miami proper. When you venture outside the city, Fort Lauderdale, Palm Beach and Boca Raton are all nearby.

In the past, people may have immediately assumed that a trip to this area was a beach vacation.

Florida has 1,200 miles of coastline, so naturally there's every kind of beach option in and around Miami. There are beaches known for their scene (like South Beach), beaches for surfing or volleyball, as well as more private and natural coastlines. On average, the temperature hits lows in the 60s and highs in the mid-80s, so you're in for beach weather pretty much year round.

In the last decade, Miami has gone from the beach scene to offering much more—it's become an art and food hub. This is due in no small part to the influence of two large Miami Beach festivals—Art Basel and the South Beach Food and Wine Festival. Both festivals are well worth a visit, but locals in Miami and Miami Beach reap the benefits of these institutions year round. Miami now is home to celebrity chefs and cutting-edge contemporary art galleries.

Outside Miami proper the surrounding cities have their own personality. Fort Lauderdale, once spring break central, now attracts a family population and is a hub for recreational boating and commercial docks. Boca Raton may not have the party vibe of Miami but you can find locals out on the golf course.

You can't talk about Palm Beach County, aka the Gold Coast, without mentioning wealth. Yes, the influence of Standard Oil's Henry Flagler remains in the area to this day, but many historic properties are open to the public.

PETER'S TOP PICKS

 STAY

Stay at the Miami River Inn to experience the city's first bed and breakfast. Affordable and centrally located, this B&B is a hidden gem in the center of the city. **Miami River Inn** (p **127**)

 Green Spaces

Green spaces in the Miami region are beach spaces. Visit the John U. Lloyd Beach State Park for wide open beaches. **John U. Lloyd Beach State Park** (p **144**)

 HISTORY

To experience a little history and check out one of my favorite restaurants, visit the Biltmore Hotel. Originally a winter retreat in the 1920s, today's elegant dining optiond are reason to continue coming back to this historic property. **Biltmore Hotel** (p **113**)

 SHOP

Head to Lincoln Road Books & Books, boutiques and the weekend open-air markets. **Lincoln Road Mall** (p **137**)

 EAT

Cafe Versailles in Little Havana is the spot to go to get a taste of the city's Cuban culture and some of my favorite Cuban food. **Cafe Versailles** (p **129**)

 ENTERTAINMENT

At the Bakehouse in the Design District, you'll get to see every aspect of the city's contemporary art scene. There are artist studios in all mediums, gallery displays and even it's own art walk night. **Like A Local Art** (p **125**)

Population: 391,355.
Michelin Map: See
inside back cover;
p101, 105, 110-111.
Info: 1901
Convention Center
Drive, Miami Beach;
℘786-276-2763;
*www.miamiand
beaches.com.*
Location: Flagler
Street divides the
city north-south;
Miami Avenue runs
east-west. The major
north-south access
routes are A1A, US 1,
I-95, US 441 and the
Florida Turnpike.
Parking: There are
parking lots and
garages, but street
metered parking is
hard to find. Take
a cab.
Don't Miss: A tour
of the Art Deco
Historic District in
South Beach.
Timing: This is a
sprawling city; allow
time to travel from
one attraction to the
next. Plan on a day to
explore Downtown
Miami sites, another
to explore sizzling
Miami Beach.
Kids: The cageless
Zoo Miami has nearly
1,000 animals roaming
in natural habitats.
Young kids will also
enjoy the exotic
animals at Jungle
Island.

MIAMI★★★ *and around*

Renowned for its tropical landscape, Miami is one of the most popular resort destinations in the US. Each year some ten million visitors from around the world pour into Greater Miami. Star-studded South Beach—"SoBe"—is a magnet for the see-and-be-seen crowd. This vibrant, sun-drenched playground boasts golf, tennis, yachting, deep-sea fishing, scuba diving beside arts and culture and a buzzy nightlife Owing to its position on the Florida Straits near the southeastern tip of the state, Miami also boasts the world's largest cruise port, accommodating passengers to and from the Caribbean and South America.

A Bit of History

Early Explorers – **Pedro Menéndez de Avilés** came ashore here in 1566. In 1567 more Spanish colonists arrived to found a short-lived Catholic mission. Disease and wars depleted the native Tequesta Indian population and when Florida became a British Colony in 1763, the remaining Tequestas fled along side the Spanish to Cuba.

The US Government established **Fort Dallas** on the north side of the Miami River in 1838. When the Second Seminole War ended in 1842, William English, platted (mapped) a town on the south side of the river. His name for this new town, Miami, is thought to derive from an Indian word meaning "sweet water."

The Mother of Miami – By the late 19C, **William and Mary Brickell** and **Julia Tuttle** were the two major landholders in the area. By 1880 the Brickell family owned all of the prime bayfront land south to Coconut Grove. Meanwhile, Julia Tuttle's campaign to put the fledgling town on the map earned the widow from Cleveland the title "Mother of Miami." She did this by seeking the help of **Henry Flagler** and his Florida East Coast Railway (FEC). In exchange for riparian rights and half of Tuttle's land, the entrepreneur laid out streets, supplied the town with water and electricity, financed a channel across the bay and donated land for community buildings.

In April 1896, the first train chugged into the village of 300 citizens, which was incorporated three months later.

Boom, Bust and Recovery

While growth corresponded directly to the development of the FEC and the federal highway system, a number of developers lured buyers with the promise of something new and different: Carl Fisher's Miami Beach; George Merrick's Mediterranean-style Coral Gables (complete with man-made canals and cos-

FLORIDA'S TURNPIKE   FORT LAUDERDALE

Miami   Gardens   Dr.
CAROL   CITY   860   I-95   NORTH MIAMI
Palmetto   Expwy.   Ancient Spanish
N.W.   826   Monastery
37th   OLETA RIVER
SP   HAULOVER
BISCAYNE   BEACH
823   Opa-locka   GARDENS   PARK
OPA-LOCKA   441   909   BAL
Ave.   North   915   HARBOUR
916   924   NORTH   MIAMI   SURFSIDE
Gratigny   N.W.   922   Museum of   Blvd.
Red   924   Pkwy.   924   Contemporary   A1A
AMELIA   Art
EARHART PARK   MIAMI   BISCAYNE
932   SHORES   PARK
HIALEAH   South   GREATER MIAMI   NORTH BAY
HIALEAH PARK   22nd   79th   NORTH   VILLAGE
RACETRACK   934
E. 25th St. N.W.   St.   LITTLE
W. 21st   E. 21st St.   441   HAITI
St.   953   9   I-95   Biscayne   Fontainebleau
27   Hilton
Airport   Expwy.   112   J. Tuttle Causeway   195
N.W. 36th   St.   MIAMI JAI   VENETIAN IS.   Collins   MIAMI
Miami   ALAI   BEACH
International   MIAMI   Ave.
Dolphin   836   Miami   OVERTOWN   STAR   A1A   South Beach
W.   S.W.   Expwy.   395   Jungle   A1A
Flagler   St.   Bayside   Island   FISHER I.
S.W.   8th   Le   St.   Marketplace   Port of
CORAL   57th   27th   LITTLE HAVANA   Miami
GABLES   Jeune   Calle Ocho   Brickell
Coral Way   S.W. 22nd   St.   Ave.   VIRGINIA KEY
Biltmore   Venetian   Dixie   Hwy.   VIZCAYA   TOLL   913
Hotel   Pool   Bayshore Dr.   Miami   ATLANTIC
959   COCONUT   Seaquarium
Univ. of   GROVE   S.   UNIV. OF MIAMI   CRANDON
Miami   Red   1   Barnacle Historic   MARINE LAB
State Park   PARK   OCEAN
Sunset   Rd.   Rd.
Dr.   KEY BISCAYNE
SOUTH   Biscayne
MIAMI   Dr.   Cutler
Kendall   MATHESON HAMMOCK   BILL BAGGS
COUNTY PARK   CAPE FLORIDA   GREATER
Rd.   Old   SP   MIAMI
Fairchild Tropical   CAPE   0   3 mi
Botanic Garden   FLORIDA   0   5 km
N

BISCAYNE NATL. PARK   MIAMI METROZOO, EVERGLADES NATL. PARK

tumed gondoliers imported from Italy); and the North Miami-Dade developments of Hialeah and Miami Springs.

By the mid-1920s the boom was over. Anti-Florida propaganda and tax investigations had already put a damper on investment when a Miami cargo embargo severely affected the state's economy. A deadly hurricane in 1926 added to the woes.

While Florida's troubles may have preceded the 1929 crash, the state's economy was also among the first in the country to revive. Ironically, Prohibition helped. Eager for tourists, officials generally turned a blind eye to illegal gambling and to rum-runners who smuggled liquor in from the Bahamas. In 1931 the state legalized pari-mutuel betting and tourists from the North poured in. Joining them were thousands of Latin American travelers arriving by sea plane.

Growing Pains – By the mid-1980s, the national recession hit Miami hard. Banks foreclosed on unfinished condos, shopping malls stood half-rented and the new billion-dollar Metrorail ran virtually empty. For a time it appeared the only people profiting in the faded resort were the illegal drug smugglers.

Modern Multicultural Metropolis – The popular television show, *Miami Vice* (1984–89), helped Miami's comeback, giving an allure to the city's pink stucco and palm trees, and even to its seamy side. A more tangible economic boost came from a new free trade center (now **World Trade Center** Miami) es-tablished in the early 1980s.

Today the city has once again re-invented itself into a boom-ing, diverse center for avant garde arts and culture, fashion and design (and frequent celebrity sightings). It's now one of the country's top vacation hot spots.

Geography

Greater Miami embraces all of Miami-Dade County and its is-lands, including Miami Beach, the long, narrow barrier island between Biscayne Bay and the Atlantic Ocean.

To the east of downtown lies 39mi-long Biscayne Bay. Seven causeways link the mainland to Miami Beach, while an eighth, Rickenbacker Causeway, brings auto traffic to Virginia Key and Key Biscayne, situated to the south.

The bustling city has a diverse mix of Latinos, Caucasians and African Americans. As a result, distinct ethnic communities ex-ist, most notably Little Havana, just west of downtown; Little Haiti, west of Biscayne Boulevard below 79th Street; and the Af-rican-American neighborhoods of Overtown, Liberty City and Brownsville. The mix is one of the things that makes Miami so interesting and culturally vibrant.

GETTING THERE

BY AIR – Miami International Airport (MIA): 7mi northwest of downtown; international and domestic flights (℘305-876-7000; www.miami-airport. com). Tourist Information Service, Central Terminal E, Level 2 (open daily year-round). Transportation to downtown: **SuperShuttle** (around $20; ℘305-871-2000; www.supershuttle.com), taxi (around $25-$30), **Metrobus** and hotel courtesy shuttles. **Rental car agencies** located near the airport.

BY TRAIN AND BUS – Amtrak **train** station: 8303 N.W. 37th Ave. (℘800-872-7245; www.amtrak.com). Greyhound **bus**: Miami International Airport: 4111 N.W. 27th St. and 700 Biscayne Blvd.; Miami Beach: 7101 Harding Ave. (reservations: ℘800-231-2222; www.greyhound.com).

GETTING AROUND

BY PUBLIC TRANSPORTATION – **Miami-Dade Transit Agency** (℘305-770-3131; www.miamidade.gov/transit) operates a public transit system connecting Greater Miami and beaches via Metrorail, Metromover and buses. **Metrorail** trains serve downtown Miami extending northwest to Hialeah and south to Kendall. **Metromover** elevated rail system links the Brickell Ave. and Omni areas, and loops around downtown. Metrorail connections at Government Center and Brickell stations, with limited nearby public parking. **Metrobus** operates county-wide. Schedules and route information, www.miamidade.gov/transit. Disabled visitors: ℘305-770-3131. **Tri-Rail** (℘800-TRI-RAIL, www.tri-rail.com) provides **commuter rail** service between Palm Beach and Greater Miami connecting to Metrorail.

BY CAR – Miami is laid out on a grid: the intersection of Flagler St. and Miami Ave. divides the city into four quadrants: southwest, northwest, southeast and northeast. Avenues and courts run north-south; streets and terraces run east-west. **Speed limit** within city: 25mph unless otherwise posted. Signs with the orange "Follow the Sun" symbol direct visitors to major tourist destinations (maps available at airport and from car rental agencies). Downtown metered **parking**: $1.50/hr. Parking lots $1.50–$3.25/1/2hr.
BY TAXI – Metro Taxi (℘305-888-8888); Yellow Cab (℘305-444-4444; www.ycab.com).

VISITOR INFORMATION

Downtown Miami Welcome Center, Olympic Theater, 174 E. Flagler St., Miami, FL 33131. ℘305 379-7070.
Miami Beach Latin Chamber of Commerce Visitor Information Center, 510 Lincoln Rd. Miami Beach, FL 33139 (Art Deco District/South Beach). ℘305-674-1414. www.miamibeach.org.
Miami Beach Visitor Information Center, 1901 Convention Center Drive, Miami Beach; ℘786-276-2763. For general information online visit www.miamiandbeaches.com.

SIGHTSEEING

For sightseeing tours go online (↺see above), or consult the Greater Miami & the Beaches Vacation Planner available from the Greater Miami Convention and Visitors Bureau. Daily **cruises** around Greater Miami and Fort Lauderdale operate from Bayside Marina and the docks at 24th St. and Collins Ave. Miami Beach Art Deco Historic District **walking and bike tours** (℘305-672-2014; www.mdpl.org). Neighborhood walking Tours are organised by HistoryMiami museum (℘305-375-1621; www.history miami.org/tours).

LOCAL PRESS

Daily news: Miami Herald; entertainment section Weekend (Friday), online at www.miamiherald.com.

Downtown

Covering 1.5sq mi, this vibrant quarter exudes the bustling atmosphere of a Latin city. The opening of the **Adrienne Arsht Center for the Performing Arts of Miami-Dade County** and the revitalization of **Bicentennial Park** has brought new energy and vitality to the downtown area.

Where the city's first wooden commercial structures once stood, is now a dense array of government and office buildings in a host of architectural styles, including Neoclassical, Art Deco, Mediterranean Revival and the stark contemporary design of the skyscrapers that illuminate Miami's night skyline.

The commercial area built by **Henry Flagler** was incorporated as the City of Miami in July 1896. Fire devoured most of the small downtown and vulnerable frontier buildings were quickly replaced with new masonry structures that adhered to a vernacular style of architecture. Downtown's best example of vernacular storefront architecture is the 1914 **Chaille Block** (Miami Ave. between N.W. 4th and N.W. 5th Sts.), now incorporated into the facade of the new federal prison. Also around this time, hotels and stores began to incorporate open walkways beneath a second-floor veranda—a style suited to the subtropics. The 1912 **Waddell Building** (24–36 N. Miami Ave.) is a notable survivor. In recent years, contemporary high-rise hotels and office buildings have arrived, most strikingly the **Miami Tower** (1985), a 47-story tiered tower *(*100 S.E. 1st St.) lit nightly by colored lights, and the 55-story **Southeast Financial Center** (1984), the tallest building in South Florida *(*200 S. Biscayne Blvd.). Downtown south of the Miami River along Brickell Avenue has emerged as an international financial district.

Bicentennial Park★

1075 Biscayne Blvd. ℘305-358-7550.
This 30-acre park, located on Biscayne Bay, is undergoing major renovation and will become a new cultural hub by 2013.
Renamed Museum Park, it will be anchored by the Jorge M. Perez Art Museum of Miami-Dade County, formerly Miami Art Museum; and The Patricia and Phillip Frost Museum of Science, formerly the Miami Science Museum.

Miami Art Museum★ (A)

Open year-round Tue–Fri 10am–5pm, weekends noon–5pm. Closed Jan 1, Thanksgiving Day, Dec 25. $8, second Sat each month free. &♿🅿 ℘305-375-3000. www.miamiartmuseum.org.
Dedicated to presenting international art of the post-World War II era—with an emphasis on art of the Americas—the museum

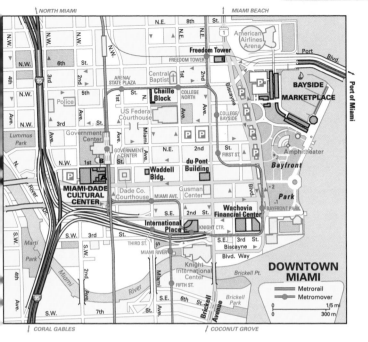

| NORTH MIAMI | MIAMI BEACH |

NORTH MIAMI   *MIAMI BEACH*

N.E. 8th St.
American Airlines Arena
Port Blvd.
Port of Miami
Freedom Tower
FREEDOM TOWER
Central Baptist
BAYSIDE MARKETPLACE
ARENA/ STATE PLAZA
Chaille Block
COLLEGE NORTH
Police
COLLEGE/ BAYSIDE
US Federal Courthouse
Amphitheater
Bayfront
Government Center
GOVERNMENT CENTER
du Pont Building
FIRST ST.
Lummus Park
MIAMI-DADE CULTURAL CENTER
Waddell Bldg.
Dade Co. Courthouse
MIAMI AVE.
Gusman Center
Park
BAYFRONT PARK
Wachovia Financial Center
S.E. 2nd St.
International Place
KNIGHT CTR.
THIRD ST.
S.E. 3rd St.
Biscayne
MIAMI RIVER
Blvd. Way
Marti Park
Miami River
Knight International Center
Brickell Pt.
DOWNTOWN MIAMI
FIFTH ST.
Brickell Park
S.E. 6th St.
Metrorail
Metromover
0   1/5 mi
0   300 m

CORAL GABLES   *COCONUT GROVE*

stages several major shows a year.

The permanent collection, a small selection of which is displayed on a rotating basis, includes 50 works by such noted contemporary artists as Christo, Alexander Calder, Jasper Johns, Robert Rauschenberg, Marcel Duchamp and Rufino Tamayo. *Plans for a new museum building, to be designed by Herzog & de Meuron, are underway. It is expected to be completed in 2013 (see above).*

HistoryMiami★★(B)

101 West Flagler St. Open year-round Tue–Fri 10am–5pm Sat–Sun noon–5pm. Closed major hols. $8. ♿ 🅿 ☎305-375-1492. www.historymiami.org.

This is the region's most important historical museum. The permanent exhibit, "Tropical Dreams: A People's History of South Florida" recounts the area's colorful past with a wealth of artifacts and mixed-media presentations including an early Tequesta Indian settlement, treasures from sunken Spanish galleons, a Conch house from the heyday of Key West's sponge trade and a 1923 trolley car. Impressive temporary exhibitions also generally focus on Miami history and folklife.

Bayfront Park

Biscayne Blvd. between N.E. 4th and S.E. 2nd Sts. Open daily year-round. 305-358-7550. www.bayfrontpark miami.com.

This 32-acre green space recently underwent a multi-million dollar renovation and reopened in 2009. In addition to its 6,500-seater amphitheater, which draws music megastars, other activities include free daily classes and a kids' playground. Cruises, tours and watersports schools are also based here.

Look for sculptures by Japanese landscape architect Isamu Noguchi, — *Challenger Memorial* (**1**), *Slide Mantra* (**2**) for children— as well as a prominent fountain and a laser light tower (**3**).

Bayside Marketplace★

401 Biscayne Blvd. Open year-round Mon–Fri 10am–10pm Sat 10am–11pm, Sun 11am–9pm. 305-577-3344. www.baysidemarketplace.com.

This hugely popular mall complex, comprising several buildings connected by plazas and open-air walkways, overlooks Biscayne Bay. Its profusion of boutiques, retail outlets, eateries and entertainment sprawls over 235,000sq ft of space and lures visitors with its ambience and vibrant nightlife.

Freedom Tower

600 Biscayne Blvd.

One of Miami-Dade County's most striking landmarks, this Spanish Renaissance Revival building consists of a three-storey base that buttresses a slim 12-storey tower. At the top is a cupola inspired by the 16C Giralda Tower in Seville, Spain.

Brickell Avenue

This broad, four-lane street is known as **"Millionaires' Row."** Signature residential high rises include **The Palace** *(no. 1541)*, recognizable by the striking stepped wing emanating from its east side; **The Imperial** *(no. 1627)*, with its red veneer, square windows and sloping roof; and **The Atlantis** *(no. 2025)*, whose much-photographed "skycourt" consists of a 37ft square-shaped hole punched out of its centre.

Sitting between The Palace and The Imperial is the 28-story **Villa Regina** *(no. 1581)*, a condominium notable for its vivid color scheme, by the acclaimed Israeli artist, Yacov Agam.

Little Havana

See map p110–111.
Immediately east of downtown, a 3.3sq mi section of Miami bounded by the Miami River (east), S.W. 37th Avenue (west), N.W. Seventh Street (north) and Coral Way (south) represents one of the city's most lively and exotic neighborhoods. Along **Calle Ocho,** or Eighth Street—Little Havana's main thoroughfare—sidewalk vendors hawk a variety of wares and ubiquitous stand-up *cafeterias* dispense tiny cups of dense black *café Cubano.*
A bewildering array of small businesses, including the diminutive *botanicas* that sell religious paraphernalia for practitioners of *Santería*, a form of voodoo, cater to a Latin clientele. English is rarely spoken.
Cuban history is remembered in places such as **José Martí Park** *(351 S.W. 4th St.).* Named for the apostle of Cuban independence (José Martí, 1853–1895), the park overlooks the western bank of the Miami River.
Visit the following sights beginning at S.W. 32nd Avenue and S.W. 8th Street, heading east. Note that at S.W. 26th Avenue, Calle Ocho becomes a one-way thoroughfare heading east. Metered parking is available on both sides of S.W. 8th Street.

Woodlawn Park Cemetery
3260 S.W. 8th St.
One of Miami's oldest burial spots (and its largest), Woodlawn Park (1913) is the final resting place for thousands of Cuban refugees. Two former exiled Cuban presidents, as well as Anastasio Somoza, longtime dictator of Nicaragua, are interred here. Gothic statuary, crypts and a mausoleum with stained-glass windows make for a somber atmosphere.

Latin Quarter
This quarter stretches along Calle Ocho between S.W. 17th and S.W. 12th Avenues. (The north-south portion of the quarter reaches from N.W. First to S.W. Ninth Streets.) Here quaint street lamps rise above brick sidewalks set with stars bearing the names of an international array of prominent Hispanic entertainers, including Julio Iglesias and Gloria Estefan.

Máximo Gómez Park
Southeast corner of S.W. 15th Ave.
For a glimpse of local color, drop by this tiny plaza, named for the Dominican Republic-born Chief of the Cuban Liberating Army, and known locally as Domino Park. As they have been doing since the early 1960s, Cubans, primarily elderly

EL CRÉDITO CIGAR FACTORY
1100 S.W. 8th St. ☎305-858-4162.
In 1969 the El Crédito company, which began in Havana in 1907, opened in Miami. Descendants of the founding Carillo family owned and operated the business until only recently; it remains one of the top hand-rolled cigar producers in Miami-Dade County. Visitors can watch the cigar-making process through glass windows looking into the factory before visiting the on-site store.

men, assemble here daily for spirited games of dominoes (introduced to the hemisphere by the Spanish), chess, cards and checkers.

Cuban Memorial Plaza (A)
In the median of S.W. 13th Ave./Cuban Memorial Blvd. and S.W. 8th St.
A hexagonal marble monument topped by a flickering eternal torch decorates this small square. Created in 1971 to honor those members of Brigade 2506 who lost their lives in the aborted invasion of Cuba in April 1961, the plaza now serves as a rallying point for political demonstrations.

Teatro Martí
420 S.W. 8th Ave., at southwest corner of S.W. 4th St.
This is one of Little Havana's oldest theaters, (founded in 1963) and is the most important, also staging films. It is housed in the Riverside Commercial Building, built by the Ku Klux Klan as its headquarters in 1926.

Templo Adventista del Septimo Dia (B)
862 S.W. 4th St. at corner of 9th Ave.
Built in 1925 by the Seventh Day Adventist Church, this stucco structure exemplifies Mission-style architecture, as erected by the Spanish in many parts of their colonial empire.

Warner House
111 S.W. 5th Ave. www.historicpreservationmiami.com.
A Neoclassical mansion built in 1912 by the Warner family, who lived here and used it as a venue for South Florida's first floral business. Fully restored, it now houses the Archaeological and Historical Conservancy. One block east of Warner House, the **Miami River Inn (C)** *(118 S.W. South River Dr.),* comprises several restored early 20C buildings that now function as a bed-and-breakfast inn (⏳*see p127*).

Coral Gables★★

♿See map p110–111

Grandest and most successful of South Florida's boomtime developments, Coral Gables covers a 12.5sq mi area just southwest of downtown Miami.

Inspired by the Garden City and City Beautiful movements of the 19C and early 20C (particularly the 1893 Columbian Exposition in Chicago), **George Merrick** (1886-1942) purchased 3,000 acres of undeveloped scrubland just outside Miami to form a comprehensively planned community in which buildings, streets, public plazas and utilities—discreetly out of sight—were conceived as a unified whole. Broad boulevards, formal entrances, sculpture and parklike landscaping associated with European cities like important components. The prevailing style was **Mediterranean Revival**, a popular early 20C design featuring elements such as clay roof tiles, small towers, wrought ironwork, breezy courtyards and loggias.

The area is bounded roughly by S.W. 57th Avenue (Red Road) on the west, S.W. 37th Avenue (Douglas Road) on the east, S.W. Eighth Street (US-41) on the north, and S.W. 72nd Street (Sunset Drive) on the south, and embraces a 6mi bayside stretch running south along Old Cutler Road. While largely residential, this city within a city also boasts the **University of Miami**, some of the area's finest Mediterranean Revival architecture, and mature tropical landscaping.

Entrances – Designed to set Coral Gables apart from surrounding areas, grand drive-through entrances welcomed visitors with suitable pomp—much in the spirit of the triumphal arches of Spanish cities like Seville and Toledo. The 1922 **Granada Entrance** (Granada Blvd. and Tamiami Tr.) is made of rough-cut coral rock; the 300ft-long gateway boasts a 40ft-high arch and flanking pergolas. **Commercial Entrance** (Alhambra Circle, Madeira Ave. and Douglas Rd.) is dominated by a 600ft curved coral-rock wall and archway marking the approach to the business section of the Gables. Costing nearly $1 million, the 1925 **Douglas Entrance** (Tamiami Tr. and Douglas Rd.), called La Puerta del Sol (Gate of the Sun), was designed with a series of arcades and complexes to suggest a Spanish *plaza*. Smaller than originally planned, it nevertheless included a 90ft clock tower, grand arch, shops, galleries, apartments and a lavish ballroom; renovated, it now houses offices. Equally elaborate is the **Country Club Prado Entrance** (Country Club Prado and Tamiami Tr.). This 1927 gateway of stuccoed concrete occupies a 240ft length of grassy median at the end of a tree-shaded boulevard. Recalling an Italian Renaissance garden, the symmetrical layout

ASK PETER...

Q: I want great food without pretension, where should I go?

A: Head straight to a place called El Carajo, which is located in a decidedly unsexy part of Miami (2465 SW 17th Ave.). You might think this restaurant looks like a 7-Eleven merged with a liquor store and a gas station. Yes, you can also buy motor oil, but you must get the tapas. Try the *coquetas de bacalao* (codfish croquettes) or the amazing *pulpo a la gallega* (octopus Galician style, from northwest Spain).

305-856-2424
www.elcarajo
internationaltapas
andwines.com

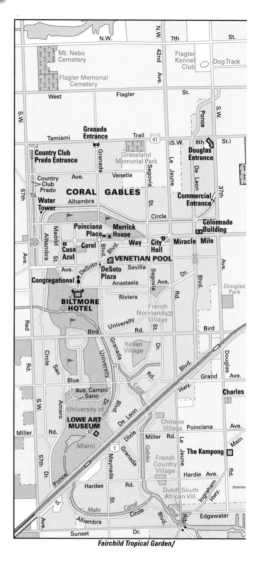

Fairchild Tropical Garden/

incorporates 20 masonry pillars topped with classical urns and pedestal fountains at each end of a reflecting pool.

Plazas – Intended to break up the predictable grid of house lots, 14 plazas were also created for Coral Gables. Many served

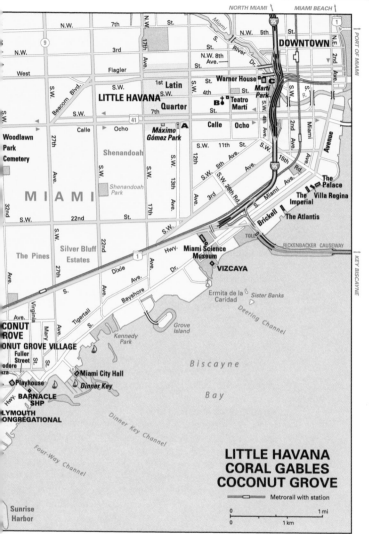

as European-style traffic circles, highlighted by fountains, such as the elaborate tiered pedestal supporting an obelisk at **DeSoto Plaza** (Sevilla Ave. and Granada and DeSoto Blvds.). To visit downtown, park on Miracle Mile (Coral Way) or Ponce

de Leon Blvd. (*metered parking*) and walk. Giralda Ave. between Ponce de Leon Blvd. and Galiano St. is notable for its trendy restaurants, and Aragon Ave. for its specialty shops. Other sights in Coral Gables are best reached by car. Street names in residential sections of Coral Gables are painted on white-washed concrete markers and placed at corners, low to the ground.

A free Coral Gables driving-tour map is available at the City Hall (*see below*) information desk. Coral Gables Chamber of Commerce is another source of information (*224 Catalonia Ave.; 305-446-1657; www.coralgables.com*).

Coral Way

This busy thoroughfare is the main east-west artery in down-town Coral Gables. The four-block (half-mile) section between Douglas and LeJeune roads is known as **Miracle Mile**. Shops range from discount stores to chic boutiques. Fronted by Corinthian columns, the two-story, coral-colored 1926 **Colonnade Building** (*no. 169*) features a baroque, Spanish-inspired arched entrance topped by spires. Used as a training center for World War II pilots, and as real-estate offices, the building now holds a restaurant. Walk inside to view the marble interior of the 75ft-high **rotunda,** connected to the Westin Colonnade Hotel tower built just north of the Colonnade Building in 1985.

Miracle Mile terminates at **City Hall** (*405 Biltmore Way*). Designed by Phineas Paist and Denman Fink, this coral-rock monument topped by a three-tiered tower cost $200,000 to build in 1927. The curved, colonnaded front bay is slightly skewed so the building aligns with angled Biltmore Way.

Coral Gables Merrick House

907 Coral Way. Grounds open daily year-round. Visit by guided tour (45min) only, year-round Wed & Sun 1pm, 2pm & 3pm. Closed major holidays. $5. &[P] 305-460-5361. www.coralgables.com.

George Merrick's two-story boyhood home was added in 1906 to the modest frame cabin that existed on the land Merrick's father purchased in 1899. Designed by Merrick's mother, Althea, the house features indigenous oolite limestone (coral rock) and Dade County pine and adapts New England architecture to the area's subtropical climate. The interior is appointed with period and Merrick family furnishings; surrounding gardens contain trees from the family's original plantation.

Houses along Coral Way between Toledo and Madrid streets represent a variety of interpretations of the area's Mediterranean Revival architecture. Three doors west of Coral Gables Merrick House is **Poinciana Place** (*937 Coral Way*), the home

George Merrick built in 1916 for his new wife. Coral Gables' first mayor, Edward "Doc" Dammers, originally lived at 1141 Coral Way. Architect H. George Fink designed the **Casa Azul** *(1254 Coral Way)*, with its blue glazed-tile roof, for himself in 1924.

Biltmore Hotel★★

1200 Anastasia Ave. Guided tours year-round Sun 1:30pm, 2:30pm & 3:30pm. ✕ ♿ 🅿 ☎ *305-445-1926 or 800-915-1926. www.biltmorehotel.com.*

The Biltmore was inaugurated in 1926 as South Florida's premier winter resort. This massive tile-roofed "wedding cake" boasted a Mediterranean Revival design by the prestigious New York architectural firm of Schultze and Weaver (designers of the Waldorf-Astoria Hotel in New York City) and formed the centerpiece of Coral Gables' 1,600-acre "Country Club Section." The 300ft-high tower with triple cupola—inspired by the 16C Giralda tower of the Cathedral of Seville, Spain—can be seen from miles around.

Its former glory fully reclaimed, the hotel is now the setting for elegant weddings, fashion photography and major motion pictures and television series (such as *CSI: Miami* and *Miami Vice*).

Directly opposite the hotel is the 1924 **Coral Gables Congregational Church** *(3010 DeSoto Blvd.)*, built on land donated by George Merrick in memory of his father, Solomon Merrick, a Congregational minister who served at Plymouth Church in Coconut Grove. With its arcaded loggias, arched bell tower and ornate baroque entry, the yellow stucco building is an excellent example of Spanish Colonial architecture and was the first church in Florida to be named on the National Register of Historic Places *(open year-round daily by appointment only;* ♿ 🅿 ☎ *305-448-7421; www.coralgablescongregational.org).*

Venetian Pool★★

2701 DeSoto Blvd. Open late-May/Jun–mid-Aug/early Sept Mon–Fri 11am–7:30pm, weekends & holidays 10am–4:30pm. Rest of the year Tue–Fri 11am–5:30pm, weekends & holidays 10am–4:30pm. Visit website to confirm all times/days when open. $11. ✕ ♿ 🅿. *Children must be a minimum of 38 inches tall and 3 years old.* ☎ *305-460-5306. www.venetianpool.com.*

A limestone quarry that supplied building materials for the area's early homes formed the base of this whimsical municipal pool. Working in tandem in 1922, artist Denman Fink and architect Phineas Paist concocted a fanciful design incorporating a casino, towers, striped light poles (inspired by those lining Venice's Grand Canal) and footbridges that crossed the free-form swimming area. The pool is drained each night and refilled

with water from underground artesian wells. Today the renovated Venetian Pool, ornamented with waterfalls and pocked with rock caves, provides a unique recreational venue for Coral Gables residents and visitors.

Lowe Art Museum★

1301 Stanford Dr., on University of Miami campus. » *Take US-1 (S. Dixie Hwy.) south to Stanford Dr.; turn right on Stanford and pass under Metrorail; museum is second building on right. Open year-round Tue–Sat 10am–4pm, Sun noon–4pm. Closed Jan 1 & Dec 25. $10.* ♿🅿 ☏*305-284-3535. www.lowemuseum.org.*

The museum, housed in a high-ceilinged, 38,600sq ft, one-story structure, showcases a permanent collection of some 8,000 works. Highlights include objects from the pre-Columbian and Greco-Roman periods, Renaissance and Baroque paintings, European masters and 19C–20C American paintings, Native American textiles and jewelry, and African and Asian art.

The new **Myrna and Sheldon Palley Pavilion for Contemporary Glass and Studio Arts** features a stunning $3.5 million glass collection with masterpieces by Dale Chihuly, Richard Jolley, William Carlson and others, as well as 3-D art by some of the world's most talented contemporary artists in this medium. Off a central garden, several smaller galleries include masks, sculpture, ceramics and beadwork from Africa, Asia and the Americas. A fine **Native American collection** of textiles, baskets and pottery from the southeast, southwest and northwest cultural areas occupies the Barton Gallery. The Green galleries and halls at the rear of the museum showcase contemporary art and changing exhibits.

Fairchild Tropical Garden★★

♿*See map p101. 10901 Old Cutler Rd.,10mi south of downtown. Open year-round daily 9:30am–4:30pm. Tram tours (40min) Mon–Fri 10am–3pm on the hr, weekends 10am–4pm on the hr. Closed Dec 25. $25.* ✕♿🅿 ☏*305-667-1651. www.fairchildgarden.org.*

Set on 83 well-tended acres studded with a series of 12 man-made lakes, the largest botanical garden in the continental US boasts more than 2,500 species of plants and trees from around the world. The gardens, named for plant explorer David Fairchild, opened in 1938. Plants here are grouped by families and arranged in spaces that vary from narrow allées to open beds.

A tram tour takes visitors past some of the garden's flora, including 500 species of **palms** and a group of rare **cycads,** a species that dates from the Cretaceous period some 100 million years ago. Tropical vegetation is maintained in a steamy greenhouse; a separate garden nurtures endangered botanical species.

Coconut Grove★★

See map p110-111.

Lush foliage and banyan trees enhance the tropical feeling of this picturesque village stretching 4mi south of Rickenbacker Causeway along Biscayne Bay. The oldest community in the Miami area, Coconut Grove retains a strong sense of history in its quiet residential neighborhoods, where many of the vine-covered bungalows and Mediterranean-style estates date to the early 20C.

By contrast, trendy bars and cafes make the downtown one of Miami's liveliest entertainment spots. Pulsing with activity at night and on weekends, the Grove is also renowned for its Saturday Farmers' Market and colorful fairs held throughout the year. To fully enjoy this area, reserve a day to see Miami Science Museum, and a second day to explore Coconut Grove proper *(avoid Tue when Vizcaya is closed)*; to shop in the village and tour The Barnacle, park on Grand Ave. or Main Hwy. (metered parking) and walk. Other sights are best visited by car. *Cocoanut Grove* (spelled with an "a" until 1919) owes its name to Horace Porter, a Connecticut doctor who started a short-lived coconut plantation here in 1873.

Vizcaya★★★

3251 S. Miami Ave. Open year-round Wed–Mon 9:30am–4:30pm. Closed Thanksgiving Day, Dec 25. $15. ✕ ♿ 🅿 ☏ *305-250-9133. www.vizcayamuseum.com.*

Overlooking the calm, blue waters of Biscayne Bay, this ornate Italian Renaissance-style villa and formal gardens embody the fantasy winter retreat of their builder, **James Deering** (1859–1925). The 35-acre estate was raised from a Florida hardwood hammock in 1916. Deering's Vizcaya (a Basque word meaning "elevated place") required 1,000 workers, $15 million and over two years to complete.

On Christmas Day 1916, Deering moved into his new 70-room mansion. Deering, who never married, lived at Vizcaya until his death in 1925. The following year, the house and gardens were badly ravaged by the legendary 1926 hurricane. The Deering family hired Paul Chalfin in 1934 to renovate the house and replant the gardens in preparation for opening the house as a museum. But public interest in Vizcaya waned, and in 1945 the family sold 130 acres to the Catholic Church to build a hospital complex. Deering's estate remained in the hands of his heirs—his brother's children—until 1952, when Dade County purchased the villa and its remaining 35 acres for $1 million. Today there are 34 rooms open to the public. The Neoclassical

Travel Tip: If you see a fleet of beds racing down the village streets of Coconut Grove, don't worry,—you're not hallucinating. It's the Great Grove Bed Race (*www.thegreatgrove bedrace.com*), an annual Labor Day tradition. Teams of four bed-pushers and one bed-rider fly down the 1/8th mile drag strip in a race against the clock. Community groups and local businesses sponsor bed-racing teams, and prizes are awarded for best theme, décor, and racing success. The event attracts 20,000 spectators and the proceeds go to a good cause: the Boys and Girls Clubs of Miami-Dade.

Tourist information:
Coconut Grove BID (☏ *305-461-5506; www.coconut grove.com*).

The Men Behind Vizcaya

In 1912 James Deering purchased 180 acres of Miami shoreline. Craving privacy, Deering envisioned a "homey" cottage on the banks of Biscayne Bay. His decorator and art advisor, Paul Chalfin, had grander ideas. A graduate of the École des Beaux-Arts in Paris and former curator at the Boston Museum of Fine Arts, Chalfin accompanied Deering to Europe, where the two men combed old European castles and Italian villas for treasures to fill the house, which had yet to be built. By the time they returned, Deering had amassed such a collection that he realized his house would have to be designed to fit its furnishings instead of the other way around. Inspired by 15C and 16C villas in the Venetian countryside, architect F. Burrall Hoffman Jr's design resulted in a triumphal merging of Italian Renaissance style with Florida's tropical landscape.

STREETS OF MAYFAIR

Located on Grand Avenue between Virginia Street and Mary Street is this fascinating mix of high-end shops, art galleries and restaurants. Its large trademark concrete building was designed in 1979 by Grove architect Kenneth Treister (whose work includes the Holocaust Memorial in Miami Beach) and originally housed boutiques reportedly used to launder South American drug money. Be sure to explore the interior courtyard (enter from Virginia St.), reminiscent of the style of architect Antonio Gaudí in Barcelona. Treister adorned this courtyard with lush greenery, multilevel walkways, tiled fountains and striking copper bird sculptures. For livelier crowds and nightlife, head across the street to CocoWalk.

entrance hall contains hand-blocked c.1814 wallpaper from the Paris workshop of Joseph Dufour. Three pairs of 1C Roman marble columns adorn the **Renaissance Hall.** The walls and ceiling of the Italian Rococo **Music Room** are covered with canvas panels hand-painted with a fanciful marine theme. Overlooking the gardens, the **Tea Room** is actually an enclosed loggia, featuring a 17C Nubian marble mantelpiece and a modeled ceiling with Neoclassical motifs. The room's stained-glass wall displays Vizcaya's emblematic sea horse and caravel. The **East Loggia,** with its striking colored-marble floor, opens onto the terrace that fronts the bay. Just off the terrace sits the **Stone Barge,** an ornamental Venetian-style breakwater where Deering once tied his luxurious 80ft yacht.

More than 10 acres of formal gardens flank the south side of the house. The garden's central axis draws the eye up a water stairway to a two-room baroque casino (garden house), atop a hill. Pools and domed gazebos define the garden's east-west axis.

Miami Science Museum

3280 S. Miami Ave., across from Vizcaya. Open year-round daily 10am–6pm. Closed Thanksgiving Day & Dec 25. $14.95.
&🅿️ ☎305-646-4200. www.miamisci.org.

Housed in a Mediterranean-style building decorated with arches and barrel tiles, the museum features over 150 exhibits that allow visitors to touch objects, climb a rock wall and dig for fossils while learning about everything from gravity to mastodon teeth. Out back, the Wildlife Center—which doubles as a rehabilitation facility for birds of prey—displays wood storks, tortoises, pythons and boa constrictors. An adjacent planetarium offers astronomy and laser shows. Special events range from experiencing hurricane force winds to discovering the physics behind yo-yos.

Miami City Hall

3500 Pan American Dr. (off S. Bayshore Dr.).

Located on **Dinner Key**, a small island attached to the mainland by landfill, this two-story Streamline Moderne gem with a flat roof and glass-block windows was designed in 1933 as the seaplane terminal for Pan American Airways. (Note the roofline frieze of winged globes, rising suns and eagles.) In the peak years of the late 1930s, flights left for 32 foreign countries and some 50,000 passengers per year passed through making this the largest international port of entry in the US. (Charles Lindbergh was one of the early pilots.) The terminal originally featured a second-story restaurant and promenade deck where spectators would watching large flying clipper ships taking off and landing in Biscayne Bay. The last flight left Dinner Key in 1945 and the building has served as the city hall since 1954.

Coconut Grove Village★

Centered on the intersection of Grand Ave. and Main Hwy.

The heart of the Grove, the downtown has undergone several transformations in recent decades. Today sidewalk cafes and clothing shops cater to the under-40 crowd, attracting local students, professionals and tourists alike.

A mélange of high-end shops and boutiques fill **Streets of Mayfair** and **CocoWalk**. Cafes line **Commodore Plaza** and the north end of Main Highway, while interesting boutiques are tucked into **Fuller Street.**

CocoWalk

3015 Grand Ave., west side of Virginia St. Daily 10am–10pm; Fri–Sat 11pm, nightclubs 3am. ☎305-444-0777. www.cocowalk.net.

This upscale retail, dining and entertainment center of bars, chain stores, clubs and movie theaters embraces an open plaza with a central cupola-topped pavilion. Pink stucco and three levels of loggias and balconies give the mall a cheerful tropical air.

Barnacle State Historic Park★★

3485 Main Hwy. Park open year-round Wed–Mon dawn–dusk. House open year-round Fri–Mon 9am–5pm. Guided tours (1hr) 10am, 11:30am, 1pm, 2:30pm. Closed Jan 1, Thanksgiving Day & Dec 25. Park $2, house $3. ☎305-442-6866. www.floridastate parks.org/thebarnacle.

This five-acre bayfront site preserves one of the last patches of tropical hardwood hammock in Coconut Grove, along with the 1891 home of **Ralph Middleton Munroe**, an accomplished sailor and yacht designer. Nicknamed "The Barnacle," for its octagonal center that tapers to a small open-air vent, the five-

Coconut Grove in the 19C

By 1890 Coconut Grove had become the largest town on the south Florida mainland, boasting the first school, library and yacht club in the region. A sizable black Bahamian community took root on the west side of town. These settlers supported themselves by salvaging shipwrecks, manufacturing coontie starch, and working in the local construction and service industries. By the early 20C, estates on the eastern and southern bayfront had become a prime winter address for society figures and affluent industrialists like James Deering. Artists, academics and writers, affiliated with the Winter Institute of Literature at the University of Miami, were drawn to the town's intellectual community. Alexander Graham Bell and Charles Lindbergh were frequent visitors. Annexed by Miami in 1925, the village has not lost its independent character and bohemian flair.

room, hip-roofed structure features a Bahamian design well-suited to the Grove's tropical climate. Virtually unchanged since Munroe's day, the house remained in the family until the 1970s and contains the original furnishings.

The 1926 **boathouse**, home to Munroe's shipbuilding tools, is also open to visitors.

Charles Avenue

Once called Evangelist Street for its many churches, this quiet road runs west through the oldest black community on mainland Florida. Known as Kebo, the area was settled in the 1880s by Bahamians who came north by way of Key West. These pioneers helped northern settlers cultivate tropical greenery in the village and brought many of the seeds for the soursops, sugar apples and Barbados cherries that thrive here today.

The avenue is notable for its early 20C **shotgun houses**. A drive west to the corner of Douglas Road brings you to one of the first cemeteries in South Florida, used since 1906.

Farther down Douglas Road, just south of Main Highway, is **The Kampong**, part of the **National Tropical Botanical Garden** *(4013 Douglas Rd.; open year-round by guided tours Wed & Sat 10.30am; twilight tours some Sats, visit website for dates; $20; ℘305-442-7169; www.ntbg.org)*, formerly the private estate and garden of the great botanist David Fairchild, who first introduced soybeans and many exotic fruits to North American soil. His original plantings are still here.

Plymouth Congregational Church★

3400 Devon Rd. Open Sun 10am (church service), other times by appt only. ♿ 🅿 ℘305-4446521. www.plymouthmiami.com.

This 1917 Spanish Colonial-style church was modeled after a 16C mission in Mexico with symmetrical bell towers flanking a curving roof parapet. Of local oolitic limestone, the building and massive cloister walls were reportedly built by a single Spanish mason using nothing more than a hatchet and a plumb line. The walnut door (c.1600) is thought to be from a monastery in the Pyrenees mountains. Tucked into the charming banyan-shaded grounds are a small meditation garden, a rose garden and a tropical cloister garden.

Moved from its original site, the one-room **schoolhouse** at the north end of the property dates back to 1887 *(open by appt only)*. Built of lumber from a salvaged shipwreck, it initially housed a Sunday school, then in 1889 it became the first public school in what is now Miami-Dade County. The bell is original.

Key Biscayne

*Tourist information: Key Biscayne Chamber of Commerce.
℘305-361-5207. www.keybiscaynechamber.org.*
In 1825 the Cape Florida Lighthouse was erected at the tip of Key Biscayne to guide ships safely through the Florida Channel. In the early 1900s, Dr. William J. Matheson dredged a yacht basin and planted thousands of coconut trees here. The Rickenbacker Causeway opened in 1947 linking Miami to the island.
Today, this 7mi-long barrier island is a haven for water sports and cycling as well as being a very desirable residential neighborhood, boasting luxury accommodations (President Richard Nixon bought a vacation home here in the 1970s) and fine restaurants. The southern end is home to two popular beachfront parks, Crandon Park and Bill Baggs Cape Florida State Park. Head west on the causeway toward Miami for spectacular **views★** of downtown (2 mi south) and Brickell Avenue.

Miami Seaquarium★

*4400 Rickenbacker Causeway, 5mi east Key Biscayne tollbooth.
Open year-round daily 9:30am–6pm (last series of shows 2:30pm).
$38.95. ✕ ᷼ 🅿 ℘305-361-5705. www.miamiseaquarium.com.*
In its late 1950s heyday, this 38-acre marine-life park served as the set for the TV series *Flipper* and was home to its eponymous star. Today, visitors can swim with dolphins (*additional charge*), watch killer whale shows, and fish and sharks being hand-fed by divers in a reef tank. Crocodile Flats houses some two-dozen Nile crocodiles. The main building provides two levels to view some 10,000 varieties of aquatic life. At the back of the park, sharks swim in an open-air channel that is crossed by several bridges. The world's first controlled manatee breeding program also takes place here.

Bill Baggs Cape Florida State Park★

1200 S. Crandon Blvd., 7mi from Key Biscayne tollbooth. Open 8am-sunset. $8 per vehicle. △ ✕ 🅿 ℘305-361-5811. www.floridastateparks.org/capeflorida.
A mile of Biscayne Bay beachfront and a 74-acre wetlands area attract locals to this secluded 412-acre park on the south end of Key Biscayne. The original 95ft-high brick **Cape Florida Lighthouse** was constructed in 1825. Tours of the keeper's quarters and kitchen follow presentation of a 14min video (*visit by guided tour only; Thu–Mon 10am & 1pm*). The light is still operational, serving as a navigational aid. A hardwood hammock borders the beach, a bicycle trail loops through the park, and a 1.5mi nature trail weaves through an adjacent 63-acre wetland.

Greater Miami North

During the boom years of the 1920s, planned subdivisions of this area, including Morningside, El Portal and Miami Shores, were developed as theme communities, often featuring Spanish or Mediterranean Revival-style architecture. Many of the other new North Miami communities stood unfinished after the bottom fell out of the real-estate market in 1926.

Today Greater Miami North is largely residential, a mix of luxury apartment houses, modern suburban developments and remnants of the older, established neighborhoods: the small farming community of Lemon City, for example, is now the Little Haiti neighborhood The fashionable district of Aventura, just north of Lehman Causeway, comprises luxury resorts and the upscale **Aventura Mall** (*www.aventuramall.com*).

Museum of Contemporary Art★

770 N.E. 125th St., North Miami. Open year-round Tue & Thu–Sat 11am–5pm, Wed 1pm–9pm, Sun noon–5pm. Last Fri each month 7pm–10pm Jazz at MOCA. Closed major holidays. $5. &♿🅿️ 📞*305-893-6211. www.mocanomi.org.*

Architect Charles Gwathmey combined cubes and cylinders in designing this simple but elegant building on palm-studded grounds. MOCA's permanent collection reflects significant artistic developments in contemporary art by emerging and established artists from the US and abroad.

Ancient Spanish Monastery★★

16711 W. Dixie Hwy., North Miami Beach. **»** *Take Biscayne Blvd. (US-1) north to N. Miami Beach Blvd. Turn left, then right on W. Dixie Hwy. Open year-round Mon–Sat 10am–4pm, Sun 11am–4pm. Tel in advance of your visit as Monastery is sometimes closed during regular business hours for private functions. Closed major holidays. $5.* ♿🅿️📞*305-945-1461. www.spanishmonastery.com.*

Nestled on a woodsy site, the Cloisters of St. Bernard of Clairvaux provides an in-depth look at a 12C monastery. This superb example of early Gothic architecture, named for the influential leader of the Cistercian Monks, was completed in the Spanish province of Segovia in 1141. Nearly eight centuries later it was disassembled and moved to the US (&*see box, opposite*) by **William Randolph Hearst**. A wealthy American newspaperman and collector extraordinaire, Hearst purchased the monastery in 1925, planning to reconstruct his "greatest art treasure" on the grounds of San Simeon, his lavish California estate. Visitors enter the Ancient Spanish Monastery, as it is locally known, through a 200-pound wrought-iron gate crowned with

---

THE WORLD'S LARGEST JIGSAW PUZZLE?

Packed in hay and shipped from Spain in numbered boxes, the stones of the monastery were quarantined by US officials (hoof-and-mouth disease had broken out in Segovia). The hay was destroyed and the haphazardly repacked stones were left in crates for over 25 years. After Hearst's death in 1951, two South Florida developers bought the stones, hoping to reconstruct the cloisters as a tourist attraction.

All 36,000 stones—some weighing 3,000 pounds—were spread over the 20-acre site. Allan Carswell, a renowned stone mason, was hired to supervise the process of fitting the stones together, using photographs that Hearst had taken of the intact monastery. Nineteen months and $1.5 million later, the reconstructed cloisters opened in 1954, only to be sold in 1964. The complex now houses an Episcopal church.

the Latin inscription meaning "These Sacred Cistercian Walls." On the southern perimeter of the lush side garden stands the entrance to a long cloister. The top of its portal is adorned with the figure of Mary, the mother of Christ, encircled by angels. A series of ribbed arches form the cloister's vault; tile now covers the floors that once consisted of small stones.

The **Chapel of St. Bernard de Clairvaux,** which served as the monks' refectory, occupies the first corridor; the small iron bell at the entrance once called the brothers to meals. Above the altar, two circular stained-glass windows, depicting scenes from the Book of Revelation written by St. John, are as old as the monastery: they represent two of only three known **telescopic windows** in existence (so-named for the three rings of receding frames that encase the windows, creating a telescopic effect). In the middle of the complex stands a **prayer well** composed of elements of an AD 1C Roman temple.

A life-size statue of King Alfonso VIII stands at the end of the first corridor; diagonally across the courtyard is a statue of his grandfather, King Alfonso VII of Castile and Leon, under whose auspices the monastery was initially built. Located midway along the second corridor, the **Chapter House** formed part of the original monastery.

The medieval pink-limestone, Gothic-style altar (at the corner past the Chapter House) was carved in Cannes, France. Ten corbels along the cloister walls—part of Hearst's art collection—portray shields of 12C Segovia noble and royal families who pledged their allegiance to both the Catholic Church and the Spanish king.

121

South Miami-Dade County

Isolated by the fringes of the Everglades, the southern portion of Miami-Dade County was among the last parts of Florida to be settled, and remains a separate community in both spirit and appearance. While the fast-growing region has its share of tract housing and new shopping malls, its rural western section is still dominated by produce farms, lime groves and tropical plant nurseries, preserving a distinctive small-town feel virtually nonexistent elsewhere in the Miami area.

Development came with the southern expansion of the Florida East Coast Railway in the early 1900s. The region's fertile soil, produced by draining the swampy Glades, proved ideal for beans, tomatoes, avocados and other cash crops. By the 1950s this was one of the top vegetable-producing areas in the US.

The agricultural economy was devastated in 1992, when Hurricane Andrew spent its full fury in and around Homestead. Recovery was aided by the $7.9 billion Hurricane Relief Bill. Funds provided a face-lift to **Homestead's Old Downtown** *(38mi southwest of downtown Miami)*, the historic business district where recently restored early-20C storefronts on Krome Avenue recapture the original character of this former railroad town.

Zoo Miami★★

12400 S.W. 152nd St. 18mi from downtown Miami.

» *Take Florida's Turnpike south to Exit 16. Go west on S.W. 152nd St. and follow signs. Open year-round daily 9:30am–5:30pm (last admission gates 4pm). Narrated Safari Tram ride ($5). $15.95.* ✗ ♿ 🄿 🕿 *305-251-0400. www.miamimetrozoo.com.*

Occupying 290 acres of landscaped park, this popular cageless zoo, one of the finest in the US, specializes in tropical species adaptable to South Florida's hot climate. Some 900 reptiles, birds and mammals, primarily from Asia, Africa and Australia, are showcased. Camouflaged moats and other inconspicuous barriers separate visitors from the animals, which appear to roam completely free in their natural habitats. An elevated monorail circuits the zoo, offering a bird's-eye view of the animals.

Among the highlights are a band of **lowland gorillas** (a walk-in viewing cave permits a close-up look) and a group of stunning **Bengal tigers,** whose habitat features a replica of Cambodia's 13C Angkor Wat ruins. Animal feedings and wildlife shows occur throughout the day *(check brochure for times)*. At the **Samburu Giraffe Feeding Station** visitors can feed the giraffes treats and get a really close-up view.

Amazon and Beyond, is dedicated to the flora and fauna of tropical America, home to species like the anaconda, giant river tters, golden lion tamarins and harpy eagles. The zoo also has children's playground and exhibit area, complete with frogs, nakes and spiders, plus a tropical free-flight aviary housing ome 300 Asian birds. The Field Research Center highlights the nk between birds and their ancestors, the dinosaurs.

Gold Coast Railroad Museum

2450 S.W. 152nd St., across the road from Metrozoo. Open year-round Mon–Fri 10am–4pm, Sat–Sun 11am–4pm. Closed major holidays. $6. Free first Sat of month, also free to Zoo Miami ticket holders. Caboose rides $6. **P** *305-253-0063. www.gcrm.org.*
A self-guided tour of this museum's grounds reveals numerous historic, renovated railroad cars, including the California Zephyr. A highlight is the Pullman car, used by several US presidents. A collection of train parts and memorabilia are also on display.

Coral Castle★

8655 S. Dixie Hwy., 30mi south of Miami (2mi north of Homestead). Open year-round daily 8am–6pm (Fri–Sat 8pm). Closed Dec 25. $12. **P** *305-248-6345. www.coralcastle.com.*
This three-acre mansion and monolithic sculpture garden is Florida's most intriguing sight. It was crafted of more than 1,100 tons of coral rock (oolitic limestone) from 1918 onwards by Ed Leedskalnin, a slight, 5ft-tall, 110-pound Latvian immigrant. Built under cover of night and in secret, no-one knows how Ed created his Coral Castle. He didn't use machinery and, when questioned, would only say that he knew "the secret of the pyramids." When he died, his secrets died with him, and to this day scientists (and talk shows) still debate Ed's methods and his reasons for building Coral Castle. Whatever, it has been listed on the National Register of Historic Places since 1984.
Most remarkable are the hinged **Nine-Ton Gate,** movable with just one finger; the **Polaris Telescope**, a 25ft-high, 30-ton rock telescope aimed toward the North Star; the 20ft-long **Florida Table**, carved in the shape of the state and surrounded by 10,000-pound coral rock chairs; the two-story tower where Leedskalnin lived in spartan quarters upstairs and labored with crude tools in the room below.

Biscayne National Park★

East end of N. Canal Dr. (S.W. 328th St.) in Homestead. 38mi south of downtown Miami. Visitor Center open year-round daily 9am–5pm; park grounds open year-round daily 7am–5:30pm. Closed Dec 25. **P** *305-230-7275. www.nps.gov/bisc.*
This is the largest marine park in the US, established in 1980 to help protect a 275sq mi area of coastal wetlands, mangrove

shorelines, coral reefs and 32 small islands. The protected waters stretch 26mi south from Key Biscayne to near Key Largo. Star attractions are the **reefs★★★**, located about 10mi offshore. Here warm Gulf Stream currents nurture some 50 species of living coral that create a hospitable environment for loggerhead turtles, spiny lobsters, sponges and flamboyant tropical fish.

Begin at the **Dante Fascell Visitor Center** at Convoy Point (park HQ and entrance), which features life-size dioramas and introductory films. Interpretive exhibits are displayed along a short bayside walking trail from which fishing is permitted. To bird-watch or explore estuaries along the main coast, you can rent a canoe from the Visitor Center.

The park's concessionaire offers canoe and kayak rentals, snorkeling the bay (*$40*) and the reef (*$45*), and cruises (*$35*) to Boca Chita Island (✆*305-230-1100; www.BiscayneUnderwater.com*).

Jungle Island★

1111 Parrot Jungle Trail. Open year-round daily 10am–5pm (weekends 6pm). $32.95. ✕ ♿ 🅿 *$8.* ✆ *305-400-7275. www.parrotjungle.com.*

This popular attraction, set on Biscayne Bay, is home to more than 1,100 exotic birds, including some 80 pink flamingos. Paths wind through lush tropical gardens and through major exhibits including a serpentarium, tortoise and crocodile ponds, aviary, penguinarium and petting barn.

There are three shows: **Winged Wonders** is a conventional bird show; **Tale of the Tiger** features a rotating cast of big cats; **Dr. Wasabi's Wild Adventures** is a "safari adventure" through the animal kingdom.

Jungle Island also has its own beach where you can relax under an umbrella and have a swim.

Fruit & Spice Park

24801 S.W. 187th Ave. at S.W. 248th St. in Homestead. 27mi southwest of downtown Miami. Open year-round daily 9am–5pm. Closed Dec 25. $8. ♿ 🅿 ✆ *305-247-5727. www.fruitandspicepark.org.*

This unusual tropical park boast hundreds of varieties of exotic fruit and nut trees, vegetables, herbs and spices, planted in geographical theme areas across its 35 acres, with mango and avocado orchards among the most interesting groves. The Park showcases 125 varieties of mango, 75 varieties of bananas, 70 bamboo varieties, and numerous other exotic edibles. Look too for such striking specimens as the Panama candle tree, with its long yellow fruit. The gift shop offers a tempting array of treats.

ART ...LIKE A LOCAL

Thanks to Art Basel, Miami has become *the* hot place for contemporary art. Don't limit yourself to museums, do as the locals and hit the galleries or join an art walk.

ART BASEL

Florida's sister event to Art Basel in Switzerland is held annually in Miami each December. While tickets go for as much as $75, public programming events let you see international art, music and culture for less. You can check out daily collection visits that are either free or ask for a small donation to a local charity. There's also free public access for both Art Basel Conversations, a series of talks with leading professionals in the art world, and Art Public: site-specific installations and public artwork in Collins Park.

Wynwood

The principal art hotspot in Miami is Wynwood. The area didn't draw many visitors until artists began renting warehouses in the Midtown renovation of the 2000s, and now it's a thriving, up-and-coming area. Today, the Wynwood Arts District is a three-block by three-block area that is the epicenter of the local art scene. There are also galleries in the Design District (where I recommend you head to shop for furniture as you wander between galleries); in Coconut Grove; in Coral Gables; and in Little Havana and the Latin Quarter, where you'll find work from primarily Latin and Cuban artists.

Art Walks

The hottest time to hit up Wynwood is during the Art Walk, a gallery-centered event with outdoor art, DJs and food trucks. On the second Saturday of the month, galleries open their doors in an event sometimes described as speed dating for art lovers. It runs from 20th St. to 36th St. and NW 2nd Ave. to NE 2nd Ave.; you'll find the food trucks on the corner of NW 23 St. & NW 2nd Ave.

Highlights

All the galleries in Wynwood are different, but Kunsthaus Miami (3312 North Miami Avenue) is consistently a standing local favorite. Also check out Wyndwood Walls, near the Wynwood Kitchen Bar and Grill, where artists from around the world have created work on the walls of six neighboring warehouses. Another space not to miss is the Bakehouse (561 NW 32nd St.). Set up in an old bakery warehouse, the building is more artists' studios than traditional gallery. The Bakehouse hosts its own art walk on the second Friday of the month. Because the gallery also serves as artists' studios, visitors get a glimpse into the artists' working space and have a chance to interact with the artist before purchasing artworks in various different media.

Little Havana

Outside of Wynwood, in Little Havana, check out the 6th St. Container (1167 SW 6th St.). This artist-run project has a contemporary feel and has monthly exhibits of unknown or lesser-known artists that work in just about every medium imaginable.

Further Research

For a comprehensive list of galleries, visit http://art-collecting.com.

ADDRESSES

For price ranges, see the Legend on the cover flap.

WHERE TO STAY

Area visitors guide including **lodging directory** available *(free)* from the **Greater Miami Convention and Visitors Bureau.** Reservation service: Greater Miami & Beaches Hotel Assn. (*℘305-531-3553 or 800-531-3553; http://gmbha.com).* Accommodations range from economy **motels** *($99–$150)* to downtown **hotels** *($125–$300),* to luxury beachfront hotels *($250 and up).* The three main Miami Beach **hostels** are the Tropics (*℘305-531-0361; www.tropicshotel.com);* the Clay Hostel *(see below)* and the South Beach Hostel (*℘305-672-2137; www.thesouthbeachhostel.com).* Shared room rates are $20–$36.

$$$$$ Biltmore Hotel – *1200 Anastasia Ave., Coral Gables.* 🛁♿🅿 *℘305-445-1926 or 800-915-1926. www.biltmore hotel.com. 276 rooms.* This massive National Historic Landmark in Coral Gables *(see p113)* looks like a Spanish palace and has attracted presidents, royalty and movie stars since 1926. The hotel is famed for its lavish Sunday champagne brunch served outdoors in a tropical setting. It also has an immaculate 18-hole golf course.

$$$$$ The Breakers – *1 S. County Rd., Palm Beach.* 🛁♿🅿 *℘561-655-6611 or 888-273-2537. www.thebreakers.com. 560 rooms.* A Palm Beach icon, this 1926 mega-resort takes its cue from Italy's Renaissance palazzos. Luxurious guest rooms are done in light woods, seaside colors and tobacco-leaf prints. The half-

mile private beach includes a new Mediterranean-style Beach Club with three oceanside pools. The resort also has two 18-hole golf courses, tennis courts, restaurants, a spa, and shopping arcade.

$$$$$ The Chesterfield – *363 Cocoanut Row, Palm Beach.* 🛁♿🅿 *℘561-659-5800.www. chesterfieldpb.com. 60 rooms.* Located around the corner from Worth Avenue, this intimate boutique white stucco property embodies quiet elegance. Guest quarters sport a singular decor, spacious closets and marble bathrooms, and have counted Oscar de la Renta, Catherine Deneuve and Margaret Thatcher among their visitors. It continues to cater to an upscale clientele with amenties such as fresh fruit in the lobby, terry robes and a gourmet basket upon arrival.

$$$$$ Delano – *1685 Collins Ave., Miami Beach.* 🛁♿🅿 *℘305-672-2000. www.delano-hotel. com. 208 rooms.* South Beach's minimalist trend started here, courtesy of Philippe Starck. Bilowing white curtains—not doors—give access to the lobby. Expect lounge areas sparsely clad with antiques, bric-a-brac, and artworks by Dalí and Man Ray, plush, white-on-white simple-chic guest quarters, and celebrities aplenty. The Blue Door restaurant, formerly co-owned by Madonna, is also a favored celebrity haunt.

$$$$ Boca Raton Resort & Club – *501 E. Camino Real.* 🛁♿🅿 *℘561-35-3000 or 888-491-2622. www.bocaresort.com. 1,070 rooms.* Grand dame of Boca Raton, this exclusive property was designed by Addison Mizner in 1926 (as the Cloister

nn). Successive additions
retained the graceful blend of
Spanish, Italian and Moorish
styles, helping to create a
well-landscaped, self-contained
paradise, to which entry is
rigidly guarded. The height of
luxury, lodgings can be reserved
in the Cloisters (the original
building), the modern 27-story
tower, the oceanfront beach
club, the Yacht Club, or at a
spacious one- or two-bedroom
golf villa.

$$$ The Hotel – 801 Collins
Ave., Miami Beach. 🛏️♿🅿️☎️305-
31-2222 or 877-843-4683. www.
thehotelofsouthbeach.com. 53
rooms. Todd Oldham designed
nearly everything in this
renovated Art-Deco gem (1936)
off South Beach's famous Ocean
Drive. A huge mirror-shaped
tile mosiac and velveteen
couches—block-patterned in
rose, green and gold—pick up
flecks of color from the lobby's
original terrazzo floor. Blue and
neon-green cottons and pale
wood furniture brighten the
bedrooms. Bask in the sun at
the neo-Mediterranean-style
rooftop pool and Spire bar,
and reserve a table at **Wish,**
the indoor-outdoor restaurant,
favored by celebrities.

$$$ Sea View Hotel –
909 Collins Ave. Bal Harbour.
♿🅿️☎️305-866-4441 or 800-
47-1010. www.seaview-hotel.com.
0 rooms. A beachfront jewel,
this upscale Euro-styled
boutique hotel was built in 1947
one of Bal Harbour's first
high rises. Remarkably spacious,
designer-appointed guest
quarters show off rich fabrics,
wicker chairs, glass-topped
metal tables and solid
the armoires.

$$$ The Pillars – 111 N. Birch
Rd., Fort Lauderdale. 🅿️🛏️☎️954-
467-9639. www.pillarshotel.
com. 22 rooms. Bordering the
Intracoastal Waterway, this
upscale oasis cultivates British
Colonial cachet complete with
grand piano and library. Rooms
are smartly appointed with
floral bedspreads, armoires and
plantation shutters.

$$$ Hotel Place St. Michel –
162 Alcazar Ave. Coral Gables.
🛏️♿☎️305-444-1666 or
800-848-hotel. www.hotel
stmichel.com. 27 rooms.
Nestled within Coral Gables'
pedestrian-friendly downtown,
this European-style bed-and-
breakfast inn has a passion
for antiques. Public areas
are reminiscent of homey
Continental inns, guest rooms
are in subdued, Old World-style
decor.

$$ A Little Inn By The Sea –
4546 El Mar Dr., Lauderdale-
By-The-Sea. 🛏️☎️954-772-
2450 or 800-492-0311. http://
alittleinnhotel.com. 29 units.
Fronting 300ft of private beach,
this Mediterranean-style bed-
and-breakfast inn is located in
a seaside village just north of
Fort Lauderdale. Family-run, it's
reminiscent of Old Florida in the
1950s. A tropical, brick-covered
courtyard overlooks the pool,
barbecue area and beach and
there's an adults-only rooftop
patio for sunning au naturel.
Rooms and suites are done in
floral patterns.

$$ Miami River Inn – 118 S.W.
South River Dr. Miami. 🛏️☎️305-
325-0045 or 800-468-3589. www.
miamiriverinn.com.40 rooms.
Listed on the National Register
of Historic Places, this downtown
bed-and-breakfast inn was

completed in 1910. Located just steps from Miami's Little Havana, the gated compound is also within walking distance of Brickell Avenue. Painted pale yellow with olive trim, the inn serves as a tropical oasis of soaring palms and native plants amid Miami's bustling downtown. Refurbished rooms, most with hardwood floors, are appointed with period antiques and spacious baths. Two cottages have a living room and fireplace. Complimentary continental breakfast, with homemade muffins, can be savored outdoors.

$ The Clay Hostel (Hostelling International Miami Beach) – *1438 Washington Ave., South Beach.* 🥤 *℘305-534-2988 or 800-379-2529. www.clayhotel.com/clay-hostel.htm. 120 private rooms; 220 dorm beds.* Located just steps from colorful Espanola Way, this ever-popular hostel in a classic Art Deco building offers good value, and has a rich history as home to Al Capone's gambling ring in the 1930s; Desi Arnaz' rumba craze in the 1950s, and the filming of the pilot for *Miami Vice.* Aside from dorms, private rooms offer baths, a/c, mini-refrigerators, TV, and phones. Laundry and kitchen.

WHERE TO EAT

$$$$ Café L'Europe – *331 S. County Rd., Palm Beach.* 🦽 *℘561-655-4020. www.cafeleurope.com.* **Continental.** French doors, beveled brick, mahogany paneling and gleaming brass lend an air of refinement to this venue. Epitomizing *la belle vie* Palm Beach-style, Café L'Europe serves more than 5,000 ounces of caviar

each year. The menu changes seasonally but you might expect dishes such as Peruvian shrimp ceviche, seafood linguine, potato-wrapped red snapper, and roasted rack of lamb. The traditional Wiener schnitzel is a signature dish.

$$$$ The Forge – *432 Arthur Godfrey Rd. (41st St. & Royal Palm Ave.), Miami Beach.* 🦽 *℘305-538-8533. www.theforge.com.* **Continental.** There's no sign on the exterior of this ornate building, but the beefy valets and sleek cars curbside are clues to the clientele. Thick carpet, plush sofas, stained glass, tapestries and art adorn the brick-walled interior. Soft piano music and candlelight add a romantic air. It has long been considered one of the best steakhouses in America and although it was recently redesigned to cater for lighter 21C dining you can't go wrong with the signature Forge Super Steak.

$$$ Cap's Place – *2765 N.E. 28 Court in Lighthouse Point. North of Pompano Beach. From Cap's Dock it's a 10min boat ride by the restaurant's motor launch.* *℘954-941-0418. www.capsplace.com.* **Seafood.** Listed on the National Register of Historic Places, this restaurant/bar is rustic, rich in history, and fun, especially for families. In the 1920s founder Cap Knight relocated several wooden shacks, floating them on a barge up the Intracoastal Waterway from Miami to Cap's Island, north of Pompano Beach. Celebrity diners have included Winston Churchill, the Vanderbilts and the Rockefeller, Errol Flynn and George Harrison. Memorable dishes include the

house-smoked fish dip, the hearts of palm salad, homemade rolls and Key Lime Pie.

$$$ Joe's Stone Crab – *11 Washington Ave., Miami Beach.* ♿ ✆*305-673-0365. www. joesstonecrab.com. Open mid-Oct to mid-May.* **Seafood.** Located at the southern end of Miami Beach, this high-energy eatery has been a Florida legend since 1913. Caught mainly off Florida's Gulf Coast between October and May, stone crabs possess the ability to grow new claws within 12 to 18 months (fishermen take just the claws, since they contain the crab's only edible meat). Medium to jumbo-size stone crab claws are conveniently cracked open and served chilled with the house mustard sauce. Sides—coleslaw and creamed spinach—are big enough for two. Expect to line up for dinner, but if you're too hungry to wait, order from Joe's adjacent take-out counter and have a surfside picnic.

$$$ Mai-Kai – *3599 N. Federal Hwy., Fort Lauderdale.* ♿ ✆*954-563-3272. www.maikai.com.* **Polynesian.** Popular for its dinner show, Mai-Kai has been attracting tourists and locals since 1956 even if its South Seas appearance—thatched roofs, tiki torches, tropical palms and cascading waterfalls—seems out of place alongside a six-lane thoroughfare. Entering the fenced "village" via a wood-plank bridge, patrons can order one of 50 specialty drinks in a dimly-lit saloon that resembles a wrecked ship. Served in intimate dining rooms or on the garden patio, expect exotic dishes such as lobster Bora Bora, roast duck Mai-Kai, filet mignon Madagascar and coconut curry bouillabaisse.

For an extra charge you can watch the Tahitian dances performed by the Islander Revue troupe, accompanied by muscular musicians.

$$ El Rancho Grande – *1626 Pennsylvania Ave., Miami Beach.* ✆*305-673-0480. www.elranch ograndemexicanrestaurant. com. Branches at North Beach (✆305-864-7404) and Kendall (✆305-382-9598.* **Mexican.** Located just off lively Lincoln Road Mall, this family-owned dining spot feels like a roomy cantina. The extensive menu offers standard Mexican dishes and sides, presented in a variety of combinations. For a sampling of several flavors, try the *plato Mexicano,* a hearty assemblage of marinated pork, chicken enchilada, *chile relleno* (green pepper stuffed with cheese), beef burrito and refried beans and rice.

$$ Cafe Versailles – *3555 S.W. 8th St., Little Havana.* ♿ ✆*305-444-0240.* **Cuban.** This may be one of the quarter's most prominent visitor attractions but Cuban ex-pats get their fix of home cooking at Versailles. Line up with the locals for hearty Cuban sandwiches and heaped plates of food from an encyclopedic menu inside the main dining room. Rib-sticking dishes, such as roast pork, and grilled *palomilla* steak with garlic and onions, come with generous portions of black beans and white rice. Specialties include *ropa vieja* (shredded beef in a tomato-based sauce) and *plátanos verdes* (fried green plantains).

$ The Floridian Restaurant – *1410 E. Las Olas Blvd., Fort Lauderdale.* ✆*954-463-4041.*

American. Inexpensive, tasty food in generous portions is what make "the Flo" popular among Las Olas regulars. It's always busy at this 24/7 diner-style eatery, where dining rooms are cheery with poster-lined red, green or blue walls. The enormous menu includes 17 types of burgers; Mexican meatloaf; a "Fat Cat" breakfast of strip steak, eggs, grits, toast and Dom Perignon for two, as well as sweet treats such as peanut-butter-chip muffins. No one leaves hungry.

$ Hamburger Heaven – *314 S. County Rd., Palm Beach.* 📞*561-655-5277.* **American.** A Palm Beach institution since 1945, this old-fashioned diner boasts the "world's greatest hamburgers" and more. At the heaving counter, diamond- and Gucci-clad millionaires are often seated next to construction workers. Red fabric booths along the wall offer more space for dining. Breakfast fare, soups, salads, cold or grilled sandwiches, and burgers fill the straightforward menu. Take your pick of hamburger toppers from jalapeño peppers, onions, smoked bacon and cheese to sauerkraut, avocado, mushrooms or homemade chili.

$ News Cafe – *800 Ocean Dr., Miami Beach.* 📞*305-538-6397.* http://newscafe.com. **American.** People-watching is a 24-hour activity at this sidewalk cafe that opened in the 1980s to give production crews and models a casual place for a quick bite any time of day or night. Everything from French toast to salads is listed on the extensive menu.

$ Tobacco Road – *626 S. Miami Ave., Miami.* 📞*305-374-1198.* http://tobacco-road.com. **American.** This neighborhood bar, one block west of Brickell Avenue in downtown Miami, holds the oldest liquor license in the county. During Prohibition, "The Road" was a speakeasy, frequented by the likes of Al Capone. During World War II, its licenses were revoked on charges of indecent behavior. Regentrified today, Tobacco Road attracts a mix of downtown yuppies, lawyers, students and bikers. It's known for offering some of Miami's best live music nightly; Blues singers B.B. King and Koko Taylor have played here. Sandwiches, burgers and steaks are on the menu items; it stays open until 5am, the kitchen until 4am.

Shopping

Downtown: Downtown Miami Shopping District, Omni International Mall and shopping district, Bayside Marketplace. **Coconut Grove:** CocoWalk, Commodore Plaza and Mayfair. **Miami Beach:** Lincoln Road Mall. **South Beach:** Collins Avenue behind waterfront Ocean Drive has something for everyone—outlet stores of famous brands for those on a budget, and chic one-of-a-kind boutiques if you want to splurge on something unique. **North Miami Beach:** Bal Harbour Shops. **Aventura:** Aventura Mall. **South Miami-Dade:** The Shops at Sunset Place. For more on Shopping See p14–15

Entertainment

Consult the What's On section in the official area websites and/or the arts and entertainment section of local newspapers for schedules of cultural events. The following are a few of the region's major theaters and concert halls.

Adrienne Arsht Centre – Miami's performing arts venue is Florida's largest, and second only to the New York City's Lincoln Center. The Cleveland Orchestra are in residence for three weeks each year; it is home to the Miami City Ballet, Florida Grand Opera and the New World Symphony. Broadway shows often tour to here *(www.arshtcenter.org)*.

American Airlines Arena – Touring shows and sporting events in Miami *(www.aaarena.com)*.

Miami-Dade County Auditorium – Greater Miami's premier performing arts center for grand opera, symphony, theater, concerts, ballets *(www.miamidade.gov)*.

Colony Theater – Miami Beach's Art Deco theater: music, dance, theater, opera, comedy, performance art and film *(www.colonyandbyrontheaters.com)*.

The Fillmore Miami Beach at the Jackie Gleason Theater – Miami City Ballet, prestigious Broadway shows, and concerts ♿*see p138*; *http://fillmoremb.com*).

Olympia Theater at the Gusman Center for the Performing Arts – This magnificently restored 1926 theater is home to live performances, films and community events *(www.gusmancenter.org)*.

Sports and Recreation

Tennis courts are plentiful; some hotels offer tennis instruction and clinics. For further information on public facilities visit *www.miamidade.gov*. Public **golf** courses: include **Miami Springs Golf and Country Club** *(www.miamispringsgolfcourse.com);* **Normandy Shores Golf Course**, Miami Beach *(www.normandyshoresgolfclub.com);* **Crandon Park Golf Course** *(www.crandongolfclub.com)*.

Spectator Sports

Thoroughbred racing at **Calder Race Course**, 21001 N.W. 27th Ave. *(🖉305-625-1311; www.calderracecourse.com)*; Gulfstream Park, 901 S. Federal Hwy., Hallandale *(🖉954-454-7000 or 800-771-TURF; www.gulfstreampark.com)*.

Greyhound racing at **Flagler Greyhound Track**, 401 N.W. 38th Court *(🖉305-649-3000; www.flaglerdogs.com)*.

Miami Dolphins (NFL) *(🖉1-888-FINS-TIX; www.miamidolphins.com)*.

♿*See p72–73 for other sporting events including basketball.*

MIAMI BEACH★★★ *and around*

Population: 87,933.
Michelin Map:
pp 101, 132.
Info: 1901
Convention Center
Drive, Miami Beach
FL 33139; ℘786-276-
2763; http://www.
miamiandbeaches.
com. www.miami
beachfl.gov/.
Location: Hwy.
195 over the Julia
Tuttle Causeway and
Hwy. 395 over the
MacArthur Causeway
provide access to
Miami Beach.
Parking: There's on-
street parking spaces,
six parking garages
and more than 60
surface parking lots—
and you'll still have
trouble finding
a space! The 13th
Street and Collins
Avenue Garage is
most convenient to
the Art Deco Historic
District.
Don't Miss: A tour
of the Art Deco
Historic District.
Timing: Allow
at least a day to
explore South Beach,
including a tour of the
Art Deco District and
time to browse shops
and people-watch.

One of the country's great tropical paradises, Miami Beach is justifiably famed for its fabulous palm-studded shoreline, Art Deco architecture and colorful local residents. Built on dreams and speculation, this is an island in perpetual transition, where the atmosphere can shift from shabby to chic in a single block. Today, Miami Beach, particularly its SoBe (South Beach) quarter are hotter than ever, with a sizzling nightlife and celebrity-studded cafes, clubs and beaches.

Geographical Notes

A separate community from Miami, the City of Miami Beach occupies a narrow barrier island (7mi long and 1.5mi wide) 2.5mi off the mainland, along with 16 islets scattered in Biscayne Bay. Dredging and land-fill have reconfigured the main island, where mangrove swamps once covered the entire area west of present-day Washington Avenue. Fisher Island, at the southern tip, was created in 1905 when the Government Cut shipping channel sliced through to link Biscayne Bay with the Atlantic.

The famous **South Beach** area *(below 23rd St.)* and **Art Deco District** are reached directly by MacArthur Causeway, which passes the exclusive residential neighborhoods on man-made Star, Palm and Hibiscus islands, and offers a great view of the enormous cruise ships that dock in the Port of Miami.

A Bit of History

In 1912 New Jersey horticulturist **John C. Collins** formed the Miami Beach Improvement Co. to raise capital for a trans-bay bridge. When funds ran short, **Carl Fisher** (an Indiana automobile magnate) stepped in with a loan. In return Fisher received 200 acres from the ocean to the bay south of the 2.5mi Collins Bridge (now the Venetian Causeway).

Two Miami bank presidents, brothers **John and James Lummus,** laid out their first subdivision, offering small lots and modest bungalows. Fisher founded his own realty company and ensured a steady stream of sunseekers by financing a paved road from Chicago to Miami; his famed **Dixie Highway** opened in 1915. That same year, Collins, Fisher and the Lummuses merged, later incorporating their land as the City of Miami Beach.

By 1921 five luxury hotels provided lodging for those who could afford it. By day polo grounds, golf courses and tennis courts offered diversion. At night locals flocked to the gambling and bootleg liquor operations hidden in the back rooms of nightclubs; **Al Capone** bought a house on Palm Island in 1928. When Wall Street crashed in 1929, so did Miami, but the area

Bal Harbour Shops, Fontainebleau Hilton /

SOUTH BEACH

☐ Art Deco Building

| 0 | | 1/5 mi |
| 0 | | 300 m |

Miami's beaches
Immortalised by the
TV series *Miami Vice*,
and dozens of movies,
the 12-mile stretch
of sugar-white sands
that make up Miami
Beach is one of the
world's most famous
playgrounds.
The island beaches
begin at South Pointe
Park. This and First
Street Beach are
very popular with
families and are busy
at weekend. Next is
the most glamorous
and buzzing of all
the beaches, South
Beach (SoBe), which
starts at 5th Steet
and is patronised
by the young, rich,
beautiful and trendy,
and is also popular
in the gay scene.
Between 21st Street,
where South Beach
ends, and 46th Street,
is family-oriented
Central Beach.
North Beach, from
46th Street to 78th
Street, is community
centered, with an old-
fashioned bandshell.
Moving further north,
upscale Bal Harbour
beach offers a palm-
shaded jogging path.
Haulover Beach,
between Sunny
Isles Beach and Bal
Harbour Beach, is
"clothing optional."

boomed again in the late 1930s due to a resurgence of tourism.
In 1936 alone, some 36 hotels and 110 apartment houses were
built in the new Art Deco style in South Miami Beach.

Miami's "Gold Coast" strip enjoyed its heyday in the 1950s and
60s, when hotels like the Fontainebleau flourished. The subsequent economic decline left many faded resorts in its wake.

Art Deco Historic District★★★

Listed on the National Register of Historic Places in 1979, this
enclave of small-scale Art Deco hotels and apartment houses,
dating from the late 1920s to the early 1940s, amounts to the
largest concentration of architecture of its kind in the world. The
official district measures about one square mile and is roughly
bounded by the Atlantic Ocean on the east, Lenox Avenue on
the west, Sixth Street on the south and Dade Boulevard north.

Architectural Preservation

As new investment focused on north Miami Beach after World
War II, the south grew increasingly shabby and economic
decline was firmly entrenched by the 1960s. In 1966 however
there was a renewal of interest in the Art Deco style, and a decade later, **Barbara Baer Capitman** and **Leonard Horowitz**,
two local design professionals, formed the Miami Design
Preservation League to identify significant architecture in
Miami Beach. The area's 1979 designation as a National Register
Historic District was remarkable in that its 800 or so Art Deco
buildings were only about 40 years old—not an age typically
considered historic. A setback was to come though. Following
the 1980 Mariel boatlift, when hundreds of Cuban prisoners
were relocated to South Beach, much of the established population fled and the Art Deco buildings—regarded as tacky and
outdated—began to crumble.

Fueled by the efforts of Capitman and Horowitz, preservation
of the Deco District began in earnest in the 1980s and continues to this day. Several exceptional buildings have been lost to
new development. Exterior changes and paint colors of new
construction are, however, subject to approval by a local review
board. The current trend for bright tropical hues is somewhat
controversial, as the original Art Deco buildings were painted
white and trimmed in primary colors.

Many Art Deco buildings here, exemplified by **1244 Ocean
Drive** (the Leslie hotel, 1937, Albert Anis) and **650 Ocean
Drive** (formerly the Imperial hotel, 1939, L. Murray Dixon)
tend to have an angular look, with symmetrical, stepped-back
facades and strong vertical banding and bas-relief decora-

ion. The 11-story St. Moritz *(1565 Collins Ave.)*, designed by Roy France in 1939, stretches upward with a soaring tower housing elevators and mechanical works.

In contrast to the angularity of these Deco structures, the later **Streamline Moderne style** featured aerodynamic imagery, horizontal racing stripes and wraparound corners, reflecting a fascination with speed and motion. In an unabashed imitation of an ocean liner, for example, a building might gain portholes, periscope-like air ducts and tubular railings, as seen in the 1930s **Beach Patrol Station** *(1001 Ocean Dr.)* designed by Robert Taylor. The patrol station now forms the rear facade of the **Oceanfront Auditorium,** which was added in the 1950s.

South Beach is best navigated on foot. Parking is by meter (quarters only) with a strictly enforced 2hr limit. The Miami Design Preservation League (MDPL) offers walking tours that depart from the Art Deco Welcome Center (near Oceanfront Auditorium), 1001 Ocean Dr. (year-round daily 10:30am except Thu 6:30pm; 1hr 30min; $20; ℘305-672-2014; www.mdpl.org). The annual Art Deco Weekend, (http://www.mdpl.org/events) featuring special programs and lectures, is held in South Beach in January.

Ocean Drive★★

Along this lively north-south boulevard bordering the Atlantic Ocean beats the heart of the SoBe scene. By day locals and tourists have snacks at shaded sidewalk cafes, while scantily clad youths streak by on in-line skates and willowy models pose for fashion shoots. At night vivid neon signs beckon revelers to some of Miami's hottest bars and dance clubs. Across the street lies fabulous **Ocean Beach★★**, refurbished and widened as part of a multimillion-dollar city project in 1982. **Lummus Park,** a magnet for teenage skaters and elderly dog-walkers alike, runs along the beach from 1st to 15th Streets. Located in the park is the nautically inspired Oceanfront Auditorium, which houses the **Art Deco Welcome Center**, an information center *(1001 Ocean Dr.; ℘305-672-2014)* stocked with books and souvenirs (**⊙***see below*).

The park offers a great **view★** of Ocean Drive and its pastel parade of Art Deco hotels. The seven-story, blue-tinted **Park Central** *(no. 640)*, designed by Henry Hohauser in 1937, displays the characteristic symmetrical facade with vertical banding, steel corner windows (designed to maximize breezes in pre-air-conditioning days) and shaded central entrance. Notable for its horizontal racing stripes and futuristic double-faced tower, the yellow-and-blue-painted **Breakwater** *(no. 940)* shares a pool with the 1935 **Edison.** This Hohauser building *(no. 960)* with a ground-floor arcade and three-story twisted colonnette,

ART DECO MEMORABILIA

If you're fond of all things Deco, or if you simply want to support a worthy cause, stop in at the beachfront shop run by the Miami Design Preservation League *(1001 Ocean Dr. at 10th St; ℘305-531-3484; www.mdpl.org)*. Inside you'll find a bounty of arty souvenirs promoting the historic district as well as Miami Beach: hotel-shaped mugs with palm-tree handles, fake flamingoes, Art Deco posters, photo postcards, picture frames, coffee-table books, model cars and toys, bakelite jewelry, journals and notecards, writing pens and logo-laden ball caps and T-shirts. There's a sizable stock of books, too. Guided tours of the area also depart from here.

recalls the area's earlier Mediterranean Revival architecture. Among the first hotels to be restored were a now-famous quartet: the **Leslie** (1937) at **no. 1244**; the **Carlyle** (1941) at **no 1250**; the **Cardozo** (1939) at **no. 1300**, now owned by singer Gloria Estefan; and the **Cavalier** (1936) next door at **no. 1320**. Among the latest to be renovated is **The Tides** (1936) at **no 1220**. This 11-story hotel is the tallest on Ocean Drive.

Jewish Museum of Florida

301 Washington Ave. OpenTue–Sun 10am–5pm. Closed Jewish holidays. $6. ♿✖. ℘305-672-5044. www.jewishmuseum.com.
Housed in the copper-domed Beth Jacob Orthodox Synagogue (1936, Henry Hohauser), some 10,000 art and artifacts relating to more than 230 years of Jewish history in the Sunshine State make up the museum's core collection. In addition, related temporary exhibits rotate three times a year.

Light streams into the large, domed room through eight colorful stained-glass windows. At the eastern end stands a marble ark, crowned by a carved Torah supported by lions.

A looped video illustrates the struggles and achievements encountered by Jews since they first landed on the Florida coast with Ponce de León to escape persecution in Spain.

The Wolfsonian-FIU★★

1001 Washington Ave. Open Thu–Tue noon–6pm (Fri 9pm). Closed holidays. $7. Free Fri 6–9pm. ♿℘305-531-1001. wolfsonian.org.
Owned and operated by Florida International University, this museum and research center holds more than 70,000 pieces of American and European decorative arts and crafts dating from 1885 to 1945. Rare books, graphics, political and propaganda artworks, architectural models, sculpture, glass, ceramics and furniture are included in the collection.

The permanent collection comprises about 300 works on display at any one time, illustrating how design has been used to help people adjust to the modern world. Focal points include design reform movements, urbanism, industrial design, transportation, world's fairs, advertising and political propaganda. Temporary exhibitions are also staged.

Washington Avenue

A busy commercial thoroughfare encompassing chic restaurants and trendy dance clubs as well as ethnic markets and Cuban coffee shops. Washington Avenue features several public buildings of note. The grand, eight-story, Mediterranean-inspired **Old City Hall** *(no. 1130)* was designed in 1927, before the Deco wave swept Miami Beach.

The **World Erotic Art Museum** at no. 1205 *(open year-round Mon–Thu 11am–10pm, Fri–Sun 11am–midnight; $15; ☎866-969-WEAM; www.weam.com. Both website and museum contains adult content and material, so you must be 18 or over to enter)*, housing the largest collection of erotic art in America.

The **US Post Office** *(no. 1300)* dates from 1939. Stripped of exterior ornament, the building displays the angular lines, glass-block window treatment and somewhat harsh overall Modernist look widely adopted for Works Project Administration (WPA) structures of the 1930s—a style sometimes called Depression Moderne. Lined with cast brass lockboxes, the central **rotunda** features a 1940 mural depicting vignettes from Florida history.

Planned as an artists' colony in the 1920s, **Espanola Way★** *(between Washington and Drexel Aves.)* breathes fresh air into an otherwise shabby area. This gas-lit enclave, with its movie backdrop ensemble of Mediterranean Revival buildings decorated in coral-colored stucco and hand-painted tiles, features cozy courtyards, pink sidewalks and chic boutiques.

Lincoln Road Mall

Lincoln Rd, Washington Ave–Alton Rd. http://lincolnroadmall.com.
This lively, lengthy pedestrian mall abounds with trendy shops, galleries and restaurants that border a central planted thoroughfare of tiled fountains and coral rock pools. Lincoln Road is the oldest commercial street on the island, laid out in 1915 by Carl Fisher. The area staged a second comeback after it was re-landscaped and closed to traffic by Morris Lapidus (a set designer-turned-architect, who designed the Fontainebleau Hotel) in the 1960s, only to be deserted in the 1970s. After a recent $16-million face-lift, its latest transition is complete. The shops *(most don't open until 11am)*, specializing in antiques, jewelry, books and designer clothes—as well as the galleries—improve

Travel Tip: If you don't want to spend the money for a night out at the symphony, don't be discouraged. Miami's New World Symphony building was designed by Frank Gehry to include a 7,000-square-foot outdoor screen, so the public can sit in an adjacent park to watch live concerts while the sound is broadcast through outdoor speakers.

in quality west of Drexel Avenue. There are plenty of restaurants, serving a wide variety of cuisine; several offer alfresco dining. Originally a cinema, the 1935 Deco **Lincoln Theatre** (nos. 555–541) was until recently the home of the city's renowned New World Symphony academy. Regular public exhibitions are on show at the **Artcenter South Florida** (nos. 800–810 and 924; www.artcentersf.org), a warren of exhibit areas and studio space for photographers, ceramic artists, painters, jewelry designers and printmakers. Across the street the two-story **Sterling Building** (no. 927) dominates the streetfront with an undulating wall of tile-studded stucco and glass block.

The Fillmore Miami Beach at the Jackie Gleason Theater

1700 Washington Ave. ✆305-673-7300. http://fillmoremb.com.
This confection of peach-colored concrete and glass block (1951, Pancoast, Hohauser and Dixon) was remodeled by Morris Lapidus in 1976, and originally hosted comedian Jackie Gleason's popular television series from 1964 to 1970. The 3,000-seat theater now stages Broadway shows alongside Russian Ballet and the likes of Woody Allen and his New Orleans Jazz Band. Look for Roy Lichtenstein's red-and-white-striped **Mermaid** (**1**) on the south lawn *(fronting 17th St.)*. Set into plaques on the adjacent yard, cement footprints of such celebrities as Julie Andrews and Don Johnson form the Walk of the Stars.

Holocaust Memorial★

Nos. 1933–1945 Meridian Ave. Open daily 9am–sunset.
♿ 🅿 ✆305-538-1663. www.holocaustmmb.org.
Set in and around a tranquil lily pond, this memorial leads visitors through a circular plaza of pale pink Jerusalem stone designed as a series of outdoor passages. Names inscribed on the walls are a simple but poignant reminder of lives lost to the Nazis during World War II. The centerpiece is Miami artist and architect Kenneth Treister's *Sculpture of Love and Anguish,* which comprises several bronze vignettes and a giant 42ft-high outstretched arm symbolizing the last reach of a dying person.

Collins Park

Between 21st Ave. and 22nd Ave. next to the ocean.
Collins Park is being expanded to include a cultural campus. Part of it is home to the **Miami City Ballet** (2200 Liberty Ave.; www.miamicityballet.org). At weekends passersby can watch the dancers practice behind huge glass windows.

Bass Museum of Art★

2121 Park Ave. Open year-round Wed-Sun noon–5pm. $8.
305-673-7530. www.bassmuseum.org.

This acclaimed regional museum maintains a permanent collection of more than 3,000 works, encompassing European, American, Asian and contemporary art. Its European holdings are rich in religious artifacts and French and Flemish tapestries. The original landmark Art Deco structure (1930, Russell Pancoast) of oolitic limestone decorated with Mayan motifs was designed as the centerpiece of a nine-acre park given to the city in 1920 by developer John Collins. First used as both a library and art center, the building was renamed in 1964 when Austrian-born New York entrepreneur John Bass donated his art collection to the city of Miami Beach.

The Bass displays European paintings, furnishings, altarpieces, sculpture and other works spanning the 15–21C. Highlights include art by masters, as well as 19C tapestries.

Collins Avenue★

Although Collins Avenue is now one of the main traffic arteries in Miami Beach, it originally knew a more affluent lifestyle, catering to pedestrians with juice bars and small boutiques. Between 16th and 23rd Streets, hotels climb to 10 stories, the maximum height allowed; below 16th they may rise higher.

Among the stars from the 1940s are the **National** *(no. 1677)*; the **Delano** *(no. 1685)*, recognizable by its finned spaceship tower; and the **Ritz Plaza** *(no. 1701)*. With their squared, stepped-back facades and quirky central towers, these local landmarks resemble a trio of oversized party-goers dressed in giant overcoats and jaunty hats. Walk west two blocks on 17th Street for the best view.

Driving north on Collins you will encounter a 13,000sq ft **mural** *(at 44th St.)* bearing the trompe l'œil image of a triumphal arch framing the **Fontainebleau Hilton** Resort and Towers, by Richard Haas. The real Fontainebleau is just around the corner *(no. 4441)* on the 20-acre site of the former Harvey Firestone estate. This 1,200-room extravaganza (1954) is the work of Morris Lapidus, who dubbed it "modern French Château Style."

To the north and west lie the exclusive residential areas of Middle Beach and Bal Harbour Village, a complex of high-rise condos and resorts (some public access to the beautiful sandy beaches), including **Bal Harbour Shops** *(www.balharbour shops.com)* a mecca of high-fashion stores and boutiques.

Population: 152,397.
Michelin Map: p.144
Info: 100 E. Broward Blvd. ℰ954-765-4466 or 800-227-8669; www.sunny.org.
Location:
Fort Lauderdale lies between Miami, 23 miles to the south and Boca Raton to the north. I-95 runs north-south, just west of downtown.
Parking: Parking garages along SW 2nd St. are the best spots for exploring the downtown and Riverwalk area.
Don't Miss: Stroll the Arts and Sciences District, including Riverwalk.
Timing: Go with the flow: allow plenty of time to browse, waterfront shops and galleries and take in a free outdoor concert or event. In downtown Hollywood you can walk the beach boardwalk, flanked by galleries, boutiques and restaurants. Bike rentals are available too.
Kids: Kids won't want to miss the Museum of Discovery and Science, which is fun for all ages.

FORT LAUDERDALE★

Fort Lauderdale is the largest city of sprawling Broward County. Straddling 300mi of natural and artificial waterways, this "Venice of America" is a boater's paradise with 40,000-plus registered yachts, many of which are moored at the Radisson **Bahia Mar Yacht Basin** on the Atlantic Intracoastal Waterway. Ranked second among Florida's busiest ports (behind Miami), **Port Everglades** handles some 23 million tons of cargo each year and is the world's third largest cruise port with close to three million people departing annually for Caribbean ports of call.

A Bit of History

The area's first residents were Tequesta natives, followed by the Spanish in the 16C and, by the early 1800s, the Seminoles, who cohabited peacefully with area settlers until the Second Seminole War. Major William Lauderdale and his detachment built an army fort atop a series of Tequesta Indian mounds here in 1838. In 1896 Henry Flagler's Florida East Coast Railway entered Fort Lauderdale en route to Miami, catalyzing the development of a busy agricultural community. Like Miami to the south, Fort Lauderdale continues to boom.

Sights

Fort Lauderdale's lively downtown **Arts and Sciences District** encompasses the Museum of Art, the Museum of Discovery and Science and the Broward Center for the Performing Arts. The latter, a contemporary complex on the river's north bank, brings world-class performances to the city. The Broward Center sits at the western terminus of **Riverwalk,** a tree-lined bricked esplanade that stretches along the north and south banks of the New River. Just east of downtown, trendy **Las Olas Boulevard** boasts a wide variety of shops, galleries and outdoor cafes.

INTERNATIONAL

Fort Lauderdale and the surrounding area has a larger international population than first meets the eye. In fact, over 100,000 people of Caribbean origin have made the area their home. And you can see the Caribbean and the British influence in Central Broward Regional Park in Lauderdale Hills, where you will find the first US Cricket Stadium. The stadium has hosted international tournaments and is also home to the Atlantic Cricket Club of Florida, which has weekly matches in season. Beyond cricket, the park is home to international soccer and rugby matches.

GETTING THERE

Fort Lauderdale/Hollywood International Airport (FLL): 4mi south of city *(information: ℘ 954-359-1200)*. A commuter line links Broward, Palm Beach and Miami-Dade counties, with free shuttles to the airport *(℘800-874-7245)* ; **taxi** service *($15–$20)* and hotel courtesy shuttles are also available. Train service to Palm Beach and Miami by **Tri-Rail** *(℘800-874-7245)*. Amtrak **train** station: 200 S.W. 21st Terr. *(℘800-872-7245; www.amtrak. com)*. Greyhound **bus** station: 515 N.E. 3rd St. *(℘800-231-2222; www.greyhound.com)*.

GETTING AROUND

Local **bus service:** Broward County Mass Transit (BCT) *($1; information: ℘954-357-8400)*. **Downtown shuttle** between Courthouse and BCT Terminal *(year-round Mon–Fri 7:30am–6pm, every 10min)* and the **TMAX Express** *(year-round Fri–Sat 6pm–1pm; ℘954-761-3543)*. If you are driving there is metered **parking** *(25¢/30 minutes)* along Andrews Ave. by the hospital and along Las Olas Blvd.

Water taxi: You haven't visited Fort Lauderdale until you've seen it from the water, along the Intracoastal Waterway and New River *(year-round daily 10am–1:30am; ℘954-467-6677; www.watertaxi.com)*. Anticipation Yachts offer daily narrated

riverfront cruises *(℘954-463-3220 or ℘800-499-2248; www.anticipation.com)*.

VISITOR INFORMATION

Greater Fort Lauderdale Convention and Visitors Bureau, 100 E. Broward Blvd., Fort Lauderdale FL 33316 *(open year-round Mon–Fri 8:30am–5pm; ℘954-765-4466 or 800-227-8669; www.sunny.org)*. A free iPhone **app**, iVisitLauderdale, can be downloaded at itunes.apple.com.

ENTERTAINMENT

Read the arts and entertainment section of the *Sun Sentinel* either in the Fri. edition or online at www.sun-sentinel. com. *Travelhost* online magazine at www. travelhost.com/fortlauderdale. Or visit the official website: www.sunny.org. The top theater in town is the **Broward Center for the Performing Arts** *(℘954-462-0222; www.browardcenter.org)*.

SPORTS AND RECREATION

Shopping: if you want upscale, head to Las Olas Blvd downtown. **Galleria Mall,** Sunrise Blvd. *(℘954-564-1015)*; **Swap Shop**, 3291 W. Sunrise Blvd. (shopping and entertainment ℘954-791-7927); **Sawgrass Mills**, 12801 W. Sunrise Blvd. (outlet mall ℘954-846-2350).

Head to the **Jai-alai stadium** in Dania to watch this ball game of Basque origin.

Stranahan House★

335 S.E. 6th Ave., 0.2mi south of Las Olas Blvd. just above New River Tunnel. Open year-round daily, by guided tour (45–60min) only, 1pm, 2pm, 3pm. Closed major holidays. $12. **P** *℘954-524-4736. http://stranahanhouse.org.*

Airy and elegant, this graceful two-story frame house skirted by wide verandas is Broward County's oldest building, and a fine example of Florida pioneer architecture. It was built on the banks of the New River in 1901 by **Frank Stranahan**—the area's first permanent white settler— who came here in 1893 from Ohio to operate a ferry. The interior boasts double-beaded wall paneling expertly crafted from Dade County pine.

Travel Tip: Consider starting and ending your trip in Fort Lauderdale. While Miami International Airport has certainly improved its facilities in recent years, it can still feel chaotic. Fort Lauderdale Hollywood International Airport, on the other hand, is just 40 minutes from Miami and has better on-time departure statistics. And you can get to over a hundred destinations from the airport. If you're headed straight to Miami, you can take the Broward Country Transit buses or the Tri-Rail commuter trains.

Museum of Art, Fort Lauderdale (MoA)★

1 E. Las Olas Blvd. Open year-round Tue–Sat 11am–5pm (Thu 8pm), Sun noon–5pm. Closed major holidays. $18.
✕ ♿ 🅿 ☏ *954-525-5500. www.moafl.org.*
This acclaimed museum comprises over 5,000 pieces ranging from a sizable collection of paintings by American Impressionist **William Glackens** to works by Andy Warhol. However, the MoA is best known for its collection of **CoBrA art★★**—the largest assemblage in the US. Born in Paris in 1948, the CoBrA movement consisted of Expressionists from **Co**penhagen, **Br**ussels and **A**msterdam, who drew their inspiration from folk art and children's drawings. Pan-African, pre-Columbian, Native American and a growing collection of contemporary Cuban art round out the museum's holdings.

Fort Lauderdale History Center

231 S.W. 2nd Ave. Open year-round Tue–Sun noon–4pm. Closed Jan 1, Jul 4, Dec 25. $10. ♿ ☏ *954-463-4431. www.oldfortlauderdale.org.*
Your visit begins in the 1905 **New River Inn,** Broward's oldest remaining hotel building, now home to the Fort Lauderdale History Center museum. This is also the ticket office for the History Center's adjacent vernacular properties, most of which are open to the public. The first property is in fact a replica, of Broward County's first **schoolhouse**, originally built in 1899. Next door the **King-Cromartie House,** built of sturdy Dade County pine with joists made from salvaged ship's timbers, was moved via river barge to its present site in 1971 *(admission by guided tour only 1pm, 2pm, 3pm).* The 1905 **Philemon Nathaniel Bryan House** features Classical Revival architectural detailing. It now houses the administrative offices of the Fort Lauderdale History Center. The **Hoch Heritage Center**, built as a post office annex in 1949, is the home of the Fort Lauderdale Historical Society housing a public research library.

Museum of Discovery and Science★★

401 S.W. 2nd St., one block south of Broward Blvd. Open year-round Mon–Sat 10am–5pm, Sun noon–6pm. $13. IMAX theater $9. Combo ticket $18. ♿ 🅿 *($3)* ☏ *954-467-6637. www.mods.org.*
This slick mega-size museum attracts people of all ages with over 200 interactive exhibits—beginning with the fantastic **gravity clock** in the atrium. **Florida EcoScapes** dominates the first floor: live trees and native plants form the setting for examples of local flora and fauna, including a colorful coral reef, an underground cave and a walk-in beehive.

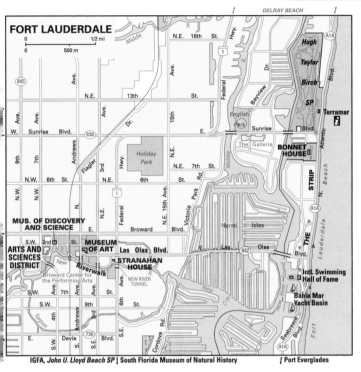

FORT LAUDERDALE

IGFA, *John U. Lloyd Beach SP* | South Florida Museum of Natural History | Port Everglades

Gizmo City is full of hands-on stations. Other highlights include **Runways to Rockets**, where you can transform yourself into a bird by putting on wings and stepping into a giant wind tunnel. A major new expansion, the **EcoDiscovery Center**, has more than doubled the Museum's exhibit space with five new areas: Otters at Play, Everglades Airboat Adventure, Prehistoric Florida, Water Mysteries and Storm Center. And of course there is the giant **IMAX** theater.

Hugh Taylor Birch State Park

3109 E. Sunrise Blvd. and A1A. Open 8 am–sunset $6 per vehicle. ⚠ ♿
🅿 ☎ *954-564-4521. www.floridastateparks.org/hughtaylorbirch.*
Canoe, hike, bike, and picnic at this 180-acre site, resting on a

DISCOVERING SOUTH FLORIDA

CORAL REEFS

Fort Lauderdale and the surrounding areas has 23 miles of coral reefs. Don't miss the Anglin Pier Reef that has bright coral and colorful tropical fish. But there's more than just natural life under the water. The area is called the "wreck capital of Florida" and there are many spots to dive. One wreck not to miss is Rodeo 25, which is an intact Dutch freighter ship, sunk in 1990. Today, its two masts rise 122 feet from the ocean floor to 52 feet from the surface.

barrier island between the Atlantic Ocean and the Intracoastal Waterway. The park faces 1.5mi of beachfront and includes a lagoon system, mangrove swamps and hardwood hammocks. Hugh Taylor Birch's former home, Terramar (c.1940), now houses the **Terramar Visitor Center** *(open 9 am–5pm Sat, Sun and hols)*.

Bonnet House★

900 N. Birch Rd. Open year-round, house by guided tour only, Tue–Sat 10am–4pm, Sun noon–4pm. $20; grounds only, $10. Closed major hols. 🅿 ☎954-563-5393. www.bonnethouse.org.

Nestled in a 35-acre green oasis, this coral rock-and-Dade County pine-house reflects the talent of its architect, Chicago muralist and art collector **Frederic Clay Bartlett** (1873–1953).

A lagoon rimmed with stately Royal Palms fronts Bartlett's 1920 interpretation of a plantation house. Named for the yellow Bonnet lilies that still bloom at the south end of the lagoon, the 30-room structure contains the family's eclectic furnishings and objets d'art. Bartlett's **studio,** with its high-beamed ceiling and two-story north window, displays his own works as well as those he collected. Also on the grounds is an orchid house.

Excursions

John U. Lloyd Beach State Park

4mi south in Dania Beach. 1mi north of intersection of Dania Beach Blvd. and A1A at 6503 N. Ocean Dr. Open 8am–sunset. $6 /vehicle. ✕⅋🅿 ☎954-923-2833. www.floridastateparks.org/lloydbeach.

This 251-acre park at the northern end of a narrow, elongated barrier island offers great views, uncrowded beaches and quiet forests. The 11,500ft-long **beach** is dotted with shaded picnic sites and sea turtle nesting areas, and extends northward to a paved fishing jetty. Whiskey Creek, a mangrove-lined tidal waterway, divides the park along its length and harbors manatees and abundant bird life. A hardwood forest and man-made wetland fill the park's interior. A self-guided walk traverses the hammock.

IGA Fishing Hall of Fame & Museum★

12mi south in Dania Beach. » From Las Olas Blvd., take I-95 south to Griffin Rd., then west to Anglers Ave. Turn left and continue to entrance at 300 Gulf Stream Way in Sportsman's Park. Open year-round Mon–Sat 10am–6pm, Sun noon–6pm. Closed Thanksgiving & Dec 25. $8. ✕ & 🅿 ✆954-922-4212. www.igfa.org.

Six museum galleries, a children's discovery room, library, museum store, cafe, the hall of fame, an outdoor marina and 3.5-acre wetlands make up this complex. In the Hall of Fame, life-size mounts of record catches dangle from the ceiling. Museum highlights include the **Catch Gallery,** where you can reel in a fish via virtual reality.

Butterfly World★

10mi north in Coconut Creek. » Take I-95 north to Sample Rd.; continue west 4mi to 3600 W. Sample Rd.; enter at Tradewinds Park, on left. Open Mon–Sat 9am–5pm, Sun 11am–5pm. Closed Thanksgiving Day & Dec 25. $24.95. ✕ & 🅿 ✆954-977-4400. www.butterflyworld.com.

Around 10,000 rainbow-colored butterflies and hundreds of birds flit around the largest butterfly house in the world, landscaped with waterfalls and bright blooms to resemble a tropical rainforest. Outside, a rose garden and vine-covered arbor surround a small pond, attracting local butterflies. A small pavilion contains specimens of exotic insects and butterflies from around the world.

Flamingo Gardens

16.5mi west in Davie. » I-595 west to Flamingo Rd.; continue 3mi south to entrance on left at 3750 Flamingo Rd. Open daily (except Mon Jun-Oct) 9:30am–5pm. Closed Thanksgiving Day & Dec 25. $18. ✕ & 🅿 ✆954-473-2955. www.flamingogardens.org.

Lush tropical plantings grace the grounds of this former citrus plantation. Paved paths traverse a mosaic of tropical plants and a narrated tram tour *(25min; $4)* takes visitors through a wetlands area and part of the original citrus grove. Displays of alligators, crocodiles, birds of prey and wading birds.

3

Population: 86,600.
Michelin Map: p147
Info: 1800 N. Dixie
Highway 561-395-
4433; www.boca
ratonchamber.com.
www.palmbeachfl.com
Location: North-
south I-95 to US 808
is the quickest way
into the city; Rte. 1
travels north-south,
parallel to the ocean
shoreline.
Parking: There are
several garages in the
city, including the
Quality Garage on
13th St. just west of
N. Dixie Hwy. Another
is just off E. Palmetto
Park Rd.
Don't Miss: Mizner
Park and the Boca
Raton Museum of Art
area with restaurants,
shops, museums,
and more.
Timing: A day or two
to explore Boca Raton
sights is plenty, then
head to the beach
or check out top
attractions in nearby
Fort Lauderdale.
Kids: Take an airboat
ride through the
northern tip of
the Everglades at
Loxahatchee National
Wildlife Refuge.

BOCA RATON★

Early mapmakers mistook this area for a similar site near
Miami's Biscayne Bay and called it by the same Spanish
name, *Boca Raton* ("mouth of the rat"). Situated halfway
between Fort Lauderdale and West Palm Beach, this prosperous community boasts 2mi of public beaches warmed
by Gulf Stream waters and has catered to the well-heeled
for more than 70 years.

Sights

Old Floresta

W. Palmetto Park Rd., Periwinkle St., N.W. 9th Ave. and N.W. 7th Ave.
Drive down Aurelia, Azalea, Hibiscus or Oleander Street for a
glimpse of one of Boca's oldest neighborhoods. Designed by
Addison Mizner for his executives in 1925, Old Floresta still
boasts 29 original houses characterized by red barrel-tile roofs
and light-colored stucco walls. Large palm and banyan trees
shade these quiet, pleasant avenues.

Boca Raton Old Town Hall★

*71 N. Federal Hwy. Open year-round Mon–Fri 10am–4pm. Closed
Dec 25–Jan 2.* 561-395-6766. www.bocahistory.org.
This elegant building was designed by Addison Mizner as Boca
Raton's first municipal edifice. Fashioned with beams and pan-
eling of pecky cypress and pine floors, it housed city officials,
and the fire and police departments until 1983.

GOLFING GUIDANCE

Boca Raton is known for its exclusive golf clubs, but no
one is forcing you to play on resort courses. Instead, for a
higher-end option, consider the Boca Greens Country Club
(*www.bocagreenscountryclub.com*), where visitors can play 18
holes on the exclusive course designed by Joe Lee, without
having to join up and become a member. The golf course is
open daily, year round, and rates vary from $40-70. If you're
looking for something a little less demanding, be sure to check
out the nine-hole Red Reef Executive Golf Course, where you
can play golf amid Boca Raton's famous red reef dunes. The
course is open to the public and all rates are under $20.

DELRAY BEACH | **Spanish River Park** |

/ DEERFIELD BEACH

Boca Express Train Museum

Open mid Jan–mid Apr first and third Fri 1pm–4pm. Call to confirm. Closed Good Fri. $5. ✆*561-395-6766. www.bocahistory.org.*
Close to the town hall, the historic F. E. C. Railway Station (also known as the Count de Hoernle Pavilion) is home to two 1947 Seaboard Air Line streamlined (Budd dining and lounge) rail cars, restored to their original splendor.

Boca Raton Museum of Art★

501 Plaza Real, in Mizner Park. Open year-round Tue–Fri 10am–5pm (Wed 9pm), Sat & Sun noon–5pm. Closed major holidays. $8. ✗ &Ⓟ✆*561-392-2500. www.bocamuseum.org.*
One of South Florida's finest cultural attractions, the Boca Raton Museum of Art presents changing exhibitions of national and international importance. Don't miss the sculpture garden.

Travel Tip: Yes, Boca Raton has a large senior population, but that doesn't mean you can't have a late night! Not all of Boca Raton's population goes to bed early. For happy hour, Boston's On The Beach, or Dubliner's attract a young crowd. Funky Buddha Lounge and Blue Martini stay open for cocktails until 2am and 4am respectively.

Beaches

Red Reef Park★

1400 N. Ocean Blvd. (A1A), 1 mi north of Palmetto Park Rd. $16–$18 per vehicle. 🅿 ℰ*561-393-7974. www.ci.boca-raton.fl.us.*
A densely vegetated dune, a boardwalk and a pleasant beach for swimming, fishing and snorkeling over an artificial reef occupy the east side of this 67-acre park. On the west side of the park, within a 20-acre swatch of tropical hammock preserved in its natural state, is the **Gumbo Limbo Nature Center** *(open year-round Mon–Sat 9am–4pm, Sun noon–4pm; closed major holidays; suggested $5.00 donation per person;* ♿ ℰ*561-338-1473; www.gumbolimbo.org).* This displays live snakes, tanks of living corals and crustaceans, and a shell collection. Large outdoor saltwater tanks allow visitors an up-close look at loggerhead turtles and other marine life. An informative short boardwalk trail winds through a tropical hammock and mangrove wetland, past strangler fig trees, paradise trees and the red-bark gumbo-limbo while a 40ft observation tower clears the forest canopy offering ocean views. A comprehensive activities schedule gives visitors the opportunity to get closer to nature.

Spanish River Park

3001 N. Ocean Blvd./A1A. Entrance on west side, just north of Gumbo Limbo Nature Center. Open year-round daily 8am–dusk. $16–$18 per vehicle. ♿🅿 ℰ*561-393-7815. www.ci.boca-raton.fl.us.*
Taking its name from a shallow freshwater stream that coursed along its western edge before the creation of the Intracoastal Waterway, the park provides oceanfront as well as coastal woodlands recreation. A nature trail beside the lagoon provides a pleasant short stroll through the forest. The picnic area is equipped with grills and tables.

Excursions

Morikami Museum and Japanese Gardens★

4000 Morikami Park Rd. 12mi northwest of Boca Raton in Delray Beach. » *Take I-95 north to Linton Blvd. and go west 3.5mi; turn south on Jog Rd. and continue 1.5mi. Open year-round Tue–Sun 10am–5pm. $13.* ✕♿🅿 ℰ*561-495-0233. www.morikami.org.*
Built on a 200-acre parcel donated to Palm Beach County by prosperous pineapple farmer George Sukeji Morikami, this complex pays homage to Japanese culture. Changing exhibits showcase art and artifacts ranging from vintage toys to laquerware, woodblock prints and textiles. In the Tea House you can

watch a Japanese **tea ceremony** *(second or third Sat of month, Oct–Jun, noon, 1pm, 2pm & 3pm; $5)*. A lakeside walk away lies **Yamato-kan★**, inspired by a Japanese imperial villa. Some 16 acres of gardens typifying traditional Japanese styles from the 9–20C feature koi ponds, waterfalls and a **bonsai garden.**

Arthur R. Marshall Loxahatchee National Wildlife Refuge★

3mi west of Boca Raton, on US-441. **»** *Take I-95 to Rte. 806/Atlantic Ave. west to US-441; go north on US-441 3mi to refuge entrance. Open year-round daily sunrise–sunset. $5 per vehicle.*
P *℘561-734-8303. www.fws.gov/loxahatchee.*

This huge refuge *(221sq mi)* at the northernmost tip of the Everglades, is home to more than 18,000 alligators and numerous species of birds and other wildlife, including the endangered snail kite and wood stork. The visitor center *(open daily 9am–4pm; closed Dec 25)* contains exhibits on local ecology. Behind the center a boardwalk *(0.4 mi)* snakes back into a bald cypress swamp. Reptiles flourish here, as do a variety of ferns and colorful bromeliads and trees. Another trail *(0.8 mi)* marked with interpretive signs circles a freshwater pond past an observation tower. Canoeists can take a 5.5mi-loop trail into the refuge.

Boca Raton Resort & Club

E. Camino Real. &℘561-395-3000. www.bocaresort.com. Visit by guided tour (1hr 30min) only, year-round Tue 2pm–3:30pm, Sat in Aug. $15 plus $10 car valet fee; reservations with Boca Raton Historical Society. ℘561-395-6766. www.bocahistory.org.

The world-class hotel that put Boca Raton on the map began life as the Cloister Inn, a 100-room Mediterranean Revival-style Inn completed in 1926 by Addison Mizner. The original part of the hotel remains as the **east wing**, decorated with pecky cypress beams and 15C Spanish furniture. Later additions came in 1929 and 1969 under different owners.

DEERFIELD BEACH

Deerfield Beach is a prime spot to catch some beach time away from the crowds, but there is more to do than mere sunbathing. Instead, once you're done soaking up the rays, be sure to check out the Quiet Waters Park *(www.broward.org)*. Quiet Waters isn't your average water park; it's almost a full-service center. There's a mini water park, a skate park, a marina with rental boats, fishing lakes, cable water skiing and mountain bike trails. *Note: the water park, Splash Adventure, is geared towards younger children. Older children should check out cable water skiing at Ski Rixen.*

Population: 10,468.
Michelin Map: p153.
Info: 400 Royal Palm
Way; ☎561-655-3282;
www.palmbeachfl.
com or www.palm
beachchamber.com.
Location: Southern
Blvd., Royal Palm and
Flagler Memorial
bridges run west-east
providing access to
Palm Beach.
Parking: There are
several public parking
garages (follow signs)
off A1A.
Don't Miss:
A driving tour along
the Atlantic to see
how and where the
rich and famous live.
Timing: Allow a half-
day or more for the
driving tour, including
a stop at the Flagler
Museum.
Kids: DivaDuck
Amphibious Tours
☎561-844-4188
or 877-844-4188;
www.divaduck.com;
$25, offers fun-filled
tours of the area.

PALM BEACH★★★ *and around*

Occupying the northern part of a 16 mile-long subtropical barrier island, this strip of real estate harbors one of the highest concentrations of multimillion-dollar mansions in the world. Though it has been a refuge for the rich for more than a century, Palm Beach attracts streams of tourists —particularly in winter—who venture across one of the bridges from the mainland to sample fine restaurants, stay in world-class hotels, shop along Worth Avenue and ogle the elegant estates bordering the ocean.

A Bit of History

When a Spanish schooner, aptly named *La Providencia*, wrecked off this coast in 1879, the area's few settlers happily inherited a windfall cargo of coconuts. They planted the spoils and met with surprising success: a flourishing grove of around 20,000 coconut palms.

This lush, tropical-looking shoreline caught the eye of **Henry M. Flagler** as he was scouting out a site for a new resort town. In Palm Beach Flagler claimed to have found "a veritable paradise." In the 1890s, Palm Beach had its first taste of the kind of development that would characterize the area for decades to come. Flagler's Royal Poinciana Hotel, now gone, opened in 1894 (the year his railroad came to town) with 540 rooms and the claim that it was the world's largest wooden structure. Flagler's indelible mark on the town is most apparent in two remaining buildings: The Breakers hotel and Whitehall, his former Palm Beach home (now the Flagler Museum).

The spectacular building boom of the late 1910s and early 20s left the town utterly changed. Early wooden seaside cottages and hotels were replaced by baronial mansions, giving Palm Beach an affluent image that lives on today. Known as the "winter Newport" (for the Rhode Island retreat of the rich and famous), Palm Beach had restaurants, shops, clubs, hotels and villas, all tailored to the tastes of the wealthiest people on both sides of the Atlantic—the Vanderbilts, the Rockefellers, the Duke and Duchess of Windsor.

When Florida real-estate speculation caved in on itself and the Depression gripped the country in the late 1920s, Palm Beach society continued to enjoy a luxurious lifestyle; the rich merely became less ostentatious.

Bastion of Elegance – Today Palm Beach remains a picture perfect island of palm-lined thoroughfares, immaculately clean streets and opulent houses manned by busy gardeners.

MILLIONS ...LIKE A LOCAL

Palm Beach is one of the wealthiest counties in Florida and in the entire United States, but that's not why it's called the "Gold Coast." In fact, Gold Coast is a reference to something else entirely. A number of Spanish Galleons sank off the coast in the 17 and 18C and the name comes from the silver and gold coins that still wash ashore from time to time.

Despite all the wealth in the community, you don't need to be a millionaire to go behind the curtain and see the high-end side of Palm Beach, all that's required is a taste for history. Learn the name Henry A. Flagler, one of the founders along with John D. Rockefeller of Standard Oil. Flagler's influence can be seen the length and breadth of Florida, especially in the Florida Keys, but Palm Beach was his home base. Start off your tour of Palm Beach by visiting Whitehall, Flagler's home, which was a wedding gift to his third wife. This 55-room, 60,000-square-foot mansion is a National Historic Landmark and is now home to the Henry Morrison Flagler Museum, which was the first museum in the state. In addition to artifacts of Flagler's work and life, including his personal railroad car, there's also changing art exhibits.

Flagler's influence can also be seen at Palm Beach's main resort—The Breakers (originally named the Palm Beach Inn). Starting in the 1880s, The Breakers has been the vacation retreat of many of the nation's wealthiest from Astors, to Rockefellers, to Andrew Carnegie and JP Morgan. However, Flagler's original Palm Beach Inn burned down and today the current building is continually renovated.

After Flagler's, the next big name in Palm Beach architecture is Addison Mizner, who moved away from New England-style buildings to a more Mediterranean style. The prime example of his work is the Everglades Club, which is sadly closed to the public, but you can see Mizner's influence in Via Mizner. Once Mizner's home, the building has since been transformed into stores and restaurants, though it remains in the national register of historic places.

Beyond architecture, check out some of the area's finer gardens at the Society of Four Arts, which houses Chinese, Spanish, rose and herb gardens that are maintained by the garden club of Palm Beach.

And if the Rolls Royces and Porches on South Ocean Boulevard get too much for you, it's time to consider a two-wheeled option. A flat and easy bike trail runs right along the Intracoastal Waterway. It'll take you from the west side of Palm Beach to the Marina in West Palm Beach. You can rent bikes right along the trail or just jog the route. You'll work up an appetite touring the area, but you don't need to cut short your tour for a meal. Curbside Gourmet (☎561-371-6565, www.curbsidegourmet. com) serves up fresh, local fare from its big green truck on weekdays, for those on bicycle—rather than chauffer-driven—budgets.

DRIVING TOUR
PALM BEACH

» *7.5mi. Start at Southern Blvd. and Ocean Blvd. (A1A) and head north. The speed limit is 35mph, though most people drive at a lower speed.*

This drive begins along the Atlantic, offering expansive **views**★★ of the ocean on the right and large, elegant houses on the left. The first mansion, partially hidden by walls and a massive gate, is **Mar-a-Lago**, so-named ("sea to lake") because it extends from the Atlantic to Lake Worth. Considered the grandest residence in Palm Beach, this 188-room Moorish fantasy, built in 1927 for cereal heiress Marjorie Merriweather Post, and owned recently by Donald Trump is now a private country club.

» *Drive north 2.6mi on Ocean Blvd. and turn left at dead end on Barton Ave. Park beside church on Barton Ave. or on Via Bethesda, one street to the north.*

Episcopal Church of Bethesda-by-the-Sea★★

141 S. County Rd. Open year-round daily 8am–5pm. Tours following 11am service on second and fourth Sun of each month. Closed major holidays. ♿🅿📷 *561-655-4554. www.bbts.org.*

This graceful structure of cast stone, built in the Gothic Revival style in 1927, features a prominent bell tower and notable ornamentations, including sculptures of the four Evangelists standing in niches in the main entrance archway.

Inside, the nave sweeps upward to wooden rafters and forward to a blue stained-glass window above the altar. Called the **Te Deum Window,** the three lancets depict the apostles St. Peter and St Paul, the risen Christ, and martyred saints Stephen and Catherine. In the south transept hangs a 17C **Madonna and Child** by Spanish painter Esteban Murillo and a suspended model ship.

A cloister to the left of the entrance leads to a courtyard and then to the small formal **Cluett Memorial Gardens**.

» *Continue 0.3mi north on County Rd.*

The Breakers★★

1 S. County Rd. Visit by guided tour (1hr) only, year-round Tue 2pm; meet in main lobby. $15. Reservations suggested. ✖♿📷 *561-655-6611 or 888-273-2537. www.thebreakers.com.*

When Henry Flagler's famous hotel burned down for the second time in 1925, his heirs put up $6 million, hired the best architects, imported 75 artisans from Italy, and employed 1,200 craftsmen to construct a palatial hotel. Eleven and a half months later, the new Breakers was complete.

Fast forward 85 years and $250 million has been spent on improvements in the last decade. The hotel roughly follows an H-shaped layout and features twin two-tiered belvedere towers with open arches, a colonnaded porte cochere and exterior relief panels. The lobby runs the entire 200ft length of the center section (the cross in the "H") with an 18ft vaulted ceiling. From the lobby extends a lush courtyard with fountains and a sunken garden.

» *Continue 0.3mi north to the southeast corner of Sunrise Ave.*

Paramount Building

139 N. County Rd.

This yellow building with green awnings, distinguished by its central entranceway and tall pointed arch, dates from 1927 when it opened as a 1,028-seat movie palace. Joseph Urban, set designer for the *Ziegfeld Follies* and architect to Austrian Emperor Franz Josef, designed the theater. Live performers included Charlie Chaplin, W.C. Fields and Glenn Miller. Women patrons wore so much jewelry that the semicircle of box seats was dubbed the "diamond horseshoe," and season tickets sold for as much as $1,000 apiece. The theater has been replaced by galleries, shops and offices.

» *Cross N. County Rd.*

Saint Edward's Church★

144 N. County Rd. Open Mon–Fri 7am– 4pm, Sat 7am–7pm, Sun 6:30am–1pm. ♿🅰☎*561-832-0400.*

Distinguished by elaborate decoration inside and out, this Roman Catholic church (1926) features a baroque entrance of cast stone, a belfry and a redtile roof. In the narthex, spiral marble pillars and wooden gates lead into a vast sanctuary vaulted with a 65ft hand-painted coffered ceiling. The main altar was carved from a single piece of Carrara marble and measures 28ft by 15ft.

» *Continue north 0.6mi on County Rd. and turn left onto Wells Rd. and left again on Bradley Pl.*

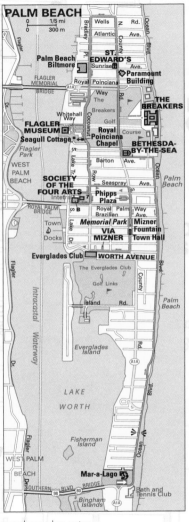

Seven blocks down on the right stands the **Palm Beach Biltmore** (*Bradley Pl. and Sunrise Ave.*), a 1927 resort hotel that closed in 1970. The building now houses luxury condominiums.

Flagler Museum★★

» *Proceed two blocks farther south and cross Royal Poinciana Way. Continue south on Coconut Row (the continuation of Bradley Pl.); take the first right onto Whitehall Way.*

Whitehall Way. Open year-round Tue–Sat 10am–5pm, Sun noon–5pm. Closed Jan 1, Thanksgiving Day, Dec 25. $18. 🅿 ✆561-655-2833. www.flaglermuseum.us.

Florida railroad magnate and Standard Oil partner **Henry Morrison Flagler** built Whitehall, this 55-room Gilded Age mansion overlooking Lake Worth, in 1901 as a wedding gift for his third wife, Mary Lily Kenan.

The mansion has been restored to its Flagler-era appearance with many of the original furnishings. The **Marble Hall** is a 110ft-by-40ft imitation of a Roman villa's atrium, decorated in seven different shades of polished marble.

The **Louis XIV Music Room** is hung with Baccarat chandeliers and paintings by 18C masters, Gainsborough and Romney.

The **ballroom** features gilt mirrors, crystal chandeliers, damask draperies and bronze fixtures hung with crystal grapes, pears and Florida bananas. The **Francis I Dining Room,** with its carved walnut woodwork and coffered plaster ceiling, saw a procession of royalty, wealth and fame with names such as Rockefeller, Astor and Vanderbilt.

Flagler's private railroad car, "Rambler," stands on the south lawn. It is open to see the sumptuous sleeping berths and kitchen. The gray-wood **Royal Poinciana Chapel** (*60 Coconut Row, just south of the museum*) was built by Flagler in 1896 for use by guests at his Royal Poinciana Hotel. Behind the chapel stands the oldest extant house in Palm Beach, **Seagull Cottage** (*not open to the public*).

Society of the Four Arts★

» *Drive south 0.7mi and turn right on Royal Palm Way; take first right into Four Arts Plaza.*

Four Arts Plaza. See below for opening times. ♿🅿 ✆561-655-7226. www.fourarts.org.

The Society of the Four Arts was established in 1936 to foster an appreciation for art, music, literature and drama.

The **Gioconda and Joseph King Library** contains more than 60,000 volumes for community use (*open Nov–May Mon–Fri 10am–5pm, Sat 10am–3pm*).

The **Esther B. O'Keeffe Gallery Building** (*open Dec–Apr Mon–Sat 10am–5pm, Sun 2–5pm*) provides space for exhibits, films, lectures and concerts.

Near the library, intimate **gardens** feature a Chinese rock garden, a rose garden and fern-rimmed pools. At the entrance is the adjoining **Philip Hulitar Sculpture Garden**.

Phipps Plaza

On N. County Rd. between Seaview Ave. and Royal Palm Way.
Planned by affluent resident socialite John S. Phipps, this peaceful Old-World cul-de-sac is a mix of residential and commercial properties. Distinctive features include belfries and walls covered with tiles taken from old buildings in Cuba, ornate iron gates, winding staircases and a densely planted central park of ficus, yucca, frangipani and golden shower trees.

« *Cross Four Arts Plaza (north), turn right on Seaview Ave. Take first left on Coconut Row, then right on Seaspray and right on N. County Rd. Take second right into Phipps Plaza.*

Town Hall

360 S. County Rd., between Australian and Chilian Aves.
Designed by Harvey and Clarke in 1924, this attractive building features beige stucco walls rising to a barrel-tile roof crowned by an enclosed bell tower.
On the north side of Town Hall, **Mizner Fountain** splashes into three basins upheld by rearing horses. Addison Mizner designed the fountain and surrounding **Memorial Park,** an oasis in the middle of busy County Road, which features cut coral-stone pavement and plantings.

« *Turn right on County Rd. and continue 3 blocks south.*

Worth Avenue★★

Between Ocean Blvd. and Coconut Row.
The East Coast's answer to Rodeo Drive in Beverly Hills, California, this upscale street acts as a magnet for well-heeled tourists and residents, as well as the merely curious, who come to eat in the fine restaurants and browse at the upscale shops. Worth Avenue's mélange of styles succeeds in creating a picturesque street with a decidedly European flair.
Addison Mizner designed many of the connecting two-story villas along the street in 1924, as well as the delightful vias, or alleyways, that thread off the main road into charming little courtyards of tile-work fountains and hanging flower baskets. Among these, **Via Mizner★** stands out for its labyrinthine passages and pastel walls of yellow, pink and aqua. Mizner's own four-story apartment dominates the skyline here. At the west end of the street sits his first Florida commission, the three-story **Everglades Club** *(no. 356)*, which embodies the ebullient, expansive spirit of pre-Depression Florida and secured his reputation as the architect of the wealthy in Palm Beach.

« *Continue two blocks south of Town Hall and turn right on Worth Ave.*

Population: 89,905.
Michelin Map: p157.
Info: 400 Royal Palm Way; ℏ561-655-3282; www.palmbeachfl. com or www.palm beachchamber.com.
Location: Two major thoroughfares (US-1 and I-95) cut through West Palm Beach, and Florida's Turnpike runs just west.
Parking: Public garages throughout downtown. Street metered parking.
Don't Miss: Norton Museum of Art.
Timing: Allow a full day to explore the Norton Museum of Art and Ann Norton Sculpture Gardens.
Kids: Take a safari through the wild 500-acre Lion Country preserve.

WEST PALM BEACH★ *and around*

It may live in the shadow of its glamorous parent, Palm Beach, and is still viewed as a commercial suburb even though it has outstripped the resort island in size, population and skyline. Nevertheless, West Palm Beach has its own charms, including one of Florida's finest art museums.

A Bit of History

The area first attracted workers who came to build the grand hotels on Palm Beach. The booming era of construction lasted most of the century through the 1980s. Today, it is again experiencing a resurgence. Bustling **CityPlace**, an entertainment and business complex, is linked to downtown's thriving Clematis Street, filled with trendy shops and eateries. Along **Flagler Drive** high-rise banks and office buildings contrast with such Palm Beach landmarks as The Breakers and Whitehall visible across Lake Worth. The **Old Northwood** neighborhood *(bounded by Flagler Dr. and Broadway Ave., 25th and 36th Sts.)* contains a number of 1920s Spanish-style homes.

Sights

Norton Museum of Art★★

1451 S. Olive Ave. Open year-round Tue–Sat 10am–5pm (second Thu of month 9pm), Sun 1pm–5pm. Closed major holidays. $12. ✕ ᕦ 🅿 ℏ*561-832-5196. www.norton.org.*
Founded in 1941 by steel tycoon **Ralph H. Norton** (1875–1953), the collection consists of over 7,000 works concentrated in European, American, Chinese, Contemporary art, and photography. In its permanent holdings, special emphasis is placed on 19–20C American and European works and Chinese art from 1700 BC to the early 1900s. Its renowned **Chinese collection** comprises archaic jade tomb carvings from as early as the third millennium BC. Highlights in the **French Impressionist** and **post-Impressionist** galleries include paintings by such notables as Cézanne, Matisse, Monet, Renoir, Gauguin and Picasso. Twentieth-century **American art** includes works by Hopper, O'Keeffe, Rauschenberg, Warhol and Pollock.

Ann Norton Sculpture Gardens

253 Barcelona Rd., north corner of Flagler Dr. Aug–Jul Wed–Sun 10am –4pm. Closed holidays. $7. ᕦ 🅿 ℏ*561-832-5328. www.ansg.org.*
This former residence of art patron Ralph Norton (€*see above)* has been converted to a display grounds for his second wife's sculptures. **Ann Weaver Norton** (1905–1982) came to the area

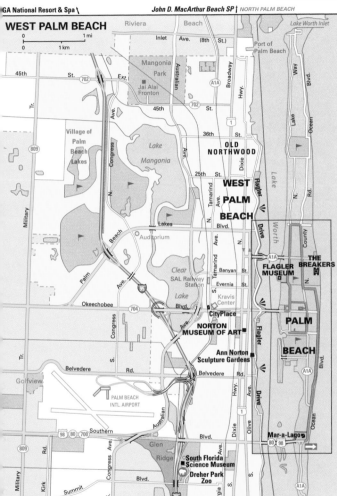

in 1942 as the Norton School of Art's first instructor in sculpture. The house contains more than 100 of Ann's works. In the garden, a walking trail leads past nine of her monumental brick and granite **abstract megaliths**, designed to suggest Tibetan shrines, mythical beasts and totemic figures. An outstanding collection of over 300 types of palm graces the property.

Palm Beach Zoo

1301 Summit Blvd., just east of I-95, accessible from Southern Blvd. or Forest Hill Blvd. exits. Open year-round daily 9am–5pm. Closed Thanksgiving Day and Dec 25. $18.95. ✕ ♿ 🅿 ℘ *561-533-0887. www.palmbeachzoo.org.*

Set on 23 acres, this small zoo is home to more than 1,500 animals representing 275 different species. Its newest attraction is its heavily themed Tropics of the Americas exhibit, an $18 million showcase for the animals and the native culture found in the Central and South American regions.

A boardwalk nature trail *(0.25mi)* leads through lush tropical foliage while on warm days, children frolic in the refreshing water jets of the Interactive Fountain.

South Florida Science Museum

4801 Dreher Trail North. Open year-round Mon–Fri 10am–5pm, Sat 10am–6pm, Sun noon–6pm. Closed Thanksgiving & Dec 25. $11.95, planetarium additional $4. Laser concerts, second Sat of month, 7pm and 8:30pm, $10. ♿ 🅿 ℘ *561-832-1988. www.sfsm.org.*

Parents and kids will enjoy themselves here with over 50 hands-on exhibits, a digital planetarium, freshwater and saltwater aquariums. Natural history exhibits include Suzie, the local Ice Age mastodon, and BUGZ! an outsized backyard garden that visitors enter with a "bugs eye"-view of the world.

Excursions

John D. MacArthur Beach State Park★

9mi north of Palm Beach, on Singer Island. ⟫ *Take US-1 north 4mi to Riviera Beach; turn right on Rte. 708 (Heron Blvd.), which becomes A1A. Follow A1A north 5mi to park entrance.*
Open 8am–sunset. $5 per vehicle. ♿ ℘ *561-624-6952. http://macarthurbeach.org.*

This natural haven encompasses 760 acres of mangrove estuary and pristine beach. The newly renovated **Nature Center** interprets the ecosystem of a barrier island while outside, the Butterfly Garden Trail offers a peaceful stroll among native flowers and the butterflies they attract. The Satinleaf Trail *(.5mi)* loops through a hardwood forest of tropical trees.

A 1,600ft wooden bridge across Lake Worth Cove provides wonderful **views★** of the mangrove estuary, home to 150 species of birdlife, mainly waterfowl but also songbirds and raptors.

OR GOLF LOVERS

ports lovers will have a field day at **PGA National Resort and
pa** *(400 Ave. of the Champions in Palm Beach Gardens; ℘561-627-
000 or 800-863-2819; www.pga-resorts.com)*, the national HQ for
e Professional Golfers of America. Billed as the "largest complex
the Western Hemisphere," it features five 18-hole tournament
purses on 2,300 acres of manicured fairways, as well as a
oquet complex. There are 339 guest rooms, 65 cottages, eight
staurants and lounges, 19 tennis courts and a 26-acre lake.
or nonsporting types or weary athletes, the spa includes an
utdoor mineral pool with Dead Sea healing waters.

ion Country Safari★★

5mi west of I-95 on Southern Blvd. (Exit 50). Pets and convertibles
ot allowed (air-conditioned sedans available for rent). Visitors drive
4mi road through the park and must remain in their cars with
indows closed. Open year-round daily 9:30am–4:30pm. $27.50.
✕ ⅃ ⼹ 🅿 ℘561-793-1084. www.lioncountrysafari.com.
orida's only drive-through safari, this 500-acre, drive-through
ame preserve features seven simulated African, Asian and
outh American habitats. You will drive past more than 900 ani-
als of over 100 different species, including lions, giant tortoises,
udu and impalas, waterbucks, wildebeests, ostriches. African
ephants, giraffes, Water buffaloes, zebras, rhinoceroses and
himpanzees, all in their relevant habitats, safely separated from
eir natural predators.
ontinue on foot through Lion Country's themed amuseument
ark with more (conventional) animal exhibits including mon-
eys, birds and reptiles.

ET IN GEAR

or all you gear heads out there, Palm Beach is a great place to
et your classic car fix and make a night out of it at the same
me. Cruising nights, where owners and fans of classic cars alike
ather to talk and admire, are increasingly popular in the area
nd happen year-round, usually taking place at the weekend.
ocations vary so check online message boards or talk to locals.
muscle cars aren't your thing, then check out the annual Ferrari
avallino Classic car show, which showcases some of the rarest
nd exotic Ferraris on the planet every January in Palm Beach.

TREASURE COAST

The aptly named Treasure Coast derives its name from the same historic event that lead to Palm Beach's moniker, the Gold Coast. In the early 18C, Spanish treasure fleets would make many runs from the silver and gold mines in Mexico back to Florida. In 1715, a hurricane caused a fleet of 12 ships to sink around the St. Lucie and Sebastian Inlet (note you can dive down to explore only one of the surviving sunken ships, the *Urca de Lima*).

The Spanish took great care to set up near the Sebastian shore in order to regain some of the wealth, however most was lost to pirates. Today, coins do wash up on shore—fewer on the Treasure Coast, though, and more on the Gold Coast.

Despite its history, I find the real treasure of this area to be the wide open spaces, which strike a direct contrast to the condominium- and development-centric areas surrounding Miami. Running along the Atlantic Ocean, the Treasure Coast officially contains Indian River, St. Lucie and Martin Counties. Though Port St. Lucie is one of the fastest-growing cities in the country, the area maintains its comparatively undeveloped beach front. Sandbars and barrier islands dot the cost, many of them national parks, which makes for remote getaways and limits development.

In addition to Port St. Lucie, Fort Pierce and Jupiter draw the largest swathe of visitors on the Treasure Coast. An old military hub, Fort Pierce was constructed in 1837 as the headquarters for the U.S. Army during the Seminole Indian War. One of the earliest Florida communities, the Fort grew after the war due to it's accessible waterways.

TREASURE HUNT

Modern treasure hunters have determined, much to their delight, that the wrecked galleons carried treasure not always reported on ship manifests. A great deal of such undeclared cargo has been found off this coast in recent decades. And pieces of eight (17C Spanish pesos) and other artifacts still occasionally wash ashore after storms churn up the ocean waters, unlocking treasures from the seabed. In contrast to the neighboring Palm Beach area, urban development has been slow. If you are traveling north-south you will be struck by the emergence of wide open natural spaces and quiet uncommercialized barrier-island beaches.

PETER'S TOP PICKS

 CULTURE

Fort Pierce began as a military base and now is home to the Navy SEAL museum, where you can check out relics from past Navy SEAL rescues. **UDT-SEAL Museum (p 162)**

 HISTORY

Go to the St. Lucie visitor's center to learn about the Ais Indians and the other pioneers of the Treasure Coast. **St. Lucie County Regional History Center (p 162)**

 GREEN SPACES

Fort Pierce State Park has beaches for surfers, sun tanners and families seeking quieter waters. **Fort Pierce Inlet State Park (p 162)**

After Henry Flagler built his railway, Fort Pierce became the commercial center of the Treasure Coast and was home to farming, fishing and local businesses. Speaking of farming, the Treasure Coast is where much of Florida's famous citrus fruit is farmed. With over 500,000 acres of orange groves in the state, the Treasure Coast boasts a third of these, and is best know for its Indian River oranges. In addition to farm land, the Treasure Coast's undeveloped coastline is preserved by several national parks, featuring animal sanctuaries, diving and undisturbed beaches.

Population: 37,841.
Michelin Map: p163.
Info: ℘772-462-1535
or 800-344-8443;
www.visitstluciefla.com.
Location: 55mi north
of West Palm Beach.
Rte. 1 snakes through
downtown and
along the shoreline.
Causeways provide
access to north-south
A1A, traveling along
Hutchinson Island.
Parking: Garage
and surface lots
available downtown;
free parking at most
beaches (metered
parking at Dollman
Beach and Fort
Pierce Inlet).
Don't Miss: Take a
scenic drive along
A1A, stopping at
beaches and parks
along the way.
Timing: Allow 2hrs
plus beach time.
Kids: The Florida
Oceanographic
Society Coastal
Centeron Hutchinson
Island has touch tanks
and nature trails.

FORT PIERCE *and Hutchinson Island*

This mid-sized town exists on two shores: the cluttered business district that lies along the west side of the Intracoastal Waterway, and the tranquil beaches on Hutchinson Island. Barrier-island beaches and 21 miles of inviting shoreline attract vacationers and second-home owners.

Sights

UDT-SEAL Museum★

3300 N. A1A, in Pepper Park (1mi north of Fort Pierce Inlet State Park). Open Jan–Apr Mon–Sat 10am–4pm, Sun noon–4pm. Rest of the year Tue–Sat 10am–4pm, Sun noon–4pm. $8. ⅙ 🄿 ℘772-595-5845. www.navysealmuseum.com.
Exhibits here vividly outline the history of the Navy SEALs (Sea, Air and Land)—the elite commando units—including life-size dioramas and films on SEAL operations, boats from World War II and the Vietnam War, and an Apollo space capsule.

Fort Pierce Inlet State Park

905 Shorewinds Dr. off A1A, south tip of North Hutchinson Island. Open 8am–sunset. $6 per vehicle. ⅙ 🄿 ℘772-468-3985. www.floridastateparks.org/fortpierceinlet.
On the north of the Inlet, this scenic park with 340 acres of beachfront and maritime hammock is a peaceful place to surf and swim, or picnic and watch pleasure craft ply the waters.

St. Lucie County Regional History Center★

414 Seaway Dr. Open year-round Tue–Sat 10am–4pm. Closed major holidays. $4. 🄿 ℘772-462-1795. www.stlucieco.gov/history.
Housed in a replica of the town's Florida East Coast Railway station, this museum tells the story of the Treasure Coast's history. Exhibits include artifacts from the Ais Indians, a 1715 treasure fleet, and early 19C pioneer life.

HUTCHINSON ISLAND

Despite major development on the south end of the island, long, unspoiled beaches remain. **The Florida Oceanographic Society Coastal Center** *(890 N.E. Ocean Blvd.; open year-round Mon–Sat 10am–5pm, Sun noon–4pm; $10; ℘772-225-0505; www.floridaocean.org)* includes a marine-education center, two trails *(1mi and 0.75mi)*, aquariums, touch tanks and computer games. **Gilbert's Bar House of Refuge** *(301 S.E. MacArthur Blvd.;*

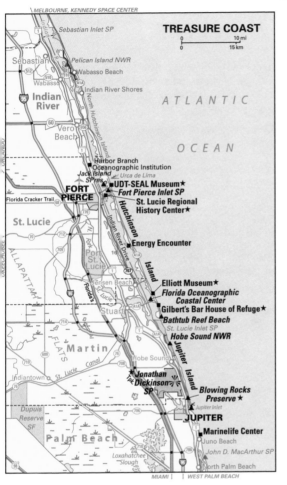

MELBOURNE, KENNEDY SPACE CENTER

TREASURE COAST

0 — 10 mi
0 — 15 km

Sebastian Inlet SP

Pelican Island NWR

Wabasso Beach

Indian River Shores

Sebastian

Wabasso

Indian River

Vero Beach

A T L A N T I C

O C E A N

North Hutchinson Island

Harbor Branch
Oceanographic Institution

Jack Island SPres.

Urca de Lima

UDT-SEAL Museum★

FORT PIERCE

Fort Pierce Inlet SP

St. Lucie Regional History Center★

Florida Cracker Trail

St. Lucie

Port St. Lucie

Hutchinson Island

Indian River Drive

Energy Encounter

Jensen Beach

Florida's

Elliott Museum★

Florida Oceanographic Coastal Center

Stuart

Gilbert's Bar House of Refuge★

Bathtub Reef Beach

St. Lucie Inlet SP

Hobe Sound NWR

Martin

Hobe Sound

St. Lucie Canal

Indiantown

Dupuis Reserve SF

Jonathan Dickinson SP

Jupiter Island

Blowing Rocks Preserve★

Jupiter Inlet

JUPITER

Marinelife Center

Juno Beach

Palm Beach

Loxahatchee Slough

John D. MacArthur SP

North Palm Beach

MIAMI | WEST PALM BEACH

✆772-225-1875; www.elliottmuseumfl.org) at the **Elliott Museum★** was erected in 1875 to aid shipwrecked sailors. The boathouse displays antique lifesaving equipment and other marine artifacts, while the main museum features a historical gallery, antique cars and vintage vehicles, and a collection of local social reformer Sterling Elliott's most notable inventions.
Bathtub Reef Beach (on MacArthur Blvd., 2.3mi south of A1A) is a favorite with families: it has a shallow wading area created by an 85-acre offshore reef.

Travel Tip: Think you're as tough as a Navy SEAL? Well, the Navy SEAL Museum gives you a good chance to size up your competition. At the museum, you can learn all about the history and the valiant missions the seals have undertaken. But check out their calendar of events to see if they have athletic fundraising events like 5ks on the schedule.

163

PRICES ...LIKE A LOCAL

Traveling like a local means you shouldn't think to pay out of pocket for every excursion and experience. Bypass the tour vans and booked excursions and take advantage of the free (or almost free) outdoor activities available throughout the area. Check out a few of my favorites.

Flamingo Heaven

The not-for-profit Flamingo Gardens in Davie has a free-flight aviary and Everglades Wildlife Sanctuary with 60 acres of lush gardens, groves, and the historic 1930s-era Wray House. The animal residents of Flamingo Gardens are all victims of human activity that wouldn't survive in the wild. A narrated trolley ride loops through the park, offering information on the flora and fauna found in the grounds. Look out for roaming peacocks, otters, bobcats, alligators, and flamingos living amongst some of Florida's rarest and most exotic plant species, including 16 Champion trees—the largest of their kind in the state. The gardens are open 9.30am–5pm, and closed Christmas Day and Thanksgiving Day.

Natural Retreat

Hugh Taylor Birch State Park sits right between the Atlantic Ocean and the Intracoastal Waterway in the middle of Fort Lauderdale. Of course there's surfing and all the other outdoor activities, but you also have the chance to catch a glimpse of some of Florida's native and migratory birds. The Terramar Visitor Center, Hugh Taylor Birch's 1940s-era Mediterranean and Art Deco home, features historical and environmental displays and is free with paid entry to the park. Visitors can enjoy one of the city's more popular beaches, investigate native and non-native plants along the coastal hammock trail, bike, walk, Segway, or boat. Located on East Sunrise Boulevard in Fort Lauderdale, off A1A; it is open 9am–5pm daily. Request a map with the $6.00 entry fee.

Archaeology

The wooden-hulled sailing ship Urca de Lima went down in a hurricane in 1715 while traveling from Cuba to Spain loaded with goods from Mexico and Manila in the Philippines. Almost 300 years later it was opened to the public as Florida's first official Underwater Archaeological Preserve. Divers will find five cement replicas of cannons and an anchor surrounding the ballast mound, which is constantly covered and revealed by sediments shifting in the currents. Located just 200 yards offshore in 10–15 feet of water about 1,000 yards north of the Fort Pierce inlet at Pepper Beach Park, the wreck is open to self-guided tours. Guides are available at local dive shops.

Sea Turtles

Half of the world's eight species of sea turtles frequent Florida's Atlantic coast, nesting between Cape Canaveral and Palm Beach. During June and July, a variety of local organizations, including the Loggerhead Marine Life Centre and the Hobe Sound Nature Center (http://hobesoundnaturecenter.com) offer guided turtle walks after dark.

JUPITER

Jupiter is a thriving community with upscale resorts, golf and yachting communities, and wide public beaches with reefs. The latter attract attract snorkelers and surfers, as well as thousands of sea turtles that nest on the shores.

Sights

Loggerhead Marinelife Center
Juno Beach Park. Open year-round daily 10am (Sun11am)–5pm. Contributions requested. ♿ ℘561-627-8280. www.marinelife.org.
Dedicated to rehabilitation and research of the area's sea turtles, the Center includes four aquariums and hands-on displays. Staff explain how injured turtles are cared for.

Jupiter Inlet Lighthouse & Museum
Captain Armour's Way. Visit by guided tour (1hr) only. Children must be at least 48in tall to climb the Lighthouse. Open May–Dec Tue–Sat (Jan–Apr daily) 10am–5pm. $9. ℘561-747-6639. www.lrhs.org.
This bright red beacon (1860) is the county's oldest surviving structure. You can climb the 105 steps to the top of the lighthouse tower for a birds-eye view of the surrounding area.

Jonathan Dickinson State Park★
7mi north of Rte. 706 on US-1. Open 8am–sunset. $6 per vehicle. ⛺ 🅿 ℘772-546-2771. www.floridastateparks.org.
This 11,500-acre tract of land and river contains the largest piece of sand-pine scrub in southeast Florida and shelters alligators, manatees, gopher tortoises and bald eagles.

ROGER DEAN STADIUM
There aren't many stadiums with a resume quite like Roger Dean Stadium in Jupiter. Aside from serving as the spring training facility for the St. Louis Cardinals and the newly founded Miami Marlins, Roger Dean is also the home to four different minor league baseball teams. The stadium is still relatively new, having opened in 1998, and can seat up to 6,800 people. A great day to go to this ball park is on family Sunday when kids get in free. Arrive early on Sunday and you can play catch on the field and after watching the game, stick around to run the bases and get some autographs.

Population: 45,100.
Michelin Map: p163.
Info: 800 North US Hw. One; ℘561-746-7111; www.jupiterfl.org.
Location: North Palm Beach County.
Parking: Parking is free along Jupiter Beach.
Don't Miss:
A boat tour on the Loxahatchee River at Jonathan Dickinson State Park through primeval wilderness (year-round Wed–Sun 9am, 11am, 1pm & 3pm; round-trip 2hrs; commentary; $14.50; 🅿 ℘561-746-1466).
Timing: Allow at least a day.
Kids: Loggerhead Marinelife Center.

ASK PETER...
Q: Which beaches are off the beaten path?
A: If you're looking for a rugged beach experience then drive a few miles out of town (5–15min drive) to Blowing Rocks Preserve on Jupiter Island. There you'll find a mile of wild, windy beaches, which are ideal for sunning and walking, if not swimming.

The Everglades might be best known for natural resources, but don't ignore the special culture that has built up around it. Locals have fought to preserve the "river of grass," building their businesses around it and pioneering the tradition of being a gladesman or a gladeswoman.

A 50 mile-wide subtropical wetland, the Everglades stretch from Lake Okeechobee to the Florida Bay. Essentially a slow moving river, the Everglades are only on average about 6 inches deep, losing elevation as they slope toward the Gulf of Mexico. Originating in the last Ice Age, it is one most the most diverse eco-systems on the planet: rare birds, mammals and reptiles, as well as plant life such as mangrove swamps, saw grass prairies, tree islands, pineland and estuaries are all to be found.

Expect heavy rains during the wet season from May to October; the landscape dries out during the winter months. This delicate environment has catered to pioneers and refugees of different stripes. The first known residents were the Calusa Indians, who called the Everglades the Pa-hay-okee, which translates as "grassy waters." Archaeologists suspect that the Calusa lived in the area for around 2,000 years, to be displaced by the Spanish in the 16C.

In the Seminole War, in the mid 1800s, some members of the Miccosukeeand Seminoles retreated to the Everglades to avoid being displaced to reservations. At that time, high heat and mosquitoes made the area uninhabitable and inhospitable.

Following the Civil War, the first settlers began to lay down roots here. John Weeks and William Smith Allen came to the area with their family after the war and struggled to farm the high ground surrounding the Allen River. In the 1920s, the area began to be developed when Barron G. Collier acquired habitable land for the headquarters of the Tamiami Trail road-building company.

The contemporary history of the Everglades is also the long-standing push and pull between development and preservation. Political pressure for agriculture and urban development is countered by a desire to preserve this ancient habitat. The Everglades National Park is the third largest park in the continental United States. The park preserves 2,500 miles of land and is also now a UNESCO World Heritage Site.

PETER'S TOP PICKS

 CULTURE

The Historic Smallwood Store is a fascinating glimpse into Everglade life in times gone by. **Historic Smallwood Store** (p **173**)

 GREEN SPACES

The Big Cypress National Preserve has the Florida National Scenic Trail. Drive the main loop and then get out and walk the unpaved Northern section. **Big Cypress National Preserve** (p **174**)

 HISTORY

Learn about the Miccosukee Indians when you visit their village. Yes, the reenactments can be a little hokey, so I say go to the museum. **Miccosukee Indian Village** (p **172**)

 STAY

Everglades Spa and Lounge is actually a B&B with a separate day spa attached. Just 'cause you're staying in the Everglades doesn't mean you have to rough it completely. **Everglades Spa and Lounge** (p **177**)

 EAT

The Rod and Gun Club began as a fishing and hunting club, but today it has morphed into an inn and restaurant. My advice, keep with the club's macho ethic, and don't get caught ordering a salad. **Rod and Gun Club** (p **173**)

Michelin Map: p168.
Info: ☎305-242-7700;
www.nps.gov/ever.
Don't Miss:
A tour boat ride
or canoe paddle
through the park's
pristine waterways.
Timing: Allow
three days to get
a good sense
of this amazing
environment.
Kids: Spotting a
'gator on the
Anhinga Trail.

SOUTHERN EVERGLADES

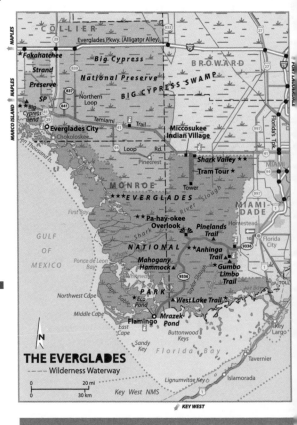

ASK PETER...

Q: Is there public
programming in
Everglades National
Park?
A: The gateway to
the park is the Ernest
Coe Visitor Center,
where programming
includes ranger-
led swamp walks,
morning bird walks,
nature films, and
starlight tours. As
you drive the park,
you'll also encounter
several observation
platforms and ponds
where you can stop
en route.

REPTILE RAP

The sluggish-looking alligator can sprint at speeds up to 15mph
for distances of 50 yards. They have been clocked swimming at
speeds of 14 knots, or 16mph. Alligators' jaws can crush their
prey with 3,000 pounds of pressure per square inch! There are six
types of poisonous snakes in Florida: pygmy rattlesnake, eastern
diamondback rattlesnake, coral snake, Florida cottonmouth
(water moccasin), and southern copperhead. The small dark
lizards you see everywhere in Florida are Cuban brown anoles, a
species introduced into the state from the West Indies. Its lesser-
seen relative, the green anole, is a Florida native.

A HAVEN FOR WILDLIFE

One of the major wetlands left on the continent, the Everglades supports some 600 species of animals, including 350 types of birds, 60 species of mosquitoes and 26 kinds of snakes, some of which are found nowhere else in the world. The southern Everglades, in fact, is the only place in the world where you'll find both alligators and crocodiles together. Birds provide the greatest spectacle in the park, with herons, egrets, ibis, cranes and other waterbirds almost always within sight. Bald eagles and ospreys nest here, and white pelicans (the largest birds on the continent, with a wingspan of 9ft) winter here.

American Alligator (Alligator mississippiensis) – Once a species with a poor prognosis for survival, the alligator has made a comeback and is often seen gliding silently through freshwater channels and marshes. Reaching lengths of up to 16ft, male alligators rank as the largest reptiles on the continent.

American Crocodile (Crocodylus acutus) – Cousin to the alligator, the endangered American crocodile has been reduced to a few hundred animals, concentrated in the salty mangrove inlets in the southern Everglades and the Keys Crocodiles can be distinguished from alligators by their lighter gray-green coloring, long pointed snout, and their protruding lower incisors.

Anhinga (Anhinga anhinga) – This long-necked denizen of the Everglades has become its symbol, often spotted in trees with its black wings outstretched. Lacking the oil covering that other birds have on their wings, the anhinga must air dry its wings in order to fly again after it has emerged from a feeding foray. To obtain food, the anhinga dives underwater and spears fish with its pointed bill. When swimming, only the bird's sinuous neck is exposed above the water; thus it is sometimes called the "snakebird."

Florida Panther (Felis concolor coryi) – Experts believe that only 50–70 of these big tawny-brown cats—designated Florida's state animal—still roam the state's wetlands, the only habitat left for them in the eastern US. The panther's birthrate of two to four kittens every other spring has been diminished by infertility caused by mercury-contaminated prey. Once widespread, these members of the cougar family have been relegated to the peninsula's tip.

Snail Kite (Rostrhamus sociabilis plumbeus) – This small, shy, gray-brown hawk survives exclusively on Pomacea, or apple, snails. With its curved beak, it extracts the snail from its shell. While snail kites are common in some parts of Central and South America, in North America these endangered birds are found only in central and southern Florida.

Roseate Spoonbill (Ajaia ajaja) – This brightest of the Everglades denizens can be seen foraging in the shallows in Florida Bay, where over 200 breeding pairs nest from November through March. Like flamingoes, with which they are sometimes confused while in flight, their pink coloration comes from a red pigment, related to Vitamin A, found in crustaceans that they eat.

DRIVING TOUR
SOUTHERN EVERGLADES

» *From Miami, take
Florida's Turnpike
(I-75) south until
it dead-ends at
Florida City. Turn
right on Rte. 1
south to Palm Dr.
(Rte. 9336). Follow
Rte. 9336 about
1.5mi and turn
left on 192nd Ave.
Continue 2mi to
376th St. S.W.
Turn right and
follow the road
5.6mi to park
entrance. Route
9336 then
continues 38mi
to its terminus in
Flamingo.*

A solitary highway cuts through the southern section of the park, east from Florida City, to the end of the road, 38 miles west, at Flamingo. En route a series of trails and visitor centers will acquaint you with the quintessential 'glades. 76mi round-trip. While you can see the highlights in a day, to best experience and understand the Everglades you must spend some time hiking its trails and boating on its waters. Sights in the southern part of the national park are organized as a driving tour, going from north to south.

Ernest Coe Visitor Center

On the right just before the park entrance. Open year-round daily 9am–5pm. ♿ *$10 per vehicle for a 7-day pass.* ♿ 🅿 ✆ *305-242-7700. www.nps.gov/ever.* Exhibits and films will enlighten you not only on the Everglades, but also on the environmental crises confronting the greater South Florida ecosystem.

Anhinga Trail★★

0.5mi. Begins at rear of Royal Palm Visitor Center. Ranger-led walks and lectures are held here several times daily. One of the park's most popular areas, this trail begins as a paved path, which follows a portion of the Old Ingraham Highway. A boardwalk then leads across Taylor Slough ("slew"), a shallow, slow-moving river that channels through a marsh dense with willow thickets and punctuated by a palm hammock. Alligators, turtles and myriad birds congregate here, particularly in the dry winter months.

» *Continue 2mi on
Rte. 9336 and turn
left at the sign for
Royal Palm Visitor
Center and the
Gumbo Limbo and
Anhinga trails.*

Gumbo Limbo Trail★

0.4mi. Begins at rear of Royal Palm Visitor Center. This trail weaves through the luxuriant vegetation of historic **Paradise Key Hammock**. A typical tropical island of hardwood trees, the Key supports a rich variety of ferns, lianas, orchids, royal palms and gumbo-limbo trees. The latter is known in Florida as the "tourist tree" because its red, peeling bark resembles sunburned skin.

» *Return to Rte. 9336
and continue 4.4mi.*

Pinelands Trail

0.3mi. A paved trail here circles through a rocky, drier landscape that supports one of the few existing forests of **Florida slash pine**, also known as Dade County pine. Highly prized for its durability, slash pine was extensively logged earlier in the 20C. That logging, and the suppression of forest fires, which allow the fire-resistant pine to compete with hardwoods, has led to the demise of the pine forests that once covered much of southern Florida. Only 20,000 acres of slash pine remain, making this species the continent's most endangered pine.

Pa-hay-okee Overlook★★

This elevated platform provides a sweeping **view★★** of the Everglades' seemingly endless saw grass prairie, interrupted only by sporadic islands of trees. Saw grass, part of the sedge family, is by far the most dominant flora in the Everglades. Though its long blades are razor-sharp, its soft roots are edible.

« Continue 6.3mi to the turn-off for Pa-hay-okee Overlook.

Mahogany Hammock

0.3mi. Tunneling through lush ferns and mahogany trees, the boardwalk trail passes the largest known mahogany tree in the country, unfortunately damaged by recent hurricanes.

« Return to Rte. 9336 and drive 7mi; turn right at sign for Mahogany Hammock.

West Lake Trail★

0.3mi. Follow the boardwalk along the edge of West Lake across a watery mangrove swamp. The dense concentration of mangroves, with their complex tangle of roots and branches, typifies Florida's coastal areas, where fresh water and salt water mix. Three types of mangroves grow in the 'glades: red, with reddish arcing roots; black, whose bases are surrounded by spiky breathing tubes; and white, generally found on drier ground.

« Return to Rte. 9336 and continue 11.3mi; turn right to parking area for West Lake.

Mrazek Pond

At dawn and dusk, grebes, herons, egrets, ibis and roseate spoonbills congregate here to feast on fish and shellfish.

« Continue 3.6mi.

Flamingo

Located at the southern terminus of Rte. 9336.
This small outpost, overlooking Florida Bay, serves as the visitor hub in the southern Everglades, providing the only food and camping facilities in this part of the park. The **Flamingo Visitor Center** (*open 9am–4:30pm, depending on staffing;* △✕&🅿☎*941-695-2945*) houses a small display area with natural history exhibits. The adjacent marina serves as the boarding point for **boat cruises★★** that tour the backcountry canals and the open waters of Florida Bay. Man-made **Eco Pond★** (*0.9mi west of visitor center; bring binoculars*) is a bird-watcher's paradise, particularly at dawn and dusk when flocks of waterfowl and wading birds gather to feed. The **observation platform** provides an excellent vantage point.

« Continue 3.5 mi to Flamingo.

171

Michelin Map: p90.
Info: ℘305-242-7700; www.nps.gov/ever.
Don't Miss:
The entertaining Tram Tour for an insight into the Everglades' natural history. (Bicycle rentals are also available here).
Kids: Gator wrestling at the Miccosukee Indian Village.

NORTHERN EVERGLADES

Completed in 1928, the Tamiami Trail (US-41) cuts across the Everglades, linking Miami with Naples. Along this strip is swampland and saw-grass prairie. The main entrance into the national park along this route is at Shark Valley.

Shark Valley (Park Entrance)★★

30mi west of Miami, US-41. Open year-round daily 8:30am–5:15pm. $10 per vehicle for a 7-day pass. ♿🅿℘305-221-8776. *www.nps.gov/ever. Maps and park information from kiosk next to parking lot.*

Named for the shallow, slow-flowing slough that empties into the brackish Shark River southwest, this shark-free "valley" is a basin that lies a few feet lower than the rest of the 'glades.

Shark Valley Tram Tour★

Tours depart from parking lot mid/late Dec–May daily hourly 9am–4pm. Rest of year daily 9:30am, 11am, 1pm, 3pm. 2hr-round trip. Reservations recommended late Dec–Apr. $19. ♿. *℘305-221-8455. www.sharkvalleytramtours.com.*

The tour follows a 15mi loop road through open fields of grassy wetland. Along the way, park naturalists point out local denizens: snail kites, egrets, herons and alligators to name a few. An **observation tower** halfway round gives expansive views.

Miccosukee Indian Village

0.5mi west of Shark Valley entrance, US-41. Open year-round daily 9am–5pm. $10 (includes optional guided tour). Airboat rides (30min) $10. ✗♿🅿℘305-223-8380. *www.miccosukeetribe.com.*

This is a re-creation of a traditional settlement of chickees—palm-thatched, open-sided structures used as shelters. Natives demonstrate crafts such as beadwork and bright patchwork.

MICCOSUKEE INDIANS

Since the mid 19C Miccosukee Indians have inhabited the Everglades. Originally a part of the Creek Confederation, this tribe shares some similarities with the Seminoles but remains a distinct group with its own language and traditions. Now numbering some 500 people, the Miccosukee are concentrated in the northern Everglades, where they maintain a residential enclave and attempt to preserve their native culture. They have however also embraced 21C tourism, with the glitzy Miccosukee Resort & Gaming complex offering 24-hour gaming and luxury rooms, dining and nightlife.

A **museum** displays reproductions of traditional clothing, tools and baskets, as well as historic photographs. In the village's **alligator arena**, wrestlers demonstrate the bare-handed way in which Miccosukee hunters once captured alligators *(11am, 12:30pm, 1:30pm, 3pm, 4:30pm)* which were tied up and kept alive until the Indians were ready to eat them.

Airboat rides include the chance to see an authentic hammock-style Indian Camp that has been owned by the same Miccosukee family for over 100 years.

Everglades City

4mi south of US-41 on Rte. 29. Gulf Coast Visitor Center (Everglades National Park information) open year-round daily 7:30am–5pm. 🅿 *℘941-695-3311. www.nps.gov/ever.*
Established in the 1920s as HQ for the building of the Tamiami Trail, this town is the gateway to the northwestern Everglades. Its most famous institution is the **Rod and Gun Club** *(200 Waterside Dr, ℘239-695-2101; www.evergladesrodandgun.com).* Serving as a fishing and hunting club since the late 19C, this rambling white-frame Victorian lodgings, with its rich interior paneling, gained world renown in the 1930s as one of the most exclusive sports clubs in the nation. It is now an inn and restaurant.

Cruises of the Ten Thousand Islands★★

Cruises depart from the ranger station on Rte. 29. » From US-41, take Rte. 29 south 4mi to traffic circle; stay on Rte. 29—3/4 turn around circle—and continue 0.5mi to Everglades National Park Gulf Coast Visitor Center on right. Open year-round daily 9/9.30am–5pm. Round-trip 1hr 30min. $26.50. ✖ & 🅿 *℘239-695-2591. http://evergladesnationalparkboattoursgulfcoast.com*
Everglades National Park Boat Tours operate cruises around **Chokoloskee Bay**. Countless small islets here are covered with one of the largest mangrove forests in the world. Look out for dolphins, manatees numerous waterbirds, including ospreys, herons, roseate spoonbills; perhaps even nesting bald eagles.
An alternative **Mangrove Wilderness Tour** explores swampy areas of the park aboard a six-passenger vessel. *(Tours last 1hr 45 min; $35/person).*

Historic Smallwood Store

360 Mamie St. » From Everglades City, continue on Rte. 29 about 3mi onto Chokoloskee Island; turn right on Smallwood Dr. and left on Mamie St.; follow Mamie to end. Open Dec–May daily 10am–5pm, rest of the year Fri-Tue 10am–4pm. $3. ℘239-695-2989. www.florida-everglades.com/chokol/smallw.htm.
From 1906 to 1982, this wooden bayfront structure was a trading

Everglades Advice and Regulations:

• Water-skiing is prohibited.
• Firearms and hunting are prohibited.
• Smoking on trails is not permitted.
• No pets on trails.
• All vehicles must stay on designated roads; off-road vehicles prohibited.
• Reduce speed in wildlife areas.
• Campfires permitted in fire rings in campground areas only.
• Do not disturb or feed wildlife.
• When hiking, advise someone of your itinerary.
• Owing to abundant wildlife in freshwater ponds and poor underwater visibility, swimming is not encouraged.
• Beware sudden weather changes that can lead to heavy thunderstorms, especially if you are boating.
• Always wear a sunscreen and protective clothing.
• Always carry mosquito repellent.
• Big Cypress Reserve is a habitat for black bears, so campers beware.

post and general store founded by "Ted" Smallwood, a Collier County pioneer. It is now a museum.

Wilderness Waterway

A paradise for boaters and canoeists, this watery inland course twists 99mi through protected rivers and bays, from Flamingo to Everglades City. Markers designate the waterway, and campsites (some furnished with chickee shelters) punctuate the route. *Pick up permit (no more than 24hrs before start of trip) and maps at the ranger station in Flamingo. ℘239-695-2945 or Gulf Coast Visitor Center (in Everglades City) ℘239-695-3311.*

Big Cypress National Preserve

Accessible from US-41 and I-75. Open daily year-round. ⚠℘239-695-1201. www.nps.gov/bicy.
Contiguous to the northern Everglades, this 729,000-acre preserve protects a portion of the 2,400sq mi **Big Cypress Swamp**, a rich variegated wetland covered with forests of bald cypress trees. A major habitat for all kinds of Everglades wildlife, Big Cypress is particularly favored by dwindling numbers of the endangered Florida panther. About 30–35 are thought to live in the park; all told, only about 80–100 panthers exist in the state. The **Oasis Visitor Center** (*19 mi west of Shark Valley on US-41; open year-round daily 8:30am–4:30pm; ℘941-695-1201*) shows a 15-min film on the geology, flora and fauna of Big Cypress. Stroll along the boardwalk for views of alligators. From here, the **Florida National Scenic Trail** leads 21mi into the preserve.
A 26mi loop road (Rte. 94 from Forty Mile Bend to Monroe Station) circles through cypress swamps in the southern part of the preserve, passing alligators, soft-shell turtles and raptors. An unpaved **northern loop** (*16.5 mi*) begins at Route 839 and goes through saw grass prairie (*Turner River Rd./Rte. 839 north 7.3mi; turn left on Rte. 837 to Birdon Rd./Rte. 841, back to US-41*).

Fakahatchee Strand Preserve State Park★

Big Cypress Bend trail parking located 7mi west of Rte. 29; park sign on right. Open year-round daily dawn–dusk. ℘239-695-4593. www.floridastateparks.org.
This "Amazon of North America. comprises a 20mi-long swamp forest, 3–5 mi wide, Its dense exotic vegetation includes the largest stand of native **royal palm** in the US, as well as the greatest concentration and diversity of **orchids** (31 threatened and endangered species); 15 species of bromeliads; and a variety of epiphytes, or air plants. A boardwalk (1 mi round-trip) at **Big Cypress Bend★★** leads through eerily beautiful virgin cypress forest, ending at a swamp frequented by alligators.

PROTECT ...LIKE A LOCAL

The Everglades of South Florida play a vital role in sustaining the state's natural wildlife as well as being a source of clean water for millions of Floridians. With modern development, the Everglades have been increasingly threatened, however awareness of environmental issues is greater than ever. If you're visiting South Florida and want to do your part in helping to protect one of the country's most stunning national parks, set aside some time to volunteer and help make a small but meaningful difference to this massively important natural asset.

National Park

There are multiple organizations that devote time and manpower to the area's wellbeing. If you're interested, a good place to start would be at the top, with the National Parks Service. The national parks service takes on all kinds of volunteers, usually between November and April, and offers a wide variety of ways to help. You can do anything from removing harmful plants to maintaining walking trails. You'll be working at the Everglades National Park, whose headquarters are in Homestead Florida, 40001 State Road (℘305-242-7700; www.nps.gov).

Wildlife Refuge

Another option is the Everglades Outpost Wildlife Refuge, which was opened in 1994 with a mission to rescue and rehabilitate hurt wildlife and endangered species.

At the refuge, you'll see exotic animals such as panthers, tigers, bears, and camels. Of course, you'll also see crocodiles, snakes, monkeys, and birds. The volunteers feed animals, clean their cages and help with park landscaping. If you're not planning to volunteer you can catch educational shows or go on a self-guided tour. You'll find the refuge in Homestead Florida, 35601 SW 192 Avenue (℘305-247-8002). There is also the Arthur R. Marshall Loxahatchee National Wildlife Refuge, which is in the Northernmost part of the Everglades, though the refuge works throughout the habitat. The refuge houses the American alligator as well as endangered species like the Everglade snail kite. Volunteers help with maintenance, as well as biological and botanical research. Visitors can

also independently take a walking bird tour or take a trail walk. Visit the refuse in Boynton Beach, 10216 Lee Road, (℘561-734-8303).

Orchid Thief

The singular environment of Fakahatchee Strand encourages the growth of rare and endangered plant species, including orchids. Fakahatchee was the scene of the John Laroche affair, in which the horticulturist was arrested for poaching the rare Ghost Orchid. He worked under the assumption that his Seminole Indian Tribe employers were beneficiaries of a loophole in state law that granted them immunity from statutes protecting endangered plants. He lost his case. The story was first told in the New Yorker and subsequently in the novel The Orchid Thief and the 2002 Spike Jonze film, Adaptation.

GETTING TO THE EVERGLADES

BY AIR – Miami International Airport (MIA): Closest commercial airport, 34mi north of Homestead (*305-876-7000; www.miami-airport.com*). Shuttle service to Homestead: **Super Shuttle** (*24hr service; one-way around $45 per passenger, for reservations: 305-871-2000; www.supershuttle.com*). Major rental car agencies are located at the airport.

BY CAR – There are two entrances to **Everglades National Park**: to reach the southern end at Flamingo, take Route 9336 east then south from Florida City. US-41 (Tamiami Trail) borders the northern part of the park. Shark Valley entrance is accessible from US-41.

BY BUS – Daily between Miami and Cutler Ridge, near Homestead. Greyhound bus station (located at a gas station next to McDonald's, 10801 Caribbean Blvd., Cutler Ridge *800-231-2222; www.greyhound.com*).

VISITOR INFORMATION

Park Headquarters, 40001 State Rd. 9336, Homestead FL 33034 (*305-242-7700; www.nps.gov/ever*). The park is open daily year-round. Entrance fee is $10/vehicle, valid at both park entrances for seven days. ⚠️♿. **Ernest F. Coe Visitor Center**: 11mi southwest of Homestead on Rte. 9336 (*open year-round daily 8am–5pm; 305-242-7700*).
Additional visitor centers: **Royal Palm** on US-41 (*open year-round daily 8am–4pm; 305-242-7700*); **Flamingo** at terminus of Rte. 9336 (*open Dec–Apr 7:30am–5pm; rest of the year daily 9am–5pm; 941-695-2945*); **Shark Valley** on US-41 (*open year-round daily 8:30am–5:15pm; 305-221-8776*) and **Gulf Coast** in Everglades City (*open year-round daily 7:30am–5pm; 239-695-3311*). Rangers lead wildlife walks, canoe trips and evening programs Dec–Apr; for schedules check the park newspaper or visitor centers.

The **Everglades Area Chamber of Commerce** Welcome Center (*open 9am–4pm*) is on SR-29 and US-41, Everglades City (*239-695-3941, www.evergladeschamber.net*). The **Tropical Everglades Visitor Assn.** (*160 Hwy. 1, Florida City, FL 33934; 305-245-9180 or 800-388-9669; www.tropicaleverglades.com*) provide good local visitor information. Florida boasts the **Great Florida Birding and Wildlife Trail**, a 2,000-mile, self-guided nature highway. If you have to choose one spot in the state to focus on, hone in on the south-central region, where the subtropical climate draw over 250 species of birds including bald eagles, cerulean warblers, sandhill cranes, bobwhite quail, and grasshopper sparrows.

WHEN TO GO

The best time to visit is **winter** during the dry season (Nov–mid-Apr), when daytime temperatures range from 60°–80°F, mosquitoes are tolerable, and wildlife is easier to spot. The busiest week is 25 Dec–1 Jan. Make lodging and tour reservations several months in advance.
In **summer** (May–Oct), the Park is, unsurprisingly less visited as temperatures often soar to 95°F and the hot, humid weather brings clouds of mosquitoes and other biting insects. Insect repellent is recommended year-round.

WHAT TO PACK

First and foremost, you must bring mosquito repellant, unless you want to risk being eaten alive. Bring sunscreen with a high SPF and a brimmed hat to protect from the sun. Consider investing in a waterproof camera or other waterproof equipment. Long pants will protect your from spiny shrubs or inhospitable critters. Wear close-toed shoes that have laces that you don't mind getting wet and muddy.

ADDRESSES

For price ranges, see the Legend on the cover flap.

WHERE TO STAY

$–$$$ Ivey House – *107 Camellia St., Everglades City. ☏239-695-3299. www.iveyhouse.com.* This 1928 house, beautifully turned out with a pool, courtyard and native plants, is run by the owners of NACT Everglades Rentals & Eco Adventures who offer guests 20 percent off rentals and tours. Lodgings include a B&B with shared baths and a guest house.

$$ Everglades Spa & Lodge – *201 Broadway W. Everglades City. ☏239-695-3151. www.bed breakfasthome.com/banksofthe everglades.* Housed in an old bank this comfy B&B whose separate day spa offers massages, facials, clay baths etc.

$ Redland Hotel – *5 S. Flagler Ave., Homestead. ☏305-246-1904 or 800-595-1904..* Built in 1904 this characterful place has also served as a mercantile store, and post office. It includes a pub and Internet cafe on site but is close to downtown.

Travel Tip:
Everglades City, Homestead and Florida City offer hotels, motels, campgrounds and RV parks. For posher accommodation options head for Naples or Miami.

Tours

The most popular type of tour in the Everglades is by **airboat**. Ironically due to their noisy nature and the disturbance they cause, airboats are banned in all designated "wilderness areas", which is in fact most parts of the 'glades. Most airboat operators are along the Tamiami Trail, where they operate either just outside the park boundary, or in park areas still awaiting "wilderness" designation. Conventional boat tours go along the mangrove coast at both Flamingo and the Gulf Coast (visit *www.nps.gov/ever/planyourvisit* for details), and **Shark Valley tram tours** offers two-hour guided road tours, narrated by park naturalists, through the heart of the "River of Grass" Shark Valley Tram Tours also rents **bicycles**. Touring the 15mi paved Shark Valley Loop Rd. typically takes 2–3 hours. Bikes are available daily on a first-come, first-served basis from 8:30am–4pm (last rental at 3pm); $7.75 per hour.

Sports and Recreation

Front Country Camping is available at Long Pine Key and Flamingo *(by reservation mid-Nov–mid-April; rest of year, first-come, first-served; ☏305-242-7873 (Long Pine Key) or 239-695-0124 (Flamingo).* The **Back Country** is only accessible by boat, canoe or on foot. A permit ($10–$30), obtainable at visitor centers, is required for all overnight trips. For all camping information visit *www.nps.gov/ever/planyourvisit.* A Florida **fishing** license, available at local bait and tackle shops, is required for fresh- and saltwater fishing. Seven **canoe** trails thread the southern park region. Rental canoes are available at Flamingo Marina *(☏239-695-3101).* Canoe the Wilderness Waterway with **North American Canoe Tours** *(http://www.evergladesadventures.com/).* **Crystal Seas** offers sea kayak tours *(Dec–Apr reservations required; ☏877-SEAS-877; www.crystalseas.com).* Several **hiking** trails fan out from Flamingo; park headquarters have trail information.

DISCOVERING
THE KEYS

The Florida Keys are easy to pigeon-hole in the lyrics of songwriter Jimmy Buffet as Florida's laid-back party island getaway; but it's not all tropical drinks and island culture. In fact, the Florida Keys stretch for 221miles and the Upper, Middle and Lower Keys all have their own individual personalities.

A mere 50 miles outside of Miami, the Florida Keys run from Biscayne Bay to the Dry Tortugas. Comprised of a thousand islets, the Florida Keys touch the Atlantic Ocean, the Florida Bay and the Gulf of Mexico. Beginning with Key Largo, the Florida Keys encompass the towns of Islamorada, Marathon, Big Pine Key and Key West.

In the Upper Keys, you'll find adventure seekers. Here's where sport fisherman, boating, kayaking and diving enthusiasts go. The Middle Keys are ideal for nature enthusiasts and were home to renowned naturalist John Audubon. Meanwhile, the Lower Keys contain rustic nature and wildlife alongside well-developed Key West, party town par excellence. Seashell stalls line roads along the archipelago.

At the turn of the 20C, the Keys were primarily accessible by boat and were a rather inhospitable collection of mosquito-plagued inlets. Henry A. Flagler, the oil magnate whose influence can also be seen in Palm Beach and throughout the state, launched his efforts to open up Florida to the public. Originally mocked as "Flagler's Folly," the tycoon fought to extend his railway through to the Keys.

Trains ran from 1912 until September 1935 when a hurricane destroyed miles of track. In place of the railway came the Overseas Highway, an extension of U.S. Route 1, which runs from Key Largo to Key West. Many of the bridges on the Overseas Highway were originally built for Flagler's railroad. Most notable is the Seven-Mile Bridge, which connects Knights Key in Marathon to the Lower Keys and the town of Little Duck Key.

Heading south across the bridge, you are not too far from Key West, the southernmost point in the Continental United States. Key West is so independent that it was home to the Conch Republic revolution, a town hall joke that became a mock secessionist movement for the entire Florida Keys in the 1980s.

Today, the Conch Republic is little more than a tourist gimmick, though the annual week-long Independence Day celebrations are lively and fun.

PETER'S TOP PICKS

 CULTURE

The Conch Republic Independence Celebration is essentially a local's pride party. Come celebrate what makes the Keys so special that they almost secede from the union. **Discovering The Keys** (p **178**)

 HISTORY

The Lighthouse and Keeper's Quarters Museums takes you back to life on the Keys before the turn of the century. **Lighthouse Keeper's Quarters and Museum** (p **197**)

 EAT

If it's good enough for Hemingway, it's good enough for me. Taste the Key's West Indian influences and dine where Hemingway used to run cock fights. **Blue Heaven** (p**201**)

 GREEN SPACES

The Bahia Honda State Park has both open beaches and vast green spaces. Take a trail walk to check out the view from the Bahia Honda bridge. **Bahia Honda State Park** (p **187**)

 STAY

There's more to the Keys than the ocean. The Gardens Hotel has only 17 units, but each one is surrounded by gardens, guaranteeing privacy at this secluded compound, which once served as a biological reserve. **Gardens Hotel** (p **200**)

 ENTERTAINMENT

Swim with the dolphins at the Dolphin Research Center. This non-for-profit facility was built by the creator of *Flipper*. **Dolphin Research Center** (p **183**)

SPORTFISHING TOURNAMENTS
General information, *www.fla-keys.com/fishing*. Late March, **Islamorada All-Tackle Spring Bonefish Tournament**, *www.inshoreworldchampionships.com*. April, **World Sailfish Championship**, Key West, *www.worldsailfish.com*. Late Apr–early May, **Tarponian Tournament**, Marathon, ☏*215-542-1492*. May, **Marathon International Tarpon Tournament**, *www.worldfishingnetwork. com*. Late June, **Gold Cup Tarpon Tournament**, Islamorada, *www.goldcuptt. com*. Late Sept, **Marathon International Bonefishing Tournament**, ☏*305-481-4571*. Nov/Dec, **Islamorada Sailfish Tournament**, *www.islamoradasail fishtournament.com*.

Population: 11,886.
Michelin Map:
p180–181.
Info: 📞305-451-1414
or 800-822-1088;
www.fla-keys.com/
keylargo.
Location: 56mi
south of Miami
International Airport.
Parking: Parking is
readily available in
Key Largo.
Don't Miss: John
Pennekamp Coral
Reef State Park, an
underwater aquatic
reserve boasting
40 species of coral
and more than 650
varieties of fish.
Timing: Plan the
length of your visit
depending upon
how much time
you want to spend
underwater. If you're
not avid snorkelers
or divers, plan a
day at the park
and a meal at the
Fish House (www.
fishhouse.com),
MM 102.4, one of
the best restaurants
around in the Keys.
Kids: A glass-
bottom boat trip
to the reef is a
great way to peek
underwater without
getting wet.

KEY LARGO★

Called *Cayo Largo*, or "Long Island," by 16C Spanish explorers, Key Largo is the first and largest—26 miles long but only
1 mile at its widest point—of the Florida Keys. Its real beauty
is to be found along its shoreline and underneath its crystal
blue waters. Immediately to the east lies the vast windswept
Atlantic Ocean; to the west, the calm shallow Florida Bay
serves as a nursery for birds and marine life.

Sights

Key Largo entered the consciousness of the nation following
the eponymous 1951 Humphrey Bogart movie. Yet it was almost entirely shot in Hollywood—the **Caribbean Club Bar**
(MM 104) is the only actual Keys location—and Key Largo, on
land at least, is something of a disappointment to most visitors.

As a token gesture to its Hollywood-Bogart success *The African Queen* is here, at the marina of the Holiday Inn at MM 100.

John Pennekamp Coral Reef State Park★★

MM 102.5. Open year-round daily 8am–dusk. $8 per vehicle plus 50c per person. ⚠🗡♿🅿✆305-451-6300. www.floridastate parks.org, www.pennekamppark.com.

Stretching along Key Largo's coastline and reaching 3mi off-shore, is America's first underwater park. Some 96 percent of it is submerged, encompassing a dazzling kaleidoscope of vivid coral and sea creatures. Informative displays (including a floor-to-ceiling aquarium) relating to the reef and its marine life in the **visitor center** *(open year-round daily 9am–5pm)*. Over 150 spe-cies of tropical fish feed here. Book a snorkeling or scuba tour; the latter (unless you have a particularly good pair of lungs), if you want to see the iconic **Statue of Christ of the Abyss**, an 8ft 6in bronze sculpture of Christ that stands in 25ft of water.

ASK PETER...
Q: How can I see Key Largo's 178 miles of corals reefs if I'm not ready to strap on scuba gear?
A: Good news, Key Largo's coral reefs are accessible to everyone. Go snorkeling, or take a trip in a glass-bottom boat to see one of the 600 local tropical fish.

Travel Tip:
Want a different hotel option? Instead of going for an ocean-front room, consider a room inside the ocean. The Jules' Undersea Lodge on Key Largo island is basically an underwater research lab which has been retro-fitted with two bedrooms to allow guests to stay overnight. To get there, you have to scuba dive 21ft. Once there, you can either relax in your quarters and watch the marine life from within, or take unlimited dives in the lagoon to explore the ocean firsthand.

*Map of the Florida Keys showing FLORIDA CITY, HOMESTEAD, MIAMI, BISCAYNE NP, MIAMI-DADE, EVERGLADES NATIONAL PARK, Card Sound Rd, Crocodile Lake NWR, Flamingo, MONROE, Wild Bird Rehabilitation Center, Key Largo, **John Pennekamp Coral Reef SP★★**, Tavernier, Plantation, Windley Key, **Lignumvitae Key Botanical SP**, **Theater of the Sea★**, **Islamorada**, Hurricane Memorial, Layton Trail, **Indian Key Historic SP**, San Pedro Preserve, Overseas Highway, Duck Key, **MIDDLE KEYS**, Grassy Key, **Long Key SP**, **Dolphin Research Center★**, STRAITS OF FLORIDA, **FLORIDA KEYS**, 20mi / 30km, N*

GETTING TO THE KEYS

BY AIR – Key West International Airport (℘305-296-5439; www.keywest internationalairport.com) is serviced by most domestic airlines, including SeaCoast Airlines (www.seacoastairlines. com) who fly from St Petersburg/ Clearwater Airport. Rental car agencies are located at and near the airport. International flights connect through Miami International Airport.

BY BOAT – The Intracoastal Waterway Key West Express operates ferries between Key West and Marco Island seasonally (Dec–mid-April), and between Key West and Fort Myers year-round. Trip from Marco Island takes 3hrs, Fort Myers 3.5hrs. Round-trip rates are $146 from either Marco Island or Fort Myers (℘888-539-2628; www.seakeywest.com).

BY CAR – Small green mile-marker **(MM)** posts mark sites along US-1 (Overseas Highway), giving distances from Key West. It begins in Florida City (MM 127). Much of the route is two-lane, and traffic can be heavy, particularly in the high season and on weekends. Allow 3hrs. The best places along US-1 to find lodging, restaurants and other amenities (marinas, recreational facilities) are: Key Largo (MM 110-87), Islamorada (MM 86-66), Marathon (MM 65-40), Big Pine Key (MM 39-9) and Key West (MM 0).

BY BUS – Greyhound **bus** makes scheduled stops in the Keys (℘800-231-2222; www.greyhound.com). A number of **shuttle** services offer transport to the Keys, including Keys Shuttle, operating from Miami International and Fort Lauderdale airports (℘888-765-9997 or 305 289-9997; www.keysshuttle.com).

WHEN TO GO

December through April is considered high season; afternoon temperatures range from 73°F to 79°F. The rest of the year they run 75°F to 85°F; annual average temperature is 77.4°F. Rainfall is considerably less than on the mainland and falls in brief thunderstorms during summer afternoons. March is Spring Break when hordes of young people descend on the Keys and Key West in particular. Travelers are likely to encounter crowds in Key West, especially on Duval Street.

FESTIVALS

There is a festival of some kind every week in the Keys. Here are three that may be worth planning your trip around; all take place in Key West.
October: **Fantasy Fest**. A Mardi Gras for gays and lesbians. www.fantasyfest.net.
April: **Conch Republic Independence Celebrations** (see p178). Around July 21: **Hemingway Days** – A celebration of the hellraising author.

VISITOR INFORMATION

FLORIDA KEYS VISITOR INFORMATION
(www.fla-keys.com; ℘800-FLA-KEYS).
Key Largo Chamber of Commerce, MM 106, 105950 Overseas Hwy., Key Largo 33037 (open daily; ℘305-451-1414 or 800-822-1088; www.fla-keys.com/keylargo).
Islamorada Chamber of Commerce, MM 83.2, PO Box 915, Islamorada FL 33036 (open daily; ℘305-664-4503 or 800-322-5397; www.islamoradachamber.com).
Marathon Chamber of Commerce, MM 53.5, 12222 Overseas Hwy., Marathon 33050 (open daily; ℘305-743-5417 or 800-262-7284; www.floridakeysmarathon.com).
Lower Keys Chamber of Commerce, MM 31, PO Box 430511, Big Pine Key 33043 (open Mon–Sat; ℘305-872-2411; www. lowerkeyschamber.com).
Greater Key West Chamber of Commerce, 510 Greene St., First Floor, Key West, FL 33040 (open daily; ℘305-294-2587 or 800-527-8539; www.keywestchamber.org).

ISLAMORADA TO MARATHON

Sportfishing enthusiasts favor these islands—especially Islamorada—for sailfish, tarpon, marlin and shark. Below MM 80, US-1 crosses a series of viaducts, causeways and bridges connecting islands. Sweeping views★★★ of the Atlantic Ocean and Florida Bay fan out to either side with the new Seven Mile Bridge affording expansive views ★★.

Sights

Theater of the Sea★

Windley Key, MM 84.5. Open year-round daily 9:30am–4pm (open 10:30am Dec 25). $26.95. 🚹🅿️ ☎305-664-2431. *www.theaterofthesea.com.*

Open-air pools at this long-established marine park house sharks, rays, sea turtles and fish. Shows feature dolphins (you can swim with them, at extra cost), parrots and sea lions.

Long Key State Park

Long Key, MM 67.5. ⛺🅿️☎305-664-4815. *www.floridastateparks.org.*

This 965-acre park offers paddling (rental kayaks), snorkeling, fishing and camping. Its **Golden Orb Trail** *(1mi)* offers views of a mangrove creek and lagoon popular with waterbirds.

Dolphin Research Center★

Grassy Key, MM 59. Open year-round daily 9am–4:30pm. Closed major holidays. $20. 🚹🅿️☎305-289-1121. *www.dolphins.org.*

This not-for-profit research facility is the brainchild of Milton Santini, creator of *Flipper.* Guides explain dolphin behavior and abilities and guests have the chance to swim alongside.

Crane Point Museums and Nature Center★

Marathon, MM 50. Open year-round Mon–Sat 9am–5pm, Sun noon–5pm. Closed major holidays. $12. 🅿️☎305-743-9100. *www.cranepoint.net.*

Trails wind through 63 acres of tropical forest connecting a **Museum**, **Children's Activities Center**, **Adderly House** (a Bahamian Conch house built 1903), and **Marathon Wild Bird Center**. Museum displays highlight local flora and fauna.

Seven-Mile Bridge★★

MM 47-40, Knight Key to Little Duck Key.

This engineering marvel is the world's longest segmental bridge with 288 135ft-long sections linking Middle and Lower Keys.

Michelin Map: pp180–181.

Info: ☎305-664-4503 or 305-743-5417; www.fla-keys.com.

Location: The stretch from Windley Key to Long Key is generally considered part of the Upper Keys (along with Key Largo and Tavernier), while the Middle Keys continue from Conch Key to the end of Seven-Mile Bridge.

Parking: Parking is fairly easy to come by here.

Don't Miss: Islamorada for serious fishing. Tell them about the one that got away at the classic, weatherbeaten 7 Mile Grill at Marathon, and catch a sunset, drink and meal at Lorelei, in Islamorada.

Timing: How long you spend here probably depends on your love of fishing, or interacting with dolphins.

Kids: The animal shows at Theater of the Sea are lively, and just the right length for small fry.

ADDRESSES

For price ranges, see the Legend on the cover flap.

WHERE TO STAY

Area visitors' guides including lodging directories are available (free) from area Chambers of Commerce.

Reservation services:
Welcome Center of Florida Keys (*℘305-296-4444 or 800-284-4482*); **Apartment and condo rentals** are available through Key West Vacation Rentals (*℘800 797-8787; www.vacationrentalskeywest.com*).

Camping and **RV parks** are located throughout the Keys and offer full hookups, and in some cases beaches, freshwater pools, marinas and rental boats. There is a KOA Kampground (*www.koa.com*) at Sugarloaf Key. The three state parks in the Keys—John Pennekamp (*see above*), Long Key (*see above*) and Bahia Honda SP (*see below*)—also offer campsites. Reserve well in advance.

A different way of staying in the Keys is to rent a **houseboat** from Houseboat Vacations, Islamorada (*3 days from $1,112, 7 days from $1,950 fully equipped; ℘305-664-4009; www.florida keys.com/houseboats*).

$$$$ Cheeca Lodge & Spa – *MM 82,Overseas Hwy., Islamorada.* ✕🚼🅿🛏℘*305-664-4651 or 800-327-2888. www.cheeca.com. 203 rooms.* Colonial Bahamian elegance permeates the grounds of this deluxe resort. Broad lawns and a 9-hole golf course surround the stucco-and-tile buildings, creating the ambience of an estate. Tennis courts, two pools and a saltwater lagoon entice adult guests, as do sailboarding and other water

activities; extensive children's programs keep young ones occupied.

$$$$ Hawk's Cay Resort – *61 Hawk's Cay Blvd., Duck Key.* ✕🚼🅿🛏℘*305-743-7000 or 800-432-2242. www.hawkscay. com. 193 rooms, 295 villas.* This 60-acre family resort offers every imaginable tropical activity, including swimming with dolphins. The complex includes a spa and five pools. Two and three-story buildings house the guest units, decorated in cool blue and white to echo Atlantic Ocean views from their balconies. Dining options range from a lobby coffee bar to The Terrace open-air dining room and classic American Indies Grill.

$$$$ Jules' Undersea Lodge – *51 Shoreland Dr., Key Largo.* 🅿℘*305-451-2353. www.jul.com. 1 unit (maximum 6 people).* You have to don scuba gear (but you don't have to be an expert diver) to reach your room at this property near John Pennekamp Coral Reef State Park. Situated 21ft below the surface of a lagoon, 100ft from shore, its the world's first undersea lodge. Tiny but well equipped guest rooms.

$$$$ Kona Kai Resort – *MM 97.8, 97802 Overseas Hwy., Key Largo.* 🚼🅿🛏℘*305-852-7200 or 800-365-7829. www.konakairesort. com. 13 rooms and suites.* Set in a small, lushly landscaped compound, this resort, gallery and botanic gardens includes single-story stucco cottages, well off the highway and overlooking Florida Bay and its spectacular sunsets. All suites feature ceiling fans, DVDs and compact kitchens. Relax in the secluded pool or hot tub.

$$$ Casa Morada – 136 Madeira Rd., Islamorada. ✕🗇 🗐🗙 ℘305-664-0044 or 888-881-3030. www.casamorada.com. 16 suites. A spa-like serenity pervades this all-suites boutique hotel. Blooming orchids, bright artwork and terrazzo floors give the property a Mediterranean-Caribbean vibe. The hoteliers who run the property get all the small details right, down to the hidden bench by the waterfall (a perfect spot for reading).

$$ Largo Lodge – MM 101.7, 101740 Overseas Hwy., Key Largo. 🗇🗐 ℘305-451-0424. www.largolodge.com. 7 cottages. Equipped with kitchens, screened porches and living rooms, Largo Lodge's rustic cottages are spacious, comfortable and economical. A private beach and boat dock offer access to the Gulf of Mexico; the under-14s policy enhances the serenity. Reserve in advance for winter weekends.

Sports and Recreation

Visitors can enjoy many activities including sailing, snorkeling, fishing, scuba diving and boating. **Diving** and snorkeling are first-rate on the Keys, thanks to good visibility, a great variety of sea life and corals, shipwrecks to explore, and amazing dive sites such as Looe Key Reef. Dive shops rent equipment and offer day trips and package deals as well as instruction. Diving in the Keys is best March–July.

Ocean Divers, MM 100, Key Largo (www.oceandivers.com).

SeaDwellersDiveShop, MM100, KeyLargo (www.seadwellers.com).

Halls Diving Center, MM 48, Marathon (www.hallsdiving.com).

Strike Zone Charters, MM 29.5, Big Pine Key (www.strikezone-charter.com).

Looe Key Reef Resort, MM 275, Ramrod Key (www.diveflakeys.com).

Snorkel Cruise: Theater of the Sea, MM 84.5; Islamorada offers an "Adventure and Snorkel Cruise" (year-round daily 8:30am and 1pm; round-trip 4hrs; purchase tickets in advance; $69 including gear rental; ℘305-664-2431; www.theaterofthesea.com).

Kayaking – Paddlers can explore pristine mangroves and remote islands that the casual traveler will never see. If you'd like to explore the **backcountry**—Key West National Wildlife Refuge and the Great White Heron National Wildlife Refuge—use a reputable guide, like Captain Bill Keogh of Big Pine Kayak Adventures. MM 30, (www.keyskayaktours.com).

Area **golf** courses: **Key West Golf Club**, MM 5 (www.keywestgolf.com); **Key Colony Beach**, MM 53.5, Marathon (www.keycolony-beach.net).

Dolphin Encounter Sites – Visitors participate in a short marine orientation seminar, followed by a swim (20–30min) with Atlantic bottlenose dolphins. Participants must generally be proficient swimmers in deep water and be experienced in the use of mask and fins. Reserve well in advance. **Dolphin Research Center** (see p179). **Theater of the Sea** (see p183).

FISHING ...LIKE A LOCAL

Throughout the year, sport fishermen flock to the Florida Keys, where nearly every species of salt water gamefish can be found. There's everything from sailfish to marlin, tuna, wahoo and king mackerel. The Keys are known as a destination for anglers. In fact, according to the International Game Fish Association, more salt-water fishing records have been set here than anywhere else on earth.

What's in the Deep?

The main draw of the Keys is that it accommodates all three distinct types of sports fishing: flats or backcountry fishing, reef or bottom fishing and deep sea fishing. The shallow fishermen go after the bonefish, tarpon, remit, snook and redfish. Reef fisherman seek snappers, grouper and mackerel. Deep sea fishermen aim for the big game, which means sailfish, marlin, dolphin (fish), tuna and wahoo, a sometimes aggressive beast with razor-sharp teeth. Not only do the waters in the Keys have an abundance of all varieties of these fish, but you'll also find potential world-record size catches.

Sport Fishing Capital

Any sport fishing trip beings in Islamorada, which has a reputation as the sport-fishing capital of the world. And it's no surprise that the leading town has the top fishing store: Bass Pro Shop's

Worldwide Sportsman (81576 Overseas Hwy., 33036; ☎305-664-4615; www.basspro.com). At the center of the store, you'll see Hemingway's 1933 boat which was the inspiration for his famous 1934 vessel, the Pilar. Customers can board the boat and use one of Hemingway's original typewriters.

Grey's Tales

Hemingway isn't the only famous writer and fisherman to call the Florida Key's home. Writer Zane Grey can be credited with popularizing flat fishing. Grey's Tales of Fishes was first published in 1919 as an ode to the sport. Grey also founded the Long Key fishing club which was active until a 1935 hurricane.

Bonefishing

In addition to the four main sport fishing styles, the Keys are also considered one of the world's best destinations for bonefishing, a form of flat fishing undertaken in the shallow waters of the backcountry. The

bonefishing season last from March through to October, but fishermen will find the biggest bonefish in September and October. Make sure you employ the services of a guide who is a specialist in bonefishing, because it requires special boats and casting techniques.

Get a Guide

For a successful introduction to sport fishing, a guide or tour is essential. To find a good guide you can consult with local hotel concierges, marinas or sport fishing stores such as the Bass Pro Shop. Having a guide or pro with you guarantees you'll know the what's, where's, when's and how's.

Stay Dry

If you're set on going solo, it's best not to head for open water. Instead, bring your rod and tackle box to the bridges between Islamorada and Marathon where you're sure to find some locals to fish alongside you.

LOWER KEYS★

Scrub and pine characterize this handful of wooded islands. The low, wet land and surrounding waters provide refuge for a variety of wildlife, including the great white heron and the diminutive Key deer. Bahia Honda boasts one of the few sand beaches in the Keys while the unusually clear waters of the reef at Looe Key are a diver's paradise.

Sights

Bahia Honda State Park★★

Bahia Honda Key, MM 36.8. ⚠ P *$8 per vehicle, plus 50c per person. www.floridastateparks.org/bahiahonda.*

This 524-acre park encompasses one of the largest stretches of sand and **beach★★** in the Keys and includes a lagoon, mangrove forest and a tropical hardwood hammock. Stroll through the **Silver Palm Trail** *(.25mi)*, where you'll glimpse specimens, such as yellow satinwood and Jamaica morning glory.

At the southern tip you can walk out on a segment of the original **Bahia Honda Bridge**, erected for Flagler's railroad and later remodeled for the Overseas Highway. From its vantage point, high over the ocean, stretch **views★** of stately palms swaying above tranquil turquoise water. Campsites on the beach (and cabins on the bay side) offer great views; reserve well in advance.

National Key Deer Refuge★

MM 30.5, on Big Pine Key. ♿ P. *www.fws.gov/nationalkeydeer.*

This National Wildlife Refuge was established to protect Key deer *(see below)*. Two trails within the refuge provide good deer sighting opportunities, particularly at dawn and dusk (feeding time). At **Blue Hole** *(west side of Key Deer Blvd., 1.25mi north of intersection with Watson Blvd.)*, look for deer drinking in this old rock quarry pond, also home to alligators, turtles and sunfish.

CONSERVATION IN THE KEYS

Voluntourism and animal conservation is alive and well in the Florida Keys, which have a rich eco system all of their own. One unique native species is the white-tailed Key Deer, the smallest of all North American deer. In 1957, the Key Deer National Wildlife Refuge was established in Big Pine Key, a 16-mi wide island. Today, the population of Key Deer has grown from 50 to close to 1,000. If you want to help the Key Deer, look into FAVOR—Friends and Volunteers of Refuges—which supports local wildlife refuges through education, preservation and advocacy for endangered Keys animals.

Michelin Map: p180-181.

Info: ☎305-872-2411; www.fla-keys.com/ lower keys.

Location: The Lower Keys run from MM 37 to MM 9.

Parking: Bahia Honda Park fills up quickly on weekends, and they close the gate when the lots are filled.

Timing: Relax here for a day or two before (or after) experiencing the comparitively crazy scene on Key West. Arrive early in the day to make sure you gain entry to the park *(see PARKING above).*

Travel Tip:

At times, the Overseas Highway is a beautiful strip of road, with views of the ocean and the bay, such as at Seven-Mile Bridge. Watch out though; the ride can go from scenic to hellish if you're stuck in traffic. To avoid weekday traffic coming into the Keys, another option is Card Sound Road in Homestead Florida; there's a $1 toll at Card Sound Bridge.

Population: 25,031.

Michelin Map: p189.

Info: ℘305-294-2587 or 800-527-8539; www.fla-keys.com/keywest.

Location: The Mile Markers in the Keys end at 0, in Key West.

Parking: Parking is hard to find and expensive in Key West. Some lodgings provide parking or discounts at municipal lots. Best advice if you're bringing a car is to park it, leave it, and walk or take taxis everywhere you want to go.

Don't Miss: The sunset celebration at Mallory Square, a Key West tradition.

Timing: Allow at least two days and two nights here.

Kids: The touch tank at tiny Key West Aquarium is a hit with kids.

Travel Tip: Key West is full of amazing sunrises and sunsets. One of the best places to catch them is the White Street Pier, a wooden pier that stretches out almost a quarter of a mile over the ocean.

KEY WEST★★★

Closer to Havana than Miami, Key West cultivates a laid-back atmosphere that welcomes an eclectic mix of residents from old-time "conch" families (descended from the island's original settlers) to a more recently arrived gay community. Well established in a lush landscape of banyan trees and palms and scented by tropical flowers, modern Key West is undeniably commercial, yet it retains its quirky charm and independent spirit that still appeals to bohemian types as well as to the droves of tourists who come here each year.

A Bit of History

When **Ponce de León** arrived in 1513, he claimed Key West for Spain and named it *Cayo Hueso* ("Island of Bones"), after the abundance of human bones he found there. In 1822 a custom house was established and soon the island became a head-quarters for **"wrecking"**—salvaging goods from ships that ran aground on the Florida reef. By the mid-19C a new industry, **cigar making**, was thriving and by 1889, the combined revenues from fishing, sponging, wrecking and cigar-making made Key West the wealthiest town per capita in the US.

Following the Civil War, which largely passed Key West by, Cuban cigar barons moved here and opened factories, attracting both Cuban workers and revolutionaries. By 1890 the largest cigar manufacturing city in the world was also a hotbed of Cuban revolutionary activity. Cuban liberator **José Martí** (1853–1895) soon headquartered himself here. In 1898 the *USS Maine* departed Key West for Havana and exploded there, precipitating the short-lived **Spanish-American War**.

In 1912 Henry Flagler's Overseas Railroad reached its terminus in Key West, connecting the island with the rest of the continent. Poor and rundown during the Depression, it still attracted the author **Ernest Hemingway** in 1931. Key West's most celebrated son bought a house here, beginning a literary tradition that includes Tennessee Williams, Robert Frost, Philip Caputo, James Merrill, Ralph Ellison and John Hersey.

Using federal funds, local volunteers transformed the shabby town into a viable tourist destination. However, a violent hurricane in 1935 destroyed the railroad to Key West and the town languished for three years before the **Overseas Highway** was completed on the old rail bed. In the 1950s President **Harry Truman** fell under the charm of Key West, escaping to his Little White House on the Navy base there. In the past several decades, the island has undergone a slow transformation from renegade outpost to fashionable resort. The town's overtly

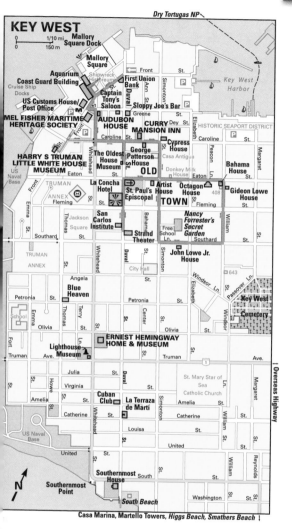

KEY WEST

Dry Tortugas NP

1/10 mi
150 m

Mallory Square Dock

Mallory Square

Aquarium

Coast Guard Building

Cruise Ship Docks

US Customs House/ Post Office

MEL FISHER MARITIME HERITAGE SOCIETY

Front St.

Shipwreck Historeum

First Union Bank

Captain Tony's Saloon

Sloppy Joe's Bar

Key West Harbor

AUDUBON HOUSE

CURRY MANSION INN

HISTORIC SEAPORT DISTRICT

Caroline St.

Caroline St.

HARRY S TRUMAN LITTLE WHITE HOUSE MUSEUM

US Naval Base

The Oldest House Museum

George Patterson House

Cypress House

Casa Antigua

Bahama House

TRUMAN ANNEX

Eaton St.

La Concha Hotel

St. Paul's Episcopal

Donkey Milk House

Eaton St.

Artist House

Octagon House

OLD

Gideon Lowe House

San Carlos Institute

TOWN

408

Fleming St.

Jackson Square

Strand Theater

Free School Ln.

Nancy Forrester's Secret Garden

Southard St.

Southard St.

TRUMAN ANNEX

John Lowe Jr. House

City Hall

Angela St.

Windsor Ln.

643

Key West Cemetery

Blue Heaven

Petronia St.

Petronia St.

Windsor

School

Olivia St.

Olivia St.

Lighthouse Museum

ERNEST HEMINGWAY HOME & MUSEUM

Truman Ave.

Truman Ave.

Overseas Highway

Julia St.

Virginia St.

St. Mary Star of the Sea Catholic Church

Amelia St.

Cuban Club

La Terraza de Martí

Amelia St.

Catherine St.

Catherine St.

Louisa St.

United St.

United St.

US Naval Base

United St.

N

Southernmost House

Southernmost Point

Southernmost South St.

South Beach

Reynolds St.

Washington St.

Casa Marina, Martello Towers, Higgs Beach, Smathers Beach

ommercial main stem, 14-block-long **Duval Street**, is named
or William Pope DuVal, the first governor of the Florida Territory.
mid the eateries, bars and boutiques that line the north end of
uval, Key West still cultivates its eccentricity. By night, live mu-
c fills the streets, spilling out of bars once known to notable
uthors, and songwriter Jimmy Buffett, among many others.

WALKING TOUR
KEY WEST

Old Town

» Begin at the intersection of Duval and Front Sts. (northwest end of Duval St.).

1.5mi. See map p189.

The 200-square-block area of the **Old Town**★★ is designated National Historic District and ranks as one of the largest in the U boasting more than 3,000 significant historic structures. In add tion there are a number of museums and attractions—some which are housed in historic buildings.

The ornate brickwork and balcony of the striking **First Uni Bank** building on the far corner (422 Front St.) reflects the o gins of the Cuban cigar manufacturers who financed its co struction in 1891.

Mallory Square

» Continue west 2 blocks on Front St., turn right on David Wolkowsky St.

Behind Mallory Market on Front St. www.mallorysquare.com.

Overlooking Key West Harbor, this former warehouse area named for Stephen Mallory, Florida's fourth US senator ar son of one of the island's oldest families. It now harbors so venir vendors, craft shops and eateries, and its adjacent do provides a berth for the large cruise ships that call at Key We Don't miss the **Sunset Celebration** *(www.sunsetcelebratio org)* ritual held every evening (weather permitting) on **Ma lory Square Dock** *(behind Mallory Square; follow Fitzpatrick . through parking lot to dock).* Here, locals and visitors gather view the spectacular Key West **sunset**★★. John James Aud bon called it "a blaze of refulgent glory (that) streams throug the portals of the west" bringing together street performe jugglers, clowns, psychics, island musicians, artists and foo vendors in a party atmosphere.

Key West Aquarium

» Return to Front St. Continue west past the intersection with Whitehead St.

Wall St. &Open year-round daily 10am–6pm. Online prices: $13.9 child $4.95. &888-544-5927. www.keywestaquarium.com.

Founded in 1934, this was the Keys' first tourist attraction. W tanks here display a variety of denizens from local waters, suc as pufferfish, grouper, angelfish and spiny lobsters. A touch tan allows tactile encounters with starfish, conchs, anemones ar other sea creatures. A highlight is the large **shark tank** whicl harbors a variety of these much-misunderstood creatures.

cognizable by its distinctive arched bays, the old Coast Guard
ilding (219 Front St.) served as the first naval storehouse in
56. The town's oldest government edifice, and the oldest
asonry building in the Keys, now holds the shops of **Clinton
quare Market**. Adjacent to the building is the Key West Mu-
um of Art and History.

ey West Museum of Art and History

1 Front St. Open year-round daily 9:30am–4:30pm. $7.
305-295-6616. www.kwahs.com.

e Custom House, built in 1891, served as a post office, court-
use and government center when wrecking helped make
y West the richest city, per capita, in the US. When Key West
·clined the building was boarded up, then abandoned. Re-
ntly renovated, it now showcases the colorful history of the
ys while gallery space features the work of local artists.

el Fisher Maritime Heritage Society★

0 Greene St., opposite Custom House. Open year-round 8:30am
ıt–Sun 9:30am)–5pm. $12.50. & ☎305-294-2633.
vw.melfisher.org.

·used in a former Navy building, the museum recounts the
ory of the discovery of the Nuestra Señora de Atocha and the
ınta Margarita, two Spanish galleons that sank in the Florida
raits in 1622. The man behind the salvage and the museum,
el Fisher, is the don of modern treasure hunters. Fisher, who
ed in 1998, spent 16 years and lost a son in his unswerving
ırsuit of the wreck. In 1985 his crew found their prize on the
·ean floor; spoils included a 77.76-carat natural emerald crys-
and a gold bar weighing over 6 troy pounds. Displays on the
st floor feature some of the fabulous gold, silver, gems and
her artifacts recovered from the dive site. The second floor is
·voted to special exhibits and traveling shows.

udubon House & Tropical Gardens★

« Cross Whitehead St.

·5 Whitehead St., across from Mel Fisher's museum. Open year-
ınd daily 9:30am–5pm. $12. & ☎305-294-2116 or 877-294-
70. www.audubonhouse.com.

ıpt. John Huling Geiger built this gracious Neoclassical house
the 1840s. Its restoration by Key West native Mitchell Wolfson
1960 sparked the island's preservation movement. Wolfson
·dicated the house to America's premiere ornithologist, **John
ımes Audubon**, who visited Key West in 1832 while working
ı his authoritative volume Birds of America. Decorated in 19C
·riod furnishings, the house is notable for its fine collection of

28 original **Audubon engravings** and for its lovely **tropic garden**. Noteworthy also is a rare collection of porcelain bir by British artist Dorothy Doughty.

Harry S Truman Little White House Museum★

111 Front St. in Truman Annex. Entrance near Hilton Hotel at the presidential gates on Whitehead St. Open year-round daily by guided tour 9am–4.30pm (last tour). Online $15. ♿ ☎305-294-9911. www.trumanlittlewhitehouse.com.

» *Continue one block south on Whitehead St. Cross Whitehead St. and enter the gates to the Truman Annex, a 44-acre private condominium development on the grounds of the former naval station. Continue for one block and turn left on Front St.*

This large, unpretentious white clapboard house, the favor retreat of America's 33rd president, **Harry S. Truman** (188- 1972), gives a rare glimpse of the personality and private life the man the press called "an uncommon common man."

Built in 1890 as a duplex for the paymaster of Key West's nav station, the unadorned dwelling, with wooden jalousies, w first visited by Truman in 1946 (his physician had persuaded hi to take a respite from official duties). Prior to Truman, Thom Edison had lived here while working on his depth charge f the Navy during World War I.

Truman found the casual atmosphere and warm climate of K West relaxing. Over his next seven years in office, he spent 1 days of "working vacations" at his "Little White House." He r the country from the desk that still sits in a corner of the livin room. Indeed, Truman came to relish his time in Key West, d claring it his favorite place in the world after his boyhood fa home in Missouri.

Tours of the house begin with a 10min video detailing the tin Truman spent here. The house is furnished much the way was during the Truman era, with most of the pieces chosen Miami decorator Haygood Lassiter in 1948. Truman's person **desk** can be seen in his bedroom upstairs.

Curry Mansion Inn★

511 Caroline St. Open year-round daily 8:30am–5pm. $5. ♿ ☎30 294-5349 or 800-253-3466. www.currymansion.com.

» *Return to Kelly's at the corner of Whitehead and Caroline Sts., and continue east on Caroline St.*

William Curry, mayor of Key West and a self-made millionai (said to be the first in Florida), completed the rear of this ram bling, white Victorian mansion before his death in 1896. His s Milton greatly expanded the house at the turn of the centu adding elaborate reception rooms and bedrooms to the fro Now an inn, the mansion retains its belle-epoque grandeur. V itors can take a self-guided tour of the house, which offers t only publicly accessible **widow's walk** *(third floor)* in Key We After your tour, relax on the wide, shady veranda.

» *Continue to the corner of Caroline and Simonton Sts.*

Built around 1889, the elegant white frame **George Patterso House** *(across from Curry Mansion at 522 Caroline St.; not op* to the public) features gables, porches and galleries adorned by delicate spindlework—all characteristic elements of the Queen Anne style.

Distinctive for its unpainted, weathered cypress exterior, the 1887 **Cypress House** (601 Caroline St.) was originally owned by the Kemp family, Bahamians who are credited with introducing the sponge industry to Key West. The low facade and simple lines of this private inn typify Bahamian architecture.

One of Old Town's best-known homes, the unique **Octagon House** (712 Eaton St.), was built in 1885 by Richard Peacon, who opened Key West's first supermarket. Renovated by acclaimed interior designer Angelo Donghia in the 1970s, the house was also briefly owned by clothing designer Calvin Klein.

Bahama House

730 Eaton St. Not open to the public.

Originally constructed on the island of Abaco, this symmetrical white pine structure was disassembled and brought to Key West by schooner in 1847 as the home of Bahamian shipbuilder John Bartlum. Its wide airy verandas on both stories, louvered windows and doors, and low-ceilinged interior rooms typify Bahamian architecture. Exterior siding incorporates boards of different widths. Note these same features on the house next door (408 William St.), which was transported from Green Turtle Cay. Note the temple form of the **Gideon Lowe House** (409 William St.), a fine mid-19C example of the Classical Revival style.

Nancy Forrester's Secret Garden

Free School Ln. Open year-round daily 10am–5pm. $10.
305-294-0015. www.nfsgarden.com.

Owner-artist Nancy Forrester has devoted more than 35 years to creating her personal one-acre tropical oasis amid the hub-bub of downtown Key West, opening it to the public in 1994. Today the lush botanical garden enamors nature lovers who wander its winding paths among ferns, heliconias and orchids, beneath a canopy of century-old hardwood trees—Spanish limes, sapodillas, gumbo-limbos—and a collection of rare palms. Adding to the ambience is a menagerie of tropical birds, cats and reptiles.

The eminent Key West surgeon, Thomas Osgood Otto built the lavender Queen Anne **Artist House** (534 Eaton St.), which is distinguished by its octagonal turret. Now a guest house, the two-story 1887 structure features wraparound verandas.

« Turn right on Simonton St. and continue one block to Eaton St. Turn left on Eaton St., then continue east on Eaton St. and cross Elizabeth St.

« Continue on Eaton St. to the corner of William St.

« Turn right on William St.

« Walk two blocks south on William to Southard St. and turn right. Continue to intersection of Simonton St.; turn right. Walk half a block north; turn right on Free School Ln. to a small gate at its end.

« Return to Simonton St. and turn right. Continue 1.5 blocks north and turn left on Eaton St.

« *Continue west to corner of Eaton and Duval St.*

St. Paul's Episcopal Church

401 Duval St. Open year-round, call or see website for services ar times. ♿ 🅿 ☎ *305-296-5142. http://stpaulskeywest.org.*

The oldest church in the Florida diocese, St. Paul's was estal lished in 1832. The current white Spanish Colonial buildir dates from 1919. The vaulted wooden ceilings inside are d signed to resemble inverted ships' hulls.

» *Turn left and walk south on Duval St.*

Opened in 1926, **La Concha Hotel** *(430 Duval; www.laconch keywest.com)* has housed such luminaries as Tennessee Williarr who wrote *Summer and Smoke* here in the mid-1940s. Stop t the hotel's rooftop bar, **The Top**, for a sunset drink and a pa oramic **view★** of the island and its surrounding waters.

» *Cross Fleming St. to the 500 block of Duval St.*

San Carlos Institute

516 Duval St. Open year-round Fri-Sun noon-6pm. Closed Jan 1, Easter Sunday, Dec 25. $3 contribution requested. ♿ ☎ *305-294-3887. www.institutosancarlos.org.*

This imposing Spanish-Colonial structure was built in 1924, b its roots date back to 1871 when it was founded as a social clu and school by Cuban exiles during the Ten Years' War.

The present building serves as school, museum, library, art ga lery and theater. Two floors of exhibits relate to Cuba's fight f independence from Spain.

Displays on the ground floor focus on **José Martí**, the Cuba independence organizer, who often spoke here. Its walls a lined with blue majolica tiles from Spain; floors incorpora checkered Cuban mosaics.

» *Continue up Duval St.*

Ripley's Believe It or Not! Key West

108 Duval St. Open daily 10am–late. $15.85, child (5–12 yrs) $12.67. ♿ ☎ *305-293-9939. www.ripleyskeywest.com.*

Occupying the former **Strand Theater** 1930 movie palac this curiously compelling collection, including a fabled whi buffalo (1 in 10 milion so it is said) and a car covered in 10,0C dimes, is a celebration of the odder things in life.

The **Cuban Club** *(1108 Duval St.)* is a two-story, white fran replica (1989) of the Key West headquarters of Sociedad Cub established in 1900 to offer education, medical care and soci activities to the Cuban émigré community. Fire destroyed th original building; the present incarnation, which incorporate the original columns, turrets and facade pediment, house shops and condominium units.

Nearby, at 1125 Duval St., the **La Te Da** (La Terraza de Mart hotel, restaurant and bar complex occupies the former hom (1892) of cigar manufacturer Teodoro Pérez. José Martí fre quently exhorted his countrymen to action from the balcony.

ETTING TO KEY WEST

Y AIR – Key West Airport (EYW):
rviced by most domestic airlines
well as charters (*305-296-5439;
ww.keywestinternationalairport.com*).
ansportation to Old Town by **taxi**
10–$20) and hotel courtesy shuttles.
ajor **rental car** agencies located here.

ETTING AROUND

cal **bus service** travels two routes
1on–Fri 6:30am–11:30pm, weekends
30am–5:30pm; $2; schedule and route
formation: *305-292-8160*). The best way
get around the Old Town is on foot,
most attractions are within walking
stance of each other. Beach cruiser or
ooter rental are available from **Keys
oped & Scooter** (*305-294-0399*).
de carefully along the narrow (often
ne-way) streets. The **Bicycle Center**
305-294-4556) rents bikes for $15 a day
nd single-seater scooters for $40 a day.
aradise Scooter Rentals (*305-293-
063; www.paradisescooterrentals.com*)
nts bikes for $13 a day and scooters
om $54 a day/single, $65/double. Small
ectric cars are another option (*http://
ratescooterrentals.com*).
axi service: Friendly Cab (*305-292-
000*); Maxi Taxi (*305-296-2222*).
arking is limited in Old Town area;
ublic parking lots average $1/hr.

VISITOR INFORMATION

Key West Chamber of Commerce
provides information on lodging,
shopping, entertainment, festivals and
recreation (510 Greene St., First Floor,
FL 33040; open year-round Mon–Fri
8:30am–6pm, weekends 8:30am–5pm;
*305-294-2587 or 800-527-8539;
www.keywestchamber.org*).

SIGHTSEEING

Conch Train Tour (*departs Mallory Square
or Roosevelt Blvd. year-round daily 9am–
4:30pm; round-trip 1hr 30min; commentary;
three stops, free re-boarding from Truval
Village only; $29; &*888-916-8687;
www.conchtourtrain.com*).
Old Town Trolley Tour (*departs from
various locations year-round daily 9am–
4:30pm; round-trip 1hr 30min; commentary;
$29 inc second day free; free re-boarding all
12 stops; *305-296-6688, www.trolleytours.
com/Key-West*). Sharon Wells of **Island City
Strolls**; (*305-294-8380; www.seekeywest.
com*) offers walking and biking tours

USEFUL NUMBERS

Police (non-emergency) Key West
(*305-294-2511*)
Florida Highway Patrol (*305-289-2300*)
**US Coast Guard Boating and Safety
Hotline** (*305-92-8700*)
Visitor Assistance Program
(*800-771-KEYS*)

ights

co-Discovery Center★

5 East Quay Rd. at end of Southard St., Truman Annex. Open Tue–
at 9am–4pm. &*305-809-4750. http://eco-discovery.com*.
his state-of-the-art, 6,400sq ft underwater ocean laboratory
lows visitors to view the Florida Reef without getting wet,
hanks to underwater cameras and touch-screen computer
isplays. Journey through other Florida Keys habitats, includ-
g mangroves and pinelands. It is modeled after Key Largo's
quarius, the only underwater ocean lab in the world.

ASK PETER...

Q: I've already been to Ernest Hemingway's home and museum, are there other landmarks?

A: Instead of seeing where Hemingway slept and wrote, check out where Hemingway drank and boxed. Try to grab a bite at the quirky Blue Heaven. The restaurant's century-old building has a history of cock fighting, gambling and boxing matches refereed by Ernest Hemingway himself. There are even roaming roosters walking around the property.

KEY LIME PIE

Don't leave the Keys without trying a slice of Key Lime Pie. With a graham-cracker crust, tart Key lime filling and a sweet whip cream top, this local classic is now a world favorite. The signature dessert of the Florida Keys was reputedly made for the first time at Curry Mansion in Key West. Since then, Key Lime Pie has been the subject of much legend, amendment and competition. Most restaurants in Key West (and far beyond) offer it for dessert; numerous delis and small grocery stores package their own versions; and an annual competition sponsored by a local radio station declares the city's best. One popular option is Pepe's Café and Steakhouse, one of the oldest restaurants in the Keys. Blue Heaven, also in Key West, boasts a meringue-style topping. They even serve it fried at Porky's barbecue in Marathon.

Fort Zachary Taylor State Park

Enter through gatehouse to Truman Annex at the west end of Southard St. Open year-round daily 8am–dusk. $6 per vehicle for 2 people plus 50¢ per additional person. 🅿 ℘*305-292-6713. www.floridastateparks.org/forttaylor.*

Remains of the three-story trapezoidal 19C brick fort started in 1845 (but never completed) form the centerpiece of this 87 acre park overlooking the Atlantic Ocean.

During the Civil War, some 800 Union soldiers were quartered here, although they saw no significant action. Today you can walk along vestiges of the fort's 5ft-thick battlements. Guided tours of the fort are available daily. Nearby, a pleasant wooded grove edges a narrow, somewhat rocky Atlantic **beach**, suitable for swimming, fishing and snorkeling.

Ernest Hemingway Home and Museum★★

907 Whitehead St. Open year-round daily 9am–5pm. $12.50. ℘305-294-1136. www.hemingwayhome.com.

Half-hidden amid lush vegetation, this gracious stucco house is where Key West's legendary resident novelist spent his most productive years.

Built by wealthy merchant Asa Tift in 1851, this one-of-a-kind house is made of coral rock mined on the property and covered with stucco. Tift brought the French Colonial-style cast-iron pillars, verandas and balusters from New Orleans. Full-length double-paned arched windows open like doors to catch island breezes. Sparsely decorated rooms contain period pieces, some of which belonged to the family. In Hemingway's bedroom, notice the **ceramic cat** made for "Papa" by Pablo Picasso. In fact

round the house there are more than 60 six- and seven-toed
(real) cats, that are, dubiously, claimed to be descendants of
Hemingway's own pets.

A wooden catwalk once connected the master bedroom to
Hemingway's **studio**, a pleasant room above the carriage house
where he wrote such classics as *Death in the Afternoon*, *For Whom
the Bell Tolls* and *To Have and Have Not*. (The character of Freddy
in the latter novel is modeled after Joe Russell, the late owner of
Sloppy Joe's Bar.) The attractive grounds contain a large **swimming pool**—the first one built on the island. Commissioned by
his second wife, Pauline, in the 1930s while Hemingway was off
covering the Spanish Civil War, the $20,000 pool infuriated "Papa"
when he returned. He reportedly railed at Pauline, declaring that
he had spent his last cent, and threw a penny on the ground to
emphasize his point. His wife had the coin embedded in the cement by the pool where it remains to this day.

Lighthouse & Keeper's Quarters Museum

*938 Whitehead St., across from Hemingway House. Open year-
round daily 9:30am–4:30pm. Closed Dec 25. $10.* 🅿 📞*305-295-
6616. www.kwahs.com.*

Built in 1846 and decommissioned in 1969, this white-brick
lighthouse now offers a sweeping **view** of the island from atop
its 92ft tower. A **lightkeeper's quarters** on the grounds, pan-
eled in gleaming Dade County pine, displays lighthouse lenses,
military artifacts and period rooms, re-creating the lifestyle of
early 20C lighthouse keepers.

City Cemetery

Margaret St. and Passover Ln. ♿*Open daily 7am-7pm (winter
6pm). Guided tours, Tue and Thu 9am, reservation required. $10 .*
📞*305-292-6718. www.keywestcity.com.*

Monuments to Key West's past can be found among the
85,000-plus headstones, which date to 1847 when the earlier
cemetery near the south coast was washed out by a hurricane.
A bronze sailor surveys marble markers commemorating seamen lost in the 1898 sinking of the USS *Maine*. Wander on your
own (a free comprehensive self-guided tour map is available
inside the cemetery's front entrance) and read headstones with
epitaphs that include "I told you I was sick" or take a guided tour.

Fort East Martello Museum & Gardens

*3501 S. Roosevelt Blvd. Open year-round daily 9:30am–4:30pm.
Closed Dec 25. $6.* 🅿 📞*305-296-3913. www.kwahs.com.*

The names of this brick tower and its counterpart, the West Martello Tower, derive from a type of fortified cylindrical tower first

built in Corsica in the Middle Ages. Begun in 1862 as back-up fortifications to nearby Union stronghold, Fort Zachary Taylor, the East Martello Tower was never completed. Yellow fever, labor strikes and wartime exigencies delayed the work, and in 1873 building ceased on the unfinished battlements.

Today, the remains of the tower house historical exhibits which range from ancient Indians to Ernest Hemingway and an exhibition entitled the **Ghosts of East Martello**. Note Robert the haunted doll, whose story is particularly creepy.

The art gallery is famous for two fine collections by reowned local folk artists:Florida's largest collections of painted wood carvings and drawings by Mario Sanchez (1908–2005); the "junkyard sculpture" of **Stanley Papio** (1941–82). Also on display is a famous **portrait of Hemingway** by Erik Smith. In the garden an 80-year-old playhouse shows how kids lived and played in old Key West

Broad, man-made **Smathers Beach**—the largest on the island—stretches for 2mi along South Roosevelt Boulevard.

West Martello Tower

White St. and Atlantic Blvd., on Higgs Memorial Beach. Gardens open year-round daily 9:30am–5pm. Closed major holidays. Free but donations very welcome. &♿❓❓*305-294-3210. www.keywestgardenclub.com.*

Companion to the East Martello Tower, this Civil War citadel served as a lookout tower during the Spanish-American War. Its brick ruins are now edged in tropical plantings beautifully maintained by the **Key West Garden Club** who have turned this into one of the island's most tranquil spots.

Adjacent, Higgs Beach is popular with the gay community.

Southernmost House

1400 Duval St.

This rambling, cream-colored brick 1899 Queen Anne manse (with pale green trim) is the southernmost house in the continental US. Now a hotel (*www.southernmosthouse.com*), the elegant structure exemplifies the Queen Anne style in Key West, modified to suit both local tastes and climate.

Small sandy shallow **South Beach** lies across from the house. Around the corner *(west end of South St.)*, a much-photographed red-black-and-yellow buoy marks what it claims is the Southernmost Point in the lower 48 states. (In fact, the true southernmost point extends from a restricted naval base just to the west.)

Dry Tortugas National Park★

69mi southwest of Key West. Accessible only by plane or boat (see below). Open year-round dawn–dusk. $5. ⚠ ☎*305-242-7700. www.nps.gov/drto.*

Encompassing 100sq mi in the Gulf of Mexico, the park protects the small cluster of reef islands called the Dry Tortugas. Spanish explorer Ponce de León named these islands *Las Tortugas* ("The Turtles") when he explored them in 1513. (The anglicized addition of the word "Dry" refers to the islands' lack of fresh water.) They remained Spanish possessions until Florida came under US control in 1821. One of the islands, 10-acre Garden Key, is the site of **Fort Jefferson**, the largest coastal stronghold built by the US in the 19C. Activities include wreck-diving, snorkeling and fishing *(information available at visitor center at fort)*. A film details the fort's history inside the visitor orientation area.

Parade grounds within the walls hold remnants of a cavernous magazine, soldiers' barracks and officers' quarters. A self-guided walk leads through the arched casemates and up onto the battlement wall, where a lighthouse (no longer functioning), still stands. From this vantage point, there's a **view★★** of the fort and nearby Bush and Loggerhead keys. The top of the surrounding moat also serves as a walkway, and a palm-fringed white-sand **beach**, ideal for snorkeling, lies on the island's west side.

If you're into birding, plan your visit from March through September, when you'll see frigates, boobies and a large number of noddy and sooty terns (100,000 terns nest here).

FROM PRISON TO PARK

Sixteen million bricks were used to form the perimeter walls of **Fort Jefferson** *(www.fortjefferson.com)*, which measures 50ft high and 8ft thick. The weight of the structure eventually caused the walls of the ill-fated fort to sink into its unstable base of sand. By the time the Civil War broke out, the brick hexagon was only two-thirds completed. Though soldiers never fired a shot in anger from Fort Jefferson, it did serve as a prison for Union deserters during the Civil War. In 1865 **Dr. Samuel Mudd** was interned here as a co-conspirator in President Lincoln's assassination. (Mudd unwittingly set the broken leg of Lincoln's fleeing assassin, John Wilkes Booth, without realizing Booth's identity.) During a yellow fever epidemic in 1867, Mudd unstintingly treated the prison's victims of the disease. His efforts won him a pardon from President Andrew Johnson and he was released in early 1869. Yellow fever struck the citadel again in the early 1870s, and four years later it was finally abandoned.

ASK PETER...
Q: Is Dry Tortugas worth the trip?
A: Absolutely— the park might be a hassle to visit, but I recommend making an effort. Its seclusion leave the bird colonies and rich marine life in peace. Book yourself on the boat or seaplane for one of the best day trips out of the Florida Keys.

Getting There
By Air - Daily from Key West Intl. Airport. 40min flight; half-day excursion $249 per person. Reservations required. Key West Seaplane Adventures, ☎*305-293-9300; www.keywestsea planecharters.com.*
By Sea - Two ferry companies depart from the Historic Seaport daily at 8am (check-in 7.30am), returning by 5/5.30pm. Both include food and snorkeling. *Yankee Freedom II* takes around 2hr 15min each way *($160; ☎305-294-7009 or 800-634-0939; www. yankeefreedom.com).*

ADDRESSES

For price ranges, see the Legend on the cover flap.

WHERE TO STAY

Most accommodations in Old Town Key West are **guest houses** and **bed-and-breakfast inns** *($85–$275).* Make reservations through the Welcome Center of Florida Keys (☎*305-296-4444).* **Youth hostel** *(rooms $28–$31; ☎305-296-5719; www.keywesthostel. com).* **Camping and RV park:** Boyd's Key West Campground *(tent camping, $55–$75; RVs, $70-$120; ☎305-294-1465; www.boydscampground.com).*

$$$$ Gardens Hotel – *526 Angela St.* ♿️🅿️🛏️☎*305-294-2661 or 800-526-2664. www. gardenshotel.com. 17 units.* The luxuriant gardens that fill much of this walled Old Town compound were once a private botanical preserve. Composed of three restored historic structures and two new additions, the complex has tastefully decorated rooms featuring wood floors and marble baths. A buffet continental breakfast is served in the sunlit garden room.

$$$$ Island City House Hotel – *411 William St.* ♿️🛏️☎*305-294-5702 or 800-634-8230. www. islandcityhouse.com. 24 units.* Small hotel encompassing 3 late-19C clapboard buildings, with exterior stairs and balconies. Some of the cozy suites include kitchenettes. The family-friendly complex encloses a palm-shaded pool with a hot tub.

$$$$ Hotel Marquesa – *600 Fleming St.* ✖️♿️🅿️🛏️ ☎*305-292-1919 or 800-869-4631. www.marquesa.com. 27 rooms.*

Comprising four 1884 Conch houses, this historic district lodging is listed on the National Historic Register. Breezy guest rooms mix tropical colors with antique pieces and West Indies wicker; several of the poolside rooms have sitting areas and patios. The hotel's sleek **Cafe Marquesa** specializes in Caribbean-inspired dishes.

$$$$ Simonton Court – *320 Simonton St.* ♿️🛏️☎*305-294-6386 or 800-944-2687. www.simontoncourt.com. 29 units.* Two blocks from Duval St., lush foliage surrounds these secluded former cigar-makers' cottages. Tropical flowers shade two small pools. Individually decorated rooms have pine furnishings and marble baths.

$$$–$$$$ Casa Marina Resort – *1500 Reynolds St.* ✖️♿️🅿️🛏️☎*305-296-3535 or 888-303-5717. www.casamarinaresort. com. 311 rooms.* Hurricane-proof stucco walls, tile roofs, and Spanish Renaissance styling mark the hotel that Henry Flagler envisioned as the endpoint resort for his Overseas Railroad. On the expansive grounds you'll find two pools, a private beach, and numerous cabanas and bars. Shuttles run guests to Old Town.

$$–$$$$ Popular House/ Key West Bed & Breakfast – *415 William St.* 🛏️☎*305-296-7274 or 800-438-6155. www.keywest bandb.com. 8 rooms.* Colorful handmade textiles and big, contemporary canvases add to a lively, artsy vibe at this stylish guesthouse. Some rooms share a bath (and none have TVs) but all guests enjoy the tropical gardens, dip pool, Jacuzzi and dry sauna, lavish Continental breakfast. No kids under age 18.

$$$ Ambrosia House – *615, 618, 622 Fleming St.* ♿🅿 ⚒ *℘305-296-9838. www. ambrosiakeywest.com. 32 units.* Rooms include suites, townhouses and cottages. Each has a private entrance and a deck, porch or patio.

$$$ Pier House Resort – *One Duval St.* ✕♿🅿⚒ *℘305-296-4600 or 800-327-8340. www.pierhouse.com. 142 rooms.* One of Key West's original landmark resorts, the attractive white buildings house airy, comfortable, spacious rooms, many of which overlook the Harbor. Full-service spa, health club, pool, private beach.

$$ Key West Hostel & Seashell Motel – *718 South St.* ♿🅿 *℘305-296-5719. www.key westhostel.com. 92 beds. 10 rooms.* One of the best budget properties near Old Town, peaceful even during Spring Break. Rooms are dorm style, but private motel rooms are also available. Free Wi-Fi.

$$ Speakeasy Inn – *1117 Duval St.* ♿🅿 *℘305-296-2680 or 800-217-4884. www.speakeasyinn.com. 10 units.* Walk to the beach from your clean but no-frills room at this characterful historic speakeasy-turned-inn.

WHERE TO EAT

$$$$ Louie's Backyard – *Vernon and Waddell Sts.* ♿ *℘305-294-1061. www.louiesbackyard. com.* Exquisite Continental cuisine matched by a sensational Atlantic views. The late-19C house containing the restaurant has been crisply refurbished; the best spots are in the backyard.

$$$ A&B Lobster House – *700 Front St.* ♿ *℘305-294-5880. www.aandblobsterhouse.com.* One of Key West's longest-established seafood restaurants, the A&B specializes in Maine and Caribbean lobster, as well as in traditional Keys favorites. Cocktail and cigar bar.

$$$ Mangoes – *700 Duval St.* ♿ *℘305-294-4606. www.mangos keywest.com/restaurant.* Nibble on wonderfully light tempura-fried ahi tuna. Dishes on the Floribbean menu include mustard-rubbed rack of lamb.

$$$ Pepe's Café – *806 Caroline St.* ♿ *℘305-294-7192. www. pepescafe.net.* At midday the vine-covered patio is a cool retreat. Great burgers, fried oyster plates and Key Lime Pie.

$$$ Seven Fish – *632 Olivia St.* ♿ *℘305-296-2777. www.7fish.com. Dinner only. Closed Tue.* Crowds gather here for rich seafood. Culinary influences range from Japanese to Italian.

$$ El Siboney – *900 Catherine St.* ♿ *℘305-296-4184. www.elsiboney restaurant.com.* In a brick building on a back street, this traditional Cuban restaurant has a down-home atmosphere, efficient service, and platters of shredded beef or pork, rice and beans and *plátanos*.

$$ Mangia Mangia– *900 Southard St.* ♿ *℘305-294-2469. www.mangia-mangia.com.* Key West's best Italian serves bountiful platters of homemade pasta with tasty sauces.

$$ Blue Heaven – *305 Petronia St.* ♿ *℘305-296-8666. http://blue heavenkw.homestead.com.* The menu here is a West Indies hybrid—think jerk chicken with brown rice.

DISCOVERING
SOUTHWEST COAST

Florida's Gulf Coast is becoming one of the state's most popular regions. Today, you'll find stretches of built-up beachfront hotels, apartments and mansions as well as unspoilt beaches and barrier islands.

Naples likes to call itself the Palm Beach of the Gulf Coast, but instead of Henry Flagler, a more colorful group of local characters can be credited with the area's development. There is Captain Bill Collier, who developed nearby Marco Island with the Marco Hotel in the late 1800s. Sarasota has John Ringling of the Ringling Brothers Barnum & Bailey Circus. In the 1920s, he established the circus' winter home outside Sarasota, where he built a palatial mansion and museum. Ringling's influence helped the area rebrand as the cultural coast. During Ringlings' heyday, Florida's east cost was growing steadily due to Flagler's railway, while the southwest portion of the state remained primarily agricultural. Today, locals and the state have made efforts to curb development and suburban sprawl. Parts of Sanibel Island are now a nature reserve, while state parks and conservation societies preserve sections of unspoilt coast line.

Collier-Seminole State Park, south of Naples is a protected wilderness and hosts Native American and Pioneer heritage days, where local crafts are sold.

Tourism continues to drive business in this part of Florida, but it's not just weekend vacationers. The golf clubs, tennis clubs, many restaurants and stores draw in the snowbird population. The area's beaches also remain a major attraction. Sanibel and Captiva Islands are known for their seashells. Old Marco Island, Captain Bill Collier's former home, attracts visitors with its deserted beaches and frontier relics. Even more beachfront history can be found in Cabbage Key, which was originally home to the Calusa Indians; today you'll see the ancient shell mounds they built along the shore.

Beyond the senior and vacation set, Major League Baseball has a second home on Florida's Southwest coast. The Grapefruit League is one of the main spring training centers for baseball. It's the spring home to the Boston Red Socks, the Baltimore Orioles, the Minnesota Twins and the Pittsburgh Pirates. After spring break, you'll find the stadiums being used by a host of minor league teams during the main season.

PETER'S TOP PICKS

 GREEN SPACES

Cayo Costa State Park has inland and beachfront activities. Start with a hike or bike expedition on one of the trails and then catch your breath on the beach. **Cayo Costa State Park** (p **211**)

 HISTORY

Visit the home and workshop of the USA's foremost inventor, Thomas Alva Edison. You can stroll through the grounds of his home-turned-museum in Fort Myers at the Edison & Ford Winter Estates. **Edison & Ford Winter Estates** (p **205**)

 STAY

Cedar Cove Resorts and Cottages are my pick for a private beach experience. Most rooms have private decks and patios that allow guests their own views of Holmes Beach. **Cedar Cove Resorts and Cottages** (p **229**)

 SHOP

Check out the galleries in Old Naples at Third Street South that sell local art and glass works. **Old Naples** (p **214**)

 EAT

The Veranda is one of Fort Myers' oldest and best known hot spots, but it remains a local go-to. The menu reflects southwest culture, blending Cajun and Southern flavors. **The Veranda** (p **208**)

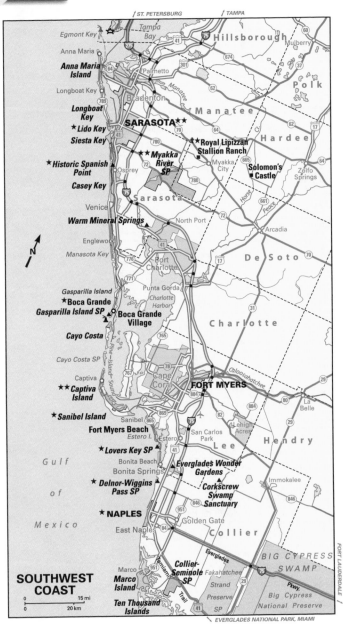

ST. PETERSBURG / TAMPA

Egmont Key
Tampa Bay
Anna Maria
Anna Maria Island
Longboat Key
Longboat Key
★ **Lido Key**
Siesta Key
★ **Historic Spanish Point**
Casey Key
Venice
Warm Mineral Springs
Englewood
Manasota Key
Gasparilla Island
★ **Boca Grande**
Gasparilla Island SP
Cayo Costa
Cayo Costa SP
Captiva
★★ **Captiva Island**
★ **Sanibel Island**
Fort Myers Beach
Estero I.
★ **Lovers Key SP**
Bonita Beach
Bonita Springs
★ **Delnor-Wiggins Pass SP**
★ **NAPLES**
East Naples
Marco
Marco Island
Ten Thousand Islands

Hillsborough
Mulberry
60
75
41
301
674
37
Palmetto
Manatee
62
Polk
64
789
Bradenton
SARASOTA ★★
70
64
★ **Royal Lipizzan Stallion Ranch**
Hardee
17
62
780
Myakka City
665
Solomon's Castle
Zolfo Springs
★★ **Myakka River SP**
72
Osprey
780
661
Horse
Peace
Sarasota
75
North Port
41
Arcadia
70
De Soto
Port Charlotte
17
31
Punta Gorda
Charlotte Harbor
Charlotte
765
Pine Island Sound
78
Caloosahatchee
767
Cape Coral
FORT MYERS
29
La Belle
884
884
80
Sanibel
865
82
San Carlos Park
29
Hendry
869
75
Lehigh Acres
Estero
Lee
Everglades Wonder Gardens
Immokalee
846
Corkscrew Swamp Sanctuary
951
846
Golden Gate
84
Collier
951
Everglades
Tamiami
Collier-Seminole SP
Fakahatchee Strand Preserve
BIG CYPRESS SWAMP
29
Pkwy.
Big Cypress National Preserve
41
Trail

Gulf
of
Mexico

N

SOUTHWEST COAST

0   15 mi
0   20 km

FORT LAUDERDALE
EVERGLADES NATIONAL PARK, MIAMI

204

FORT MYERS

A city of royal palms and tropical flowers, Fort Myers curves along the shore of the gentle Caloosahatchee River. Though recent development has sprawled the urban area out past I-75 and into the communities of North Fort Myers and Cape Coral, a renewed downtown offers historic houses and a scenic waterfront. Just south on Estero Island, Fort Myers Beach is the center of the local sun-and-fun scene.

A Bit of History

Fort Myers was established when relations between settlers and Native Americans flared up after the Second Seminole War. In 1885 Fort Myers incorporated, elected a mayor and received a very important visitor. Newly widowed and in poor health, **Thomas Alva Edison** traveled from New Jersey to Florida to look for a winter home in which to recuperate. He bought a 14-acre estate in Fort Myers and set up shop, developing some of the world's earliest lighting, phonographic, cinematic and telegraphic equipment, plus other domestic appliances. An active member of the community, Edison imported royal palms from Cuba to line his property along **McGregor Boulevard**. The city took up where he left off, and now some 14mi of the city's signature avenue are edged with palms. The publicity that followed America's most famous inventor gave a boost to Fort Myers; by the 1920s building boom, the city was off and running.

Sights

Edison & Ford Winter Estates★★

2350 McGregor Blvd. &(Edison's Home). Open year-round daily 9am–5:30pm. Closed Thanksgiving Day & Dec 25. Homes & Gardens Tour $20. Botanical Tour $24. Laboratory & Museum only, $12. ☐✗☎*239-334-7418. www.efwefla.org.*
Situated on the Caloosahatchee River, this complex holds the winter homes and tropical gardens of **Thomas Edison** (1847–1931) and **Henry Ford** (1863–1947). Edison bought his property in 1885 and designed two connecting cottages, some of the first prefabricated houses in the country. In his laboratory and botanical gardens, he perfected the light bulb, the phonograph, the movie camera and projector, and the storage battery.
In 1896 Edison met Henry Ford, then working at Edison Illuminating Co. in Detroit, and encouraged Ford to follow his dream of building cars. The men became friends, and in 1916 Ford bought an adjacent house to spend winters near his mentor.
Edison's Home – The star attraction of the estate, Edison's

Population: 50,575.
Map: p206
Info: 2310 Edwards Drive; ☎800-366-3622 or 239-332-3624; www.fortmyers.org.
Location: I-75 and Hwy. 41 provide north-south access. Hwy 867 crosses the bay to Sanibel and Captiva islands.
Don't Miss: Edison Ford Winter Estates and Edison Museum.
Kids: Look for 'gators and manatees at Lovers Key State Park.

Travel Tip: Start your day with the locals in Fort Myers at Bennett's Fresh Roast. The coffee shop serves a full menu that includes lunch and dessert but the real draw are the fresh donuts, which are hand cut and made from scratch. Run by long-time radio personality C. David Bennett, the downtown shop has become a local institution.

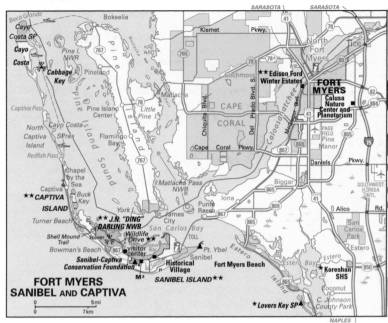

FORT MYERS
SANIBEL AND CAPTIVA

The Shell Factory

2787 US-41, north of Littleton Rd. in North Fort Myers.Open winter daily 10am-6pm, summer Wed-Sun 10am-6pm. ☎239-995-2141 or 800-282-5805. www.shell factory.com. Tired of sifting through broken shells? This huge store is your answer with shells from many countries, along with shell jewelry, shell lamps and myriad other shell souvenirs.

spacious house nestles amid tropical fauna and towering bamboo—all part of the botanical gardens the inventor used for his experiments. Tours wend along garden paths and enter the "double house," as the two connected structures are called.

Ford's Home – Ford bought "Mangoes" (1911), a relatively modest cottage, for $20,000 in 1916. Outside, a garage houses vintage Ford automobiles. A paved path connects the properties, curving by the river where Ford and Edison used to fish.

The Botanic Research Laboratory – Outfitted with the original apparatus and equipment this is one of the highlights of the estate. When rubber prices soared in the late 1920s, Edison, Ford and Harvey Firestone combined their efforts in search of a natural source for rubber. Together they established the Edison Botanic Research Company and discovered that Goldenrod, a common weed, could be cultivated to yield 12 percent latex.

The adjacent **Edison Museum** houses six rooms filled with thousands of items, including more than 200 Edison phonographs—his favorite invention. Outside the laboratory, the **banyan tree**, which tire magnate Harvey Firestone brought back from India for Edison in 1925, has grown to measure some 400ft around its myriad trunks, and ranks as the world's third largest banyan.

Southwest Florida Museum of History

2300 Peck St., at Jackson St. Open year-round Tue–Sat 10am–5pm, Closed major holidays. $9.50. ♿ 🅿 ☎239-321-7430. www.swflmuseumofhistory.com.

Housed in a 1924 railroad depot, the museum features exhibits on the Calusa and Seminole Indians, Spanish explorers and white settlers. Among the indoor displays is a saber-toothed cat skeleton found in central Florida. Outside is the **Esperanza**, an 84ft private railcar—the longest and one of the last built by George Pullman.

Calusa Nature Center and Planetarium

3450 Ortiz Ave. Open year-round 9am (Sat 10am, Sun 11am)–5pm. $10. ♿ 🅿 ☎239-275-3435. www.calusanature.com.

Live turtles, fish and snakes occupy the indoor exhibits; outside there's an aviary for injured raptors. Three miles of interpretive boardwalk trails weave through hammocks of pine and cypress frequented by raccoons, otters, lizards and other animals. At the end of one trail sits a replica of a Seminole village.

Lovers Key State Park★

30mi south on Lovers Key. Open 8am-sunset. $8 per vehicle. 🅿 ☎239-463-4588. www.floridastateparks.org/loverskey.

Occupying a gorgeous stretch of undeveloped barrier island, Lovers Key encompasses 712 acres of tidal lagoons, mangrove estuary and white-sand beach. Wildlife includes roseate spoonbills, egrets, alligators and manatees. A boardwalk to the beach crosses two peaceful lagoons, enjoyed by fishermen.

RUBBER WEED

If you're looking to see Thomas Edison's innovations, don't just visit the Edison Botanic Research laboratory of the Edison Estates. Instead, take a closer look at the grounds. In the heyday of the estates, during World War I, the price of rubber spiked. Edison set out to find a domestic source of rubber and a latex producing plant. His Fort Myers estate has about 2,200 specimens, which were sent by friends and followers of his quest. The winning plant was goldenrod, a common weed, which eventually became the focus of 1,090 patents to commercialize it as a source of rubber. Another relic from Edison's rubber quest is the enormous banyan tree at the entrance to the estate. The tree was a gift from tire manufacturer Harvey Firestone, who was also invested in Edison's quest for natural rubber.

Paddling the back waters

Canoe or kayak the backbay estuaries on a naturalist-guided tour departing from Lovers Key State Park to discover the rich ecosystems of the area, or sign up for a guided paddle trip to Mound Key and hike to native American shell mounds. Pontoon cruises for novice anglers (equipment provided) or for leisurely viewing of the backbay are also offered along with overnight paddling excursions. The park also rents canoes and kayaks (including sea kayaks), as well as rod and reels on an hourly, half-day or full-day basis. Call for fees, schedules and reservations, ☎239-463-4588.

Boca Grande★

This charming **village** of sun-splashed houses, pastel-colored shops and a handful of restored early 20C buildings perches at the southern end of 7mi-long **Gasparilla Island**, separated from the mainland by a 2-mi toll bridge and causeway. Relax on the sparkling white beach of its **State Park** *(www.florid-astateparks.org/gasparillaisland)* and visit the two-story **Boca Grande Lighthouse** *(open daily Nov–Apr 10am–4pm, May–Jun & Sept Wed–Sun 10am–4pm; www.barrierislandparkssociety.org).* Vacationers come for the island's lovely peaceful beaches, while fishermen cast their lines in the waters of Boca Grande Pass, in the hope of netting tarpons weighing up to 300lbs.

ADDRESSES

For price ranges, see the Legend on the cover flap.

WHERE TO STAY

$$$$$ Sanibel Harbour Resort & Spa – *17260 Harbour Pointe Dr., Fort Myers.* ✗🕭🅿🛎 *℘941-466-4000 or 800-767-7777. www.sanibel-resort.com. 347 rooms, 70 condos.* This modern Marriott mega-resort includes three hotel/condominium high rises, a 40,000sq ft spa/fitness center, fishing pier and marina, six swimming pools, three restaurants and a berth for its private yacht. The state-of-the-art tennis facilities have hosted two Davis Cup tournaments. Dining choices range from spa cuisine to dinner cruises and Sunday brunch aboard a 100ft private yacht.

$$$$ Bokeelia Tarpon Inn – *8241 Main St., Bokeelia.* 🕭🅿 *℘239-283-8961 or 866-827-7662. www.tarponinn.com. 5 rooms.* It's worth heading off the beaten path to this ultra-luxury B&B,

reminiscent of the days when millionaire Barron Collier came to the area to fish. Built on the shore of Charlotte Harbor, the 1914 house still lures renowned anglers and those seeking seclusion. The Chart Room sports a fly-tying bench and rod-and-reel adorned walls. Overlooking the water, the second-story screened porch is a coveted spot. Guests can tour the island in the inn's golf cart or bicycles (kayaks available, too) and fish from the private pier.

WHERE TO EAT

$$$ The Veranda – *2122 Second St. (at Broadway), Fort Myers.* 🕭*℘239-332-2065. www.verandarestaurant.com.* **Continental.** Gracious Southern hospitality awaits at this "dressy casual" restaurant. Tastes of Dixie flavor the chef's take on old favorites: Cajun grilled sea scallops; Southern grit cakes with pepper jack cheese and andouille sausage; Bourbon Street filet medallions in a smoky sour-mash whisky sauce.

SANIBEL AND CAPTIVA ISLANDS★★

A paradise for shell collectors, these popular barrier islands, connected by causeways to each other and to the mainland, form a 20-mi arc into the Gulf of Mexico, southwest of Fort Myers. Though winter brings a steady stream of traffic, there are still pockets of tranquillity and beauty on both islands. The main thoroughfare passes boutique-and-restaurant complexes on Sanibel's south end, then traverses a long stretch of bayside wilderness before crossing to Captiva for the 3.5mi drive to the end. Occasionally affording a glimpse of sea, the road mostly passes through dense greenery shielding resorts and expensive houses.

Population: 6,102.
Michelin Map: p206.
Info: 1159 Causeway Road, Sanibel Island; ☎239-472-1080; www.sanib-captiva.org.
Location: Periwinkle Way and Sanibel-Captiva Road traverse the islands.
Don't Miss: J.N. Ding Darling National Wildlife Refuge; take a guided tram or kayak tour.
Timing: Allow at least a couple of nights here.
Kids: Take a boat trip over to Cayo Costa beach.

A Bit of History

The Spanish navigators who discovered Sanibel and Captiva in the 16C never settled here, leaving the islands to the Calusa Indians. Pioneers attempted to settle Sanibel as early as 1833 but development proceeded slowly until 1963 when the causeway was built, at which time the floodgates opened to tourism. Conservation groups rallied to protect their island from rampant development, the most noteworthy result of their efforts being the J.N. "Ding" Darling National Wildlife Refuge, which today preserves more than one-third of Sanibel's total acreage.

Sights

Bailey-Matthews Shell Museum
3075 Sanibel–Captiva Rd. Open year-round daily 10am–5pm. Closed major holidays. $9. ♿🅿☎239-395-2233 or 888-679-6450. www.shellmuseum.org.

A must for conchologists, this attractive stucco building houses a reference collection of some two million shells. Displays range from shells worldwide to the many mollusks that can be found on Sanibel and Captiva. The museum explores, among other things, the role of shells in tribal art, medicine and as a food source. Note the 19C **Sailors' Valentines**, octagonal boxes of mosaic designs created from shells, made for seamen on the New England-Caribbean route, to give to their sweethearts.

Sanibel Historical Village and Museum
950 Dunlop Rd., off Periwinkle Way in the government complex. Visit by guided tour (1hr) only, Nov–Apr Wed–Sat 10am–4pm, May–early Aug Wed–Sat 10am–1pm. $5. ♿🅿☎239-472-4648.

Travel Tip: The
Periwinkle Park and
Campground (*1119
Periwinkle Way, FL
33957; ℰ239-472-1433;
www.sanibelcamping.
com*) is open for
camping and RVs
but there's another
draw for visitors. The
grounds are home to
a huge aviary which
houses exotic and
local species of birds.
There are toucans,
macaws, lemurs,
ducks and more.

www.sanibelmuseum.org.
Set up as a pioneer village, this local history museum-village
comprised of eight buildings (the old tea room, the 1926 San
bel post office, Bailey's General Store), brought from elsewhe
on the island. In the 1913 Cracker house there is a dining roor
parlor and kitchen furnished to depict early island life. Additior
al rooms contain fossil and shell displays, Spanish shipwreck a
tifacts and 2,000-year-old remains of the Calusa Indian culture

Sanibel-Captiva Conservation Foundation
*3333 Sanibel-Captiva Rd. (1mi southeast of J.N. "Ding" Darling
Refuge entrance). Nature Center open year-round Mon–Fri
8:30am–4pm (Jun–Sept 3pm); Dec–Apr Sat 10am–3pm. Closed
major holidays. $5. ▣ ℰ239-472-2329. www.sccf.org.*
This 247-acre site surrounds a nature center containing a touc
tank, a butterfly house and displays on wetlands ecolog
Outside is a native plant nursery and nearly 5mi of boardwa
trails winding through wetland and upland habitats. One wa
(0.3mi) leads to a 30ft observation tower that provides fir
views of the Sanibel River and forest canopy.

J.N. "Ding" Darling National Wildlife Refuge★★
*1 Wildlife Dr., off Sanibel-Captiva Rd. Education Center open 9am
4pm (Jan–Apr 5pm). Wildlife Drive open Sat-Thu 7am/7:30am to
half-hour before sunset. Closed major hols. Wildlife Drive $5 (exac
money please). ♿▣ ℰ239-472-1100. www.fws.gov/dingdarling.*
A showcase of barrier island wildlife abounds here in canal
inlets, mangrove swamps and upland forests. Begin at th
Education Center to learn about the 6,300-acre refuge an
its natural history. Then take the (one-way, unpaved) 4mi-lon
Wildlife Drive, which offers virtually guaranteed sighting
of water birds and other animals, including alligator. En rout
a 20-ft high observation tower offers **views** of herons, egret

EXPLORING THE "DING"
If you want to take a closer look at the local flora and fauna in
the J.N. "Ding" Darling National Wildlife Refuge, you can hike the
refuge's 4mi of interpretive trails, or paddle the 6mi of marked
canoe courses. Canoes, bicycles and fishing equipment are all
available for rent. Guided kayak and canoe tours are available
from Canoe Adventures along the Drive (ℰ239-472-5218) and
in Tarpon Bay with Tarpon Bay Explorers (ℰ239-472-8900;
http://tarponbayexplorers.com), who also offer tram tours along
Wildlife Drive, guided by experienced naturalists ($13).

THE SANIBEL STOOP

The islands' unusual east-west orientation intersects with the junction of gulf currents, acting as a natural catchment for over 400 species of mollusks that inhabit the Gulf of Mexico's shallow continental shelf. A common "affliction" here is the Sanibel Stoop, the bent-over posture assumed by serious conchologists, or shell collectors. For best finds, arrive an hour before low tide; tides are especially low at new and full moons. Two days after a northwesterly wind is the optimum time to discover the largest assortment churned up on the beach from deep waters. Lovely Bowman's Beach *(3mi north of "Ding" Darling Refuge entrance; turn left on Bowman's Beach Rd.)* and Turner Beach *(at Blind Pass between the islands)* are popular starting places for beginner shell collectors.

roseate spoonbills, ospreys etc. For the best bird-watching, visit near dawn, at sunset or at low tide, when mud flats are exposed. Near the end of the drive, the **Shell Mound Trail** loops through lush vegetation over an ancient Calusa shell mound.

Cayo Costa

Accessible by boat only. Reservations needed. Full day $45, half-day $35. **P** *Captiva Cruise, ℘239-472-5300. www.captivacruises.com.*
Cayo Costa (Spanish for "key by the coast") is owned by the state park department and protected from development. The 1,600-acre island maintains its pre-European appearance, dense with palmetto brush and pine. **Cayo Costa State Park** occupies the north part of the island *(open 8am-sunset; ⚠$2; ℘239-964-0375; www.floridastateparks.org/cayocosta)*. Visitors may hike or bike the 5mi of inland trails, or stroll the deserted shell-strewn beach and watch pelicans and dolphins at play. In summer, loggerhead turtles come to the island's shores to lay their eggs.

Cabbage Key

Accessible by boat only. Reservations required. Full-day $35. **P**. *Captiva Cruises. ℘239-472-5300. www.captivacruises.com. www.cabbagekey.com.*
This tiny island harks back to the earliest days of Florida tourism. The weathered **Cabbage Key Inn** was built in 1938 on a Calusa Indian shell mound as a winter residence for the son of mystery writer, Mary Roberts Rinehart. Now a restaurant, which serves good, simple fare, some 25,000 dollar bills, signed by patrons, hang from its ceiling. You can take a half-mile nature trail through dense mangroves, strangler figs and sea grapes. A 30ft water tower provides a **view** of the surrounding islands.

ASK PETER...

Q: Do you know any interesting places for souvenirs?
A: The Bailey-Matthews Shell Museum is more than just a seashell gift shop. The museum aims to educate visitors about shells and molluscs and in so doing it furthers research in the the Gulf Coast and beyond. The gift shop has everything from shell art to identification guides.

GETTING TO THE ISLANDS

Southwest Florida International Airport (RSW): Fort Myers, (26mi east) *www.flylcpa.com).* Transportation to Sanibel/Captiva: airport **shuttle** *($56; reservations:* ☎239-472-0007 *or* 800-395-9524)*; **taxi** *($56–$75).* Visitor booth in baggage claim area,(☎239-338-3500 *or* 800-237-6444).* **Rental car agencies** located at airport and in Fort Myers. Nearest Amtrak **train** station is in Tampa, with Greyhound/Trailways **bus** connection to Fort Myers (☎800-231-2222; *www.greyhound.com).* **Major access roads:** I-75, US-41 and Route 869 south to Sanibel Causeway; toll in-bound.

GETTING AROUND

Sanibel **Taxi** (☎239-472-4160 *or* 888-527-7806; *www.sanibeltaxi.com)* is the only taxi on the island. The best way to get around is by bicycle. Captiva is less attractive to cyclists because of its narrow winding roads. **Bicycle rental shops:** Finnimore's Cycle Shop, The Winds Cente 2353 Periwinkle Way (☎239-472-5577; *www.finnimores.com);* Billy's Rentals *(1470 Periwinkle Way;* ☎239-472-5248 *or* 800-575-8717; *www.billysrentals.com)* offer all kinds of bike, motor scooters and even **Segway tours**. Yolo Watersports (☎239-472-1296 *www.yolo-jims.com)* offer Scoot Coupes (small 3-wheeler automobiles) , golf carts, motor scooters and bikes.

VISITOR INFORMATION

Lee County Visitor and Convention Bureau, 2180 W. First St., Fort Myers FL 33901 *(open Mon–Fri;* ☎239-338-3500 *or* 800-237-6444; *www.fortmyers-sanibel.com)* **Sanibel-Captiva Islands Chamber of Commerce**, 1159 Causeway Rd., Sanibel FL 33957 *(open daily; www. sanibel-captiva.org;* ☎239-472-1080).

ADDRESSES

For price ranges, see the Legend on the cover flap

WHERE TO STAY

Camping: Periwinkle Park *(tents and RVs;* ☎239-472-1433; *www.sanibelcamping.com).* Cayo Costa State Park (🚫*see above).*

$$$$ 'Tween Waters Inn – *15951 Captiva Rd., Captiva Island.* ✕🚫🅿🏊☎239-472-5161 *or* 800-223-5865. *www.tween-waters.com. 138 rooms.* Framed by the Gulf and calm waters of Pine Island Sound, contemporary quarters built on stilts offer great water views. Tennis clinics, an Olympic-size pool, spa, fitness center and marina.

$$$ Jensen's Twin Palms Cottages – *15107 Captiva Dr., Captiva Island.* 🚫🅿🏊 ☎239-472-5800. *www.jensen-captiva. com. 14 units.* Laid-back resort right on the waters of Pine Island Sound, beside the beach. Modest Old Florida cottages (and apartments) sit between coconut palms.

$$$ Sunshine Island Inn – *642 East Gulf Dr., Sanibel Island.* 🚫🅿🏊☎239-395-2500. *www. sunshineislandinn.com. 6 rooms.* Guest rooms are light and cheery. Laundry facilities and barbecue grill. Located in a quie neighborhood across the street from the beach and a short bike ride from the pier.

WHERE TO EAT

$$ RC Otters – *11506 Andy Rosse Lane, Captiva Island.* 🚫☎239-395-1142. *http://captivaislandinn.com* **American**. Feel the island spirit in this intimate shiplap-constructed cottage, decked with paintings by local artists, or dine al fresco on the front porch or brick patio.

SEAFOOD ...LIKE A LOCAL

Dinner on Sanibel Island requires some planning. Most of the population descends upon the island's restaurants at the same time and most don't take reservations.

Fish Market

...mbers Restaurant and ...sh Market specializes ...n fresh seafood—their ...am chowder is hugely ...opular. Arrive early ...o beat the the rush, ...nce the restaurant is ...rowded, even in the ...ff-season. How do you ...now the food is fresh ...ere? The local fish ...arket is just next door.

Doc Ford's

...he novelist-turned-...estaurateur Randy ...Vayne White made his ...haracter, Doc Ford, ...omething of a reality ...hen he opened a Rum ...ar and Grille in his ...ame. Doc Ford's is like ... sports bar straight out ...f Margaritaville. With ...ndoor and outdoor ...eating—don't forget ...ug spray for the ...osquitoes—it has ...n island vibe, plus 27 ...creens playing sports. ...he place could get ...y on the reputation ...f its Yucatán shrimp ...lone, but don't miss the ...aw Bar and the bar's ...election of premium ...ums.

Gramma Dot's

...or a taste of history, ...ead to Gramma Dot's. ...orothy Stearns came

to Sanibel in 1963, by then a seasoned sailor who had traveled across the world by boat with her family. She landed in Sanibel when it was just a sleepy island with a few friendly locals. She's the namesake of Gramma Dot's Seaside Saloon, which serves lunch and dinner seven days a week at the Sanibel Marina. Diners arrive by land or sea—check in with the Dockmaster for a lunch slip—for the menu of fresh seafood. Dot's is a local favorite, so much so that it has been the winner of the Taste of the Island People's Choice Award seven years in a row. For dinner, be sure to arrive before 8pm.

Lazy Flamingo

For family-friendly casual dining and Sanibel staples, head to The Lazy Flamingo II. The second location of the local hangout boasts a popular grilled grouper platter in addition to a solid selection of seafood and bar food. Skip the conch fritters and go with the flavorful conch chowder instead. The raw bar has a solid

selection of fresh fish and seafood, and the bar features beers on tap, including the elusive Yuengling.

Cabbage Key

For a taste of what Sanibel Island might have been like prior to the construction of the Sanibel causeway, check out the tiny island of Cabbage Key. Cabbage Key is a postage-stamp-size island that is accessible only by boat, ferry or sea plane. The small island has no cars and just a few permanent residents. The main center of life on the island is the Cabbage Key Inn, whose restaurant is known for its cheese burgers. The Inn is the former home of mystery writer Mary Roberts Rinehart. Dollar bills line the wall—rumor has it that the wallpaper is worth $25,000.

Did you know?

The Spanish labeled the islands Puerto de Nivel del Sur (port of the south plain) and Boca del Cautivo (captives' entrance). Over the years these names became Sanibel and Captiva.

Population: 21,709.
Michelin Map: p215.
Info: 2800 Horseshoe
Dr.; ℘239-403-2384
or 800-688-3600;
www.paradise
coast.com.
Location: Hwy. 41
runs north-south
through the city;
Gulf Shore Blvd.
skirts the waterfront.
Don't Miss:
Browsing shops and
dining in historic
Old Naples.
Timing: A day in
downtown plus a day
on the island beaches.
Return for shopping
and dining in the city.
Kids: Spotting
crcodiles, alligators
and even panthers,
at the Everglades
Wonder Garden.

NAPLES★ *and around*

Just west of Big Cypress Swamp and north of the Eve
glades, Naples marks the edge of civilization at the south
west end of Florida. Like a small-scale Palm Beach, it boast
fine dining and hotels, upscale shops, plus the 1,200-sea
Philharmonic Center for the Arts, more than 40 golf cour
es and nine miles of beaches. Many vacationers sample th
area known as the Ten Thousand Islands archipelago t
the south; at the northern tip, Marco Island offers moder
resort life on one end and the charming maritime village c
Goodland on the other.

A Bit of History

Impressed by the area's beaches and subtropical foliage, Wa
ter S. Haldeman, owner of the *Louisville Courier-Journal*, bega
building Naples (its name probably derives from early compar
sons with its Italian namesake) in 1887. Accessible only by boa
or ox cart, it attracted well-to-do families and reclusive millior
aires who erected impressive estates along the beach. Real pros
perity arrived in the 1920s, with the railroad and the completio
of the Tamiami Trail in 1928—the latter financed largely by loc
landowner **Barron G. Collier** (1873–1939). Today Collier Count
remains one of the richest and fastest-growing areas in Florida.

Sights

Scenic Drive★

6mi. ≫ *Follow Mooring Line Dr. (north of downtown, off US-41)*
south as it becomes Gulf Shore Blvd.; turn left on 19th Ave., go one
block to Gordon Dr.; turn right, follow to dead end at Gordon Pass
Driving south on Gulf Shore Boulevard, and then Gordon Driv
you will pass some of the finest houses in Naples. Built in 1888
the 600ft wooden **Naples Pier** *(at 12th Ave. S.)* marks wher
vacationers used to disembark. Opposite on 12th Ave. is **Palm**
Cottage *(visit by guided tour only; open May–Oct Wed & Sc*
1pm–4pm; Nov–Apr Tue-Sat 1pm-4pm; closed major holidays; $1(
&℘239-261-8164; www.napleshistoricalsociety.org).* Constructe(
of tabby mortar (burnt seashells), it is Naples' oldest residenc
and serves as headquarters for the Naples Historical Society.

Old Naples★

5th Ave. S. and 3rd St. S.
The historic downtown offers chic shops and restaurants tha
open onto palm-lined streets, as well as shaded courtyards. Ga

eries along **Third Street South** sell original paintings, sculpture, prints and glass objects. For other shops, stroll down **Fifth Avenue South** between Third and Ninth streets.

Across Fifth Avenue stands the Mediterranean-style **Naples Depot** *(1051 5th Ave. S.)*, built in 1927 as the southern terminus of Seaboard Air Line Railway's west coast line. It is now an office and shops complex and **museum** *(open Mon–Fri 9am–5pm, Sat 9am–4pm; ℘239-262-6525)*. Seminole dugout canoes, a mule wagon, antique swamp buggy, restored rail cars and interactive exhibits tell the story of how trade and travel transformed Naples. There is an extensive model railroad layout and miniature train rides for kids.

Conservancy Nature Center

1450 Merrihue Dr., off 14th Ave. N. (adjacent to Naples Zoo and Caribbean Gardens). Open year-round Mon–Sat 9am–4:30pm, Sun noon–4pm. Closed major holidays. $9. ♿ 🅿 ℘239-262-0304. www.conservancy.org.
The Conservancy Nature Center is closed for major refurbishment in 2011 with a phased-in re-opening planned for early 2012. When it re-opens, this 15-acre preserve will boast hands-on displays, live snakes and other exhibits on southwest Florida's various ecosystems. Outside, a boardwalk trail loops through a mangrove swamp and past a wildlife rehabilitation center, where injured pelicans and other birds recover. A boat ride on the Gordon River is included in the admission; canoes and kayaks are for rent.

Naples Museum of Art★

833 Pelican Bay Blvd. Open Oct–Jun Tue–Sat 10am–4pm, Sun noon–4pm. Closed major holidays. $8. ♿ 🅿 ℘239-597-1900. www.thephil.org.
Visitors enter this striking three-story gallery via a massive granite portico with 16ft metal gates and step into an outdoor sculpture court. Inside the domed conservatory, a stunning 10ft red glass chandelier by **Dale Chihuly** is an eye-catching centerpiece. The Gow Collection of Ancient Chinese Art spans 550BC to the 19C, while American art from 1900 to 1955 include works by Jackson Pollock and Marsden Hartley.

Beaches Tip: The beaches near the pier on Fifth Street South can get very crowded. Also, try to avoid anything on the northern end of town—too many hotels and few locals. Instead, a great option is by 18th Avenue South, which is the last downtown street with direct access. Parking is hard to come by, so consider walking from Gordon Drive. Make time for a beach walk to check out some of Naples' over-the-top beachfront mansions.

Excursions

Delnor-Wiggins Pass State Park★

Bluebill Ave., off US-41. Open 8am–sunset. $6 per vehicle. ♿ **P** *239-597-6196. www.floridastateparks.org/delnorwiggins.*
Punctuating the heavily developed shoreline north of Naples more than a mile of unspoiled white sugar sand, backed by se grapes, sea oats, cabbage palms and mangroves, rated as on of the best beaches in the nation.

Everglades Wonder Gardens

14mi north, Bonita Springs. Open daily 9am–5pm. Closed Dec 25. $15, child (3–10 yrs) $8. ♿ **P** *239-992-2591.*
Established in 1936 and redolent of bygone Florida tourism, th old-fashioned attraction exhibits some 2,000 species of plant and animals from Florida, Asia, and Central and South Americ Included are crocodiles, alligators, panthers and flamingoe housed in animal enclosures set amid lush gardens. Shows an tours are included, too.

Collier-Seminole State Park

17mi southeast on US-41. Open 8am–sunset. $5 per vehicle. △ ♿ **P** *239-394-3397. www.floridastateparks.org/collierseminole.*
This 6,400-acre preserve boasts a wide diversity of plants an wildlife. A 6.5mi trail offers the promise of wood storks, bald ea gles, black bears and Florida panthers. Canoe rentals available.

ADDRESSES

For price ranges, see the Legend on the cover flap.

WHERE TO STAY

$$$$ Hotel Escalante – *290 Fifth Ave. S., Naples.* ♿ **P** *239-659-3466 or 877-485-3466. www. hotelescalante.com. 10 rooms.* This Mediterranean-style complex includes generous, ground-level guest quarters with mahogany armoires, ceiling fans, spacious bathrooms, and French doors opening onto a garden or poolside patio.

WHERE TO EAT

$$$ Bistro 821 – *821 Fifth Ave. S., Naples.* ♿ *239-261-5821. www.bistro821.com. Dinner only.*
Continental. Start with jumbo prawns served with sweet chili-Thai basil butter or rock lobster satay. Then try specialties, like miso-sake roasted seabass, or Chef Jess's "Pot Roast."

$$ The Dock – *845 12th Ave. S. (next to City Dock), Naples.* ♿ *941-263-9940. www.dockcraytoncove.com.*
Caribbean. This Old Naples institution (est. 1976) has diners waiting in line, especially on weekends, for great seafood, specialty sandwiches and "docktails." Order Bahamian conch fritters or rock shrimp nachos to start, then pineapple-glazed sea bass or banana macadamia nut-crusted groupe

SARASOTA *and around* ★★

Lying on the Gulf Coast just south of Bradenton, Sarasota offers one of Florida's best-balanced menus of attractions. Here you'll find the finest art museum, a host of cultural and sports activities, shopping districts that rival the swankiest in Palm Beach, restaurants catering to all palates and budgets, and a 35-mile stretch of world-class beach.

A Bit of History

The area's pioneers began arriving in the late 1860s and the town elected its first mayor, in 1902. The most famous and arguably most influential city father was **John Ringling**, (of **Ringling Bros. and Barnum & Bailey Circus** fame) who bought a house in Sarasota in 1912. Ringling not only shaped the famous circus into what it is today, he also helped shaped Sarasota with his real estate interest in the city; for example, linking the barrier islands—once his personal property—to the mainland.

In 1927 he moved his circus' winter headquarters to Sarasota, providing a much-needed injection to the local economy and began construction of his magnificent Ca d'Zan to house their paintings.

In the late 1940s Arthur Vining Davis' Arvida Corp. changed Lido, St. Armands, Longboat and other keys into bastions of high-toned houses, shops and resorts. Neighborhoods like **Indian Beach**, just south of the Ringling Museum, showcase older houses from Mediterranean Revival to Craftsman bungalows; . The Ringling complex, the adjacent **Florida State University Center for the Performing Arts** and the purple shell-shaped **Van Wezel Performing Arts Hall** cover the cultural spectrum, presenting art, music, dance and theater. Other options include the Sarasota Ballet, Sarasota Opera Association, Florida West Coast Symphony, and a number of small theaters and annual film festivals.

YOUR OWN BEACH

Sarasota has more than 150 miles of beaches that embody the authentic Florida beach experience: think volleyball, hot sand and bathers young and old. But, if you want to escape the crowds, head to Sarasota's northern neighborhood and to Anna Maria Village, which is on the top of the area's narrow peninsula. Park in the residential area, follow the narrow path and you'll find yourself transported to the old Florida beaches, rich in natural beauty and with few crowds.

Population: 54,349.
Michelin Map: p218-219.
Info: 701 North Tamiami Trail Sarasota; ☎800-800-3906; www.sarasotafl.org.
Location: Highways 41 and 301 travel north-south through the city. East-west Hwy. 789 crosses Sarasota Bay to Longboat Key. Once over the bridge, Gulf of Mexico Blvd. runs north-south from Anna Maria Island to Lido Key.
Parking: Street parking in downtown Sarasota can be a hassle. Avoid Main St.; look for parking garages and lots.
Don't Miss: The Ringling museums, including the Museum of Art and Circus Museum.
Timing: Allow a day to explore the Ringling Museum complex and visit the Art District.
Kids: An airboat ride at Myakka River State Park.

Travel Tip: Want to eat something other than Florida seafood? This might surprise you, but Florida has a significant Amish population. For authentic Amish food visit Yoder's restaurant (3434 Bahia Vista Street, Sarasota). There's comfort food dishes as well as four different kinds of cream pie. And not just any kind of cream pie. Don't leave without sampling the famous peanut butter cream pie.

The Mainland

Sarasota's museums and many of its other sights are concentrated along US-41 north of downtown. Begin with the Ringling Museum and work your way south to the Downtown Art District.

John and Mable Ringling Museum of Art★★

5401 Bayshore Rd. Tickets include admission to Ringling Museum, Cà d'Zan, and Circus Museum. Open year-round daily 10am–5pm. Museum of Art and Circus Museum: Open until 8pm on Thu. Closed Jan 1, Thanksgiving Day, Dec 25. $25 ($10 after 5pm Thu). Docent-led tours of the art museum, mansion and circus museum (free, 30min) are offered throughout the day. ✗ ⚹ 🅿 ✆941-359-5700. www.ringling.org.

A treasury of European culture, this complex, comprising art museum, the newly renovated circus museum, the Ringlings' mansion, the historic Asolo Theater, and Mrs. Ringling's rose garden, is the artistic triumph of southwest Florida and the 16th largest museum in the US. Complemented by magnificent architecture, the Ringling concentrates on paintings of the late Renaissance and Baroque periods (1550–1750), including significant works by Rubens, Van Dyck, Velázquez and Poussin. The **Baroque Collection** is considered one of the finest in the US. Ringling's museum is the Greatest Show on Earth in formal attire. Where Ringling, the man, was quiet, the Ringling museum is flamboyant. The majestic entrance shouts its Italian-villa influence with three soaring arches crowned by a balustrade upon which stand four larger-than-life figures representing music, sculpture, architecture and painting.

Galleries

More than 1,000 paintings, 2,500 prints and drawings, and 1,500 decorative art objects are exhibited here. Inside and out, the building displays an abundance of architectural flourishes and ornamentations that Ringling found in his travels. These elements accentuate—sometimes overshadow—the paintings.

A wing of 11 rooms, the **North Galleries** *(galleries 1-11)* takes in late Medieval through early Baroque art of Italy and northern Europe, with emphasis on 16C and 17C Italian works.

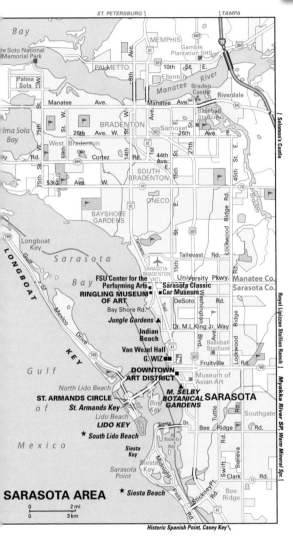

The **Rubens Galleries** center on four huge paintings by Rubens and his assistants, executed around 1625. With their brilliant colors, their dramatic scenes and their breathtaking size, they manifest the appeal that the Baroque period had for Ringling. The second Rubens gallery occupies a vast chamber with clerestory windows more than 30ft above the ground. Other

Baroque masterpieces in this wing include works by Lucas Cranach the Elder, Piero di Cosimo, and Francesco del Cairo.

A graceful central **courtyard** extends from a marble-paved bridge linking the two wings. From the bridge you can admire the formal plantings and sculpture in the elegant garden, lined by parallel vaulted loggias. On the other side of the bridge stretches a lovely view of Sarasota Bay.

The **South Galleries** survey 17C–19C European and 18C–19C American art with major works by Poussin, Vouet, Van Dyck, Jordaens and Tiepolo. The **West Galleries** *(off gallery 12)* display changing exhibits of contemporary art. Galleries 19 and 20 showcase the **decorative arts**. Furnished in the styles of Louis XV and Louis XIV, respectively, these rooms were purchased from the New York City mansion of Mrs. William Backhouse Astor. The sumptuous interiors are typical of those favored by American aristocrats in the late 19C.

Cà d'Zan

Hours as museum. Guided tours ($5) daily, on the hour 11am-4pm.
Ringling built this sprawling, extravagant Venetian-style palace (Cà d'Zan means "House of John") as a winter residence in 1926. With its terracotta walls and red-tiled roof, its balconies and grand turret, it incorporates Italian and French Renaissance, Venetian Gothic, Baroque and even modern architectural elements. Note the 30ft-high **court room** with painted cypress

---

THE SHOWMAN'S ART

John Ringling (1866–1936), one of the founding partners of the Ringling Bros. and Barnum & Bailey Circus, first visited Sarasota in 1911, lured by reports from land speculators. The following year, he bought property north of Sarasota and built a winter home. He and his beloved wife, Mable, lived primarily in New York City at that time, and traveled abroad several times a year looking for new acts for the show. During these trips they began buying paintings, turning their passion for fine art into a dedicated connoisseurship. By the 1920s they had amassed hundreds of objets d'art, including the world's largest private collection of works by Baroque master **Peter Paul Rubens** (1577–1640). The Ringlings soon envisioned plans for a palatial repository for their holdings. They hired architect **John H. Phillips**, previously known for his design work, and construction of the art museum began in 1927. Two years later, just before the museum's opening, Mable died. Ringling's fortunes declined from then until his own death, seven years later. The museum complex is his gift to Sarasota, a legacy to his adopted state.

GETTING TO SARASOTA AND AROUND

BY AIR – **Sarasota Bradenton International Airport (SRQ)**: 3mi north of city *(information: ☎359-5200; www.srq-airport.com)*. Transportation to downtown: Regal **Limo** *(☎941-351-2547 or 800-600-2547; www.regal-limousine. com)* and Diplomat Taxi/West Coast Executive Sedan *(☎877-859-8933; www. diplomattaxi.com)*, 24hr reservations suggested *(around $40)*; and taxi *(around $15–$40)*. **Amtrak bus** connection to Tampa leaves from 1995 Main St. (next to movie complex) *(☎800-872-7245; www. amtrak.com)*. **Greyhound bus** station: 575 N. Washington Blvd. *(☎800-231-2222; www.greyhound.com)*.

BY BUS – Local **bus service**: Sarasota County Area Transit *(Mon–Sat 5:30am–7pm; 50¢)*; for bus schedule and route information *(☎941-861-1234; www.scgov.net)*.

BY CAR – **Rental car agencies** are located at airport. Downtown metered **parking** *(50¢/hr)* garages and lots are available.

BY TAXI – Yellow Cab *(☎941-366-3333 or 888-459-7827; http://yellowcabfla.com)*; Diplomat *(☎877-859-8933; www.diplomat taxi.com)*.

VISITOR INFORMATION
Sarasota Convention and Visitors Bureau, 701 North Tamiami Trail (US 41) Sarasota FL 34236 *(open year-round Mon–Sat 10am–5pm; ☎800-800-3906; www.sarasotafl.org)*. This organization provides information on shopping, entertainment, festivals and recreation.

ACCOMMODATIONS
Area visitors' guide including lodging directory available free from Sarasota Convention and Visitors Bureau. Accommodations range from luxury **hotels** and resorts (around $150–$800) to moderate motels (around $125–$200) and **bed-and-breakfast inns** (around $150–$250). *Rates quoted are average prices per night for a double room and are subject to seasonal variations.*

beams, the stained glass in the **tap room**, Ringling's eight-piece mahogany bedroom suite and his Siena marble bathtub. Ceiling panels in the **ballroom** were painted by Willy Pogany, set designer for the New York Ziegfeld Follies. Walk out on the **marble terrace** for a sweeping **view** of Sarasota Bay.

Circus Museum
Hours as museum. Guided tours (free) daily noon, 1pm, 2pm & 3pm. The recently renovated museum boasts the largest miniature circus in the world. The Howard Bros. Circus model is a replica of Ringling Bros. and Barnum & Bailey Circus from 1919–1938. Complete with eight main tents, 152 wagons, 1,300 circus performers and workers, more than 800 animals and a 59-car train, the model occupies 3,800 square feet. It was created over a period of more than 50 years by master model builder Howard Tibbals. Circus posters and photographs, antique circus wagons and calliopes, and a hodgepodge of other memorabilia depict the old days of the big top.

Sarasota Classic Car Museum

5500 N. US-41; across from Ringling Museum. Open year-round daily 9am–6pm. Closed Dec 25. $9.85. ♿ 🅿 ✆ *941-355-6228. www.sarasotacarmuseum.org.*

Established in 1953 this is the second oldest car museum in the US. Over 100 classic and antique automobiles include such makes as Rolls-Royce, Mercedes and Pierce Arrow. Highlighting the collection are four cars owned by circus magnate John Ringling, John Lennon's psychedelic-painted 1956 Bentley and Paul McCartney's Mini Cooper. Classic and muscle cars are on display side by side, including Don Garlits' *Dragster Number Two.* The museum also exhibits antique arcade games, so bring dimes and quarters to play.

G.WIZ

1001 Blvd. of the Arts. Open year-round Tue–Sat (Mon during school hols) 10am–5pm, Sun noon–5pm. Closed major holidays. $10. ♿ 🅿 ✆ *941-309-4949. www.gwiz.org.*

The initials stand for Gulfcoast Wonder and Imagination Zone, and this hands-on facility offers good educational fun for children of all ages. Equipped with bubblemakers, funhouse mirrors, touchable reptiles, a beehive and lots more—over 100 hands-on exhibits in all—the museum also includes a butterfly-filled habitat, a kids' lab and an outdoor science area.

Sarasota Jungle Gardens

3701 Bay Shore Rd. Open year-round daily 10am–5pm. Closed Dec 25. $15. ✖ ♿ 🅿 ✆ *941-355-1112 (ext 306) or 877-861-6547. www.sarasotajunglegardens.com.*

Brick paths wind through a 10-acre dense jungle of coconut palms, viburnum, rubber trees and other fauna. Bridges cross lakes and lagoons loud with the calls of flamingos and the rush of waterfalls. An enchanting wonderland for children, the gardens also include a petting zoo and playground. Reptile and bird shows are scheduled throughout the day.

Downtown Art District★

Palm & Pineapple Aves. & Main St.

Along these three streets beats the heart of downtown Sarasota. Main Street maintains the charm of old-time Sarasota, even if these days it is lined with sidewalk cafes, French bakeries, art galleries, gourmet markets and chic boutiques. On Saturday mornings a **farmers' market** *(7am–noon)* is held at Main and Lemon streets. A stroll down Pineapple Avenue encompasses the Selby Library, with its artful mobiles and archway aquarium. The red-tiled 1926 **Sarasota Opera House** *(one block north of*

TENNIS ...LIKE A LOCAL

Sarasota has plenty of tennis pros, but you don't have to go to a tennis resort to serve a set or two. Instead, consider the town's public courts and clinics. Also, if you're visiting in April, you'll be able to catch the Sarasota Open, the premier men's open and women's invitational on the west coast of Florida.

Sarasota YAC

Sarasota Youth Athletic Complex has four illuminated tennis courts located at the complex's northwest corner. Built in 1976, the courts were originally painted red, white, and blue in honor of America's Bicentennial. You can also find illuminated courts at Arlington Park, Potter Park, and Siesta Beach. The beach is known for its pure white sand and shallow shoreline waters.

Public Courts

You'll find twin court facilities at BeeRidge Park, Colonial Oaks Park, Fruitville Park, Longwood Park, Newtown Community Center and Newtown Estates, Pinebrook Park, and Twin Lakes Park. Gillespie Park and Pioneer Park have three courts each, while there's a single court on Coconut Avenue. The Riverview Tennis Courts at Riverview High School on Ram Way, has eight illuminated courts that are open to the public in the evenings

and on weekends. The courts at these parks are all free and available on a first-come-first-served basis. Free here means that you'll need to come prepared. Bring your own racket and balls.

Payne Park

The larger facilities at Payne Park Tennis Center on Adams Lane feature nine green clay tennis courts with lights and 12 Har Tru Hydrogrid courts, as well as canopy-covered bench seating, locker rooms with showers, a hitting wall, and courtside tables. The facilities are situated on the site of a tennis complex opened back in 1938 by the City of Sarasota. The courts at Payne Park are also first-come-first-served, but there is a fee to use them. It's $8 for one hour or $10 for an hour and a half per player. Payne Park also has certified teaching pros onsite who are available for one-on-one lessons and clinics by appointment. Programs for juniors, adults and seniors take place year-round.

Fancy something a little less tiring?

Siesta Key, scientifically proven to be the best beach in America, is known for its pure white sand, ideal for sandsculpting. The 99 percent quartz crystal sand makes for intense competition at the annual Siesta Key Crystal Classic Master Sandsculpting Contest. The November event is free to the public, though VIP passes are available for $5 and afford up-close access to the sculptures. The event features group and individual contests for master sculptors, as well as lessons and demonstrations for amateurs. There is also live music, food and retail vendors, a pro volleyball tournament, and environmental education booths. Proceeds from the Siesta Key Crystal Classic benefit sea turtle research, rehabilitation and conservation at Mote Marine Laboratory and Aquarium.

Main St.), once hosted vaudeville acts and minstrel shows; Will Rogers and Elvis Presley performed here. Pineapple Avenue is the city's antique center as well as the setting for several popular al fresco cafes. Palm Avenue is lined with art galleries.

At the northern end of downtown, framed by Morrill Street and US 301, Towles Court is a full block of Caribbean-colored old Sarasota houses, transformed into galleries and artists' studios; its centerpiece is an imaginative sculpture garden.

South of downtown lies **Sarasota Quay** *(US-41 at Fruitville Rd.)*, an attractive bayfront park. Escape the bustle of downtown at the quay's boat docks and watch the shorebirds. At night restaurants and nightclubs pick up the pace.

Marie Selby Botanical Gardens★

811 S. Palm Ave. Open year-round daily 10am–5pm.
Closed Dec 25. $17. ♿ 🅿 ✆*941-366-5731. www.selby.org.*

Occupying a nine-acre peninsula on the downtown waterfront, these lovely gardens display over 20,000 tropical plants, including 6,000 orchids. The **Tropical Display House**, just beyond the entrance, is widely known for its **epiphytes**, and also features a large collection of orchids and bromeliads.

Garden areas include the cycad collection (a class of plants that date from the age of dinosaurs); the cactus and succulent garden; the shady banyan grove, and a native plant community. Here an elevated walkway will take you along a lush grove of palms and bamboo, past a mangrove swamp, to an idyllic **view** of Sarasota Bay, framed by a spreading pipal fig tree, known to Buddhists as the bodhi tree, or tree of enlightenment.

The **Mansion**, built as a private residence in 1935, now hosts changing exhibits of art and photography with a botanical theme. Nearby you'll find the tropical food and medicinal plant gardens, as well as the butterfly garden.

RINGLING MUSEUM OF ART

Stop for a bizarre experience at this 30-room mansion-museum. The Florentine style building, modeled after the Uffizi Gallery in Florence, Italy, was specifically designed to suit Mrs. Ringling's tastes and to house the Ringling collection of European art. The couple accumulated a vast array of art during trips to Europe in search of new circus acts. The resulting museum features a courtyard filled with bronze replicas of Greek and Roman sculpture, including a bronze cast of Michelangelo's David, the Ringling's personal train car, and an exhibit on the history of circus posters.

Sarasota's Barrier Islands

Flung out north and south along Sarasota's Gulf Coast lie several idyllic barrier islands, linked to the mainland by causeways.

Anna Maria Island

Northwest of Sarasota. » *From Longboat Key, follow Gulf of Mexico Dr. north to Anna Maria Island.*

This "Margaritaville" of the Gulf Coast barrier islands is coveted for its laid-back lifestyle, cottage-style residences, and its three fishing piers laden with waterside restaurants. Though heavily developed, Anna Maria is worth the drive, especially for the parks north and south. Southwest, attractive **Coquina Beach** provides picnic tables, a beach cafe, playground, a wide expanse of white sand and inviting Gulf water. South of the Route 684 causeway, **Bradenton Beach** is a quaint lively seaside town.

Drive east across the causeway to **Cortez** *(south of Cortez Rd./ Rte. 684 at 119th St.)* to see one of Florida's few remaining early fishing villages. This Manatee County Historic District contains a good sprinkling of vernacular structures, one of the last working fish houses in Florida, and casual waterfront restaurants.

The hub of Anna Maria Island is **Holmes Beach**, known for its antique shops, pancake breakfasts on the beach and uncrowded stretches of sand. At the northern end of the island, **Anna Maria Bayfront Park** *(northeast end of Pine Ave. at Bay Blvd.)* holds a 1,000ft expanse of shoreline running just north of City Pier. Built in 1911, the pier extends 678ft into Tampa Bay and tempts visitors with a no-frills oyster bar.

St. Armands Key

Across the John Ringling Causeway from downtown Sarasota.

Named after its original homesteader Charles St. Armand, this key began as a mangrove island and is rumored to have been won by John Ringling in a poker game. Today it is home to Sarasota's most famous shopping district, **St. Armands Circle★**, built by John Ringling who explained it thus: "Now Mable won't have to go to Palm Beach to shop." Set at the end of the John Ringling Causeway, the circle and the streets that radiate from it encompass over 150 specialty shops, galleries, restaurants and businesses. The circle's hub is an oasis of palms, bougainvillea and hibiscus; around its edge, plaques honor great circus performers of the past. Beware, peak-season traffic is very heavy.

Mote Marine Laboratory

1600 Ken Thompson Pkwy., 2.2mi north of St. Armands Circle.

Open year-round daily 10am–5pm. $17. ✕ ♿ 🅿 ℘ 941-388-4441 or 800-691-6683. www.mote.org.

Mote combines marine research with public outreach through an aquarium that features sea turtles, skates, moray eels and other denizens of Sarasota Bay and the Gulf of Mexico. A huge shark tank, offers both above- and below-water viewing areas. A 30ft touch tank allows visitors an opportunity to handle living sea creatures, while a preserved 25ft giant squid, is the center-piece of the mollusk section. At Sharktracker, you can learn how researchers track sharks using high-tech sensing equipment.

Lido Key★

Just west of St. Armands Key via Ringling Causeway.

Home to some of the area's most prestigious real estate Lido Key was developed by John Ringling in the late 1920s; his circus elephants transported timber for the causeways. Posh hotels, condominiums and homes share the narrow island with popular Lido Beach, pine-fringed North Lido Beach and lovely **South Lido Beach**⚲, flanked by mangroves on its bay side.

Siesta Key

6mi southwest of Sarasota. » From downtown, take US-41 south to Siesta Dr. (Rte. 758); go west on Siesta Dr. 1mi to Siesta Key.

This popular barrier island, with its clutch of white high-rise condominiums, is highly regarded for its soft white-sand beaches. **Siesta Beach**⚲ , voted top beach in the US in 2011 (👓 *see p.12 and p.223*) , sports 2,400ft of sparkling shoreline and a seaside pavilion with a snack bar, souvenir shop and rental stand.

Excursions

Historic Spanish Point★

8mi south, Osprey, via US-41. Open year-round Mon–Sat 9am–5pm, Sun noon–5pm. Closed Jan 1, Easter Sun, Thanksgiving Day,

---

BIG CATS

Big Cat Habitat and Gulf Coast Sanctuary is home to Siberian Tigers, Royal Bengal Tigers, African Lions and rare White Tigers. Featuring indoor and outdoor complexes and habitats, this is a family-run operation. Kay Rosaire and her son Clayton have been committed to the care and preservation of their animal charges for more than 20 years, nearly double the expected life spans in the wild of these big cats. The sanctuary welcomes visitors Wed–Sun 12.30–4pm. Watch the demonstration at 1.30pm, when a man sticks his head in a lion's mouth.

Dec 25. $10. 🄿 ☎941-966-5214. www.historicspanishpoint.org.
Jutting into scenic Little Sarasota Bay, this peaceful 30-acre site
illuminates the lives of prehistoric Indians and early pioneers.
Tours follow a path through a landscape varying from mangrove estuary to live oak forest to formal gardens (after the tour,
visitors are free to stroll the grounds on their own).
The path winds past a burial mound, a packing house, a chapel,
graveyard, and an archaeology dig within a 15ft-high shell midden, one of the largest intact prehistoric villages in southwest
Florida. The **Window to the Past** exhibit allows visitors to actually see the shells, bones and shards in the midden, while video
footage and other displays explain the sleuth work of archaeologists. The grounds also hold the largest **butterfly garden**
on the Gulf Coast, while the restored gardens of former Chicago
socialite Bertha Honoré Palmer, Sarasota County's leading lady
in the early 1900s, are another highlight.

Myakka River State Park★★

*14mi east in Myakka via Rte. 72 (Clark Rd.). Open 8am-sunset.
$6 per vehicle. △✕♿🄿 ☎941-361-6511. www.floridastateparks.
org/myakkariver.*
This 28,875-acre parcel stretches along the primeval protected
Myakka River for 12mi and encompasses a wide variety of fauna
and flora. Deer and bobcat favor the palm hammocks, pine
flatwoods and dry prairies, while alligators and numerous species of wading birds inhabit Upper Myakka Lake and its grassy
marshes. Hiking trails traverse the park, as does a flat road suitable for bicycling. The **Canopy Walk**, an 85ft-long suspension
bridge, sways some 25ft high among the treetops. Popular
tram and airboat tours give visitors a different perspective
*(airboat tours operate year-round daily, tram tours operate mid-
Dec-May: arrive early to guarantee a seat $12; ♿🄿; ☎941-365-
0100, http://myakkawildlife.com).* The concessionaire at the boat
basin sells fishing, camping and picnicking supplies and rents
boats, bicycles and canoes.

South Florida Museum/Parker Manatee
Aquarium/Bishop Planetarium

*» Take US 301 north to Manatee Ave. W (Hwy. 64 W). Turn left,
continue .5mi. Turn right on 10th St. West. Open Jan–Apr & Jul
Mon–Sat 10am–5pm, Sun noon to 5pm. Rest of year Tue–Sat
10am–5pm, Sun noon–5pm. Closed all major hols. $15.95.
♿🄿 ☎941-746-4131. www.southfloridamuseum.org.*
Located on the banks of the Manatee River, this newly expanded and renovated museum and aquarium complex traces the
cultural and natural history of the Florida Gulf Coast. Life-size

Travel Tip: You might not expect something with Ritz-Carlton in the address to be a local haunt, but locals successfully fought to preserve the Lido Key Tiki Bar (originally known as the Azure Tides Beach Bar) when this institution was facing demolition from the Ritz-Carlton Members Beach Club. This beach bar is right on the water and has everything you'd expect—strong drinks, bar food, live music—as well as some surprises. The bar's signature Green Flash Cocktail has flashing ice cubes.

dioramas, casts of Ice Age mammals, and an impressive collection of artifacts and fossils are showcased, but the biggest draw is **Snooty**, arguably the world's most recognized manatee watch him frolicking and feeding in his 60,000-gallon pool.

The **Bishop Planetarium** is a multipurpose state-of-the-art domed theater, boasting one of the most advanced all-digital projection systems in the world.

Herrmanns' Royal Lipizzan Stallions★

23mi east in Myakka City. » *Take Fruitville Rd. (Rte. 780) east 17.5mi to Verna Rd. Turn left and continue 1.1mi to Singletary Rd. Turn right and go 4.3mi to ranch (entrance on left) at 32755. Training sessions (90min) open to the public. Check website for times and dates. Arrive early to get choice seats. Min. contribution $5 requested.* &⬛🅿 🕿*941-322-1501. www.hlipizzans.com.*

Bred from Arabian and Andalusian stallions, these "aristocrats of the horse world" perform spectacular feats, such as the capriole in which the horse jumps up and kicks his hind legs out parallel to the ground. These originated more than 300 years ago as battle maneuvers, use by mounted riders to terrorise foot soldiers. You can watch them here in Myakka in their winter training camp, as they prepare for a rigorous annual US tour.

Solomon's Castle

4533 Solomon Rd. Open Oct–Jun Tue–Sun 11am–4pm; $10 (cash only). 🕿*863-494-6077. www.solomonscastle.com.*

Local artist and sculptor, Howard Solomon, built his 12,000sq ft home in the 1970s to resemble a medieval castle, complete with turrets and drawbridge. Wacky but impressive, the castle and its 300 pieces of original sculpture were made entirely from discarded materials. The castle's siding, for example, incorporates shiny aluminum printing plates from a local newspaper. Visitors take a pun-filled 30min tour of the interior. A 60ft replica Spanish galleon, handmade by Solomon, contains a restaurant.

The Springs at Warm Mineral Springs

30mi southeast in Warm Mineral Springs. » *Take I-75 south to Exit 34; go 5mi south to US-41. Turn left on US-41 and continue 2.5mi to Ortiz Blvd.; turn left on Ortiz and follow 1mi to springs' entrance on right. Open year-round daily 9am–5pm. Closed Thanksgiving, Dec 25 & Jan 1. $20, includes free classes.* ✕&🅿 🕿*941-426-1692. www.warmmineralsprings.com.*

Indians knew of the 87°F warm mineral springs here for perhaps 10,000 years before an English hunter discovered the area in 1874. The springs were not developed for tourists until the 1930s and today it is a spa resort.

ADDRESSES

For price ranges, see the Legend on the cover flap.

WHERE TO STAY

$$$$$ Ritz Carlton, Sarasota– 1111 Ritz-Carlton Drive, Sarasota. ✕ ♿ 🅿 🛏 𝄢941-309-2000. www.ritzcarlton.com. 266 rooms. Rooms are spacious and plush with private balconies. Spa, 18-hole golf, tennis courts. A private beach club is located at Lido Key.

$$$$ Longboat Key Club & Resort – 301 Gulf of Mexico Dr., Longboat Key. ✕ ♿ 🅿 🛏 𝄢941-383-8821 or 888-237-8821. www.longboatkeyclub.com. 215 rooms. This exclusive 410-acre resort with spacious rooms and suites has a private beach. 45 holes of golf and 38 tennis courts.

$$$ The Cypress – 621 Gulfstream Ave. S., Sarasota. ♿ 🅿 𝄢941-955-4683. www.cypressbb.com. 5 rooms. Built of cypress wood in 1940, this B&B nestles in an oasis of green. Interiors boast art and antiques.

$ Cedar Cove Resort & Cottages – 12710 Gulf Dr., Anna Maria Island. ♿ 🅿 🛏 𝄢941-778-1010 or 800-206-6293. www.cedarcoveresort.com. 19 units. This cozy, comfy beach resort sits on pretty Holmes Beach. One- and two-bedroom suites have private decks or patios.

$ Tides Inn Motel – 1800 Stickney Point Rd., Sarasota. ♿ 🅿 🛏 𝄢941-924-7541 or 800-823-8594. www.myplanet.net/tidesinn. 12 rooms. Good value, clean and simply appointed. Siesta Key beach 8 blocks away.

WHERE TO EAT

$$$$ Beach Bistro – 6600 Gulf Dr., Holmes Beach, Anna Maria Island. ♿ 𝄢941-778-6444. http://www.beachbistro.com. Dinner only. **American/Continental.** Tiny bistro right on a white, sandy beach. The best seating faces the waters of the Gulf of Mexico and the setting sun.

$$ Bangkok – 4791 Swift Rd., Sarasota. ♿ 𝄢941-922-0703. www.bangkoksarasota.com. **Thai.** A serene setting for authentic Thai cuisine.

$$ Moore's Stone Crab Restaurant – 800 Broadway, Longboat Key. ♿ 𝄢941-383-1748. www.mooresstonecrab.com. **Seafood.** A Longboat Key institution, this unpretentious, family-owned place offers stunning views of Sarasota Bay and serves the fresh stone crabs.

$$ Sharky's on the Pier – 1600 S. Harbor Dr., Venice. ♿ 𝄢941-488-1456. www.sharkysonthepier.com. **American.** Thatched-roofed Tiki shelters and sturdy palms sprout from the spacious deck. Expect conch fritters, fish & chips, gulf shrimp, steaks and baby ribs.

$ Old Salty Dog – 1601 Ken Thompson Pkwy., City Island, Sarasota (also at Siesta Key). ♿ 𝄢941-388-4311. www.theoldsaltydog.com. **American.** This fun spot combines an Old Florida nautical look with the casual atmosphere of boater hang-outs. The Salty Dog is a quarter-pound hot dog deep fried in batter, topped with sauerkraut or cheese.

$ Anna Maria Island Beach Cafe – 4000 Gulf Dr. in Holmes Beach on Anna Maria Island. 𝄢941-778-0784. http://amibeachcafe.com. The all-you-can-eat pancake breakfast is the biggest draw.

INDEX

MAP LEGEND

★★★ **Worth the trip**
★★ **Worth a detour**
★ **Interesting**

Sight Symbols

Recommended itineraries with departure point

Church, chapel – Synagogue   Building described

Town described   Other building

AZ **B** Map co-ordinates locating sights   Small building, statue

Other points of interest   Fountain – Ruins

Mine – Cave   Visitor information

Windmill – Lighthouse   Ship – Shipwreck

Fort – Mission   Panorama – View

Other Symbols

Interstate highway (USA)   US highway   Other route

Trans-Canada highway   Canadian highway   Mexican federal highway

Highway, bridge   Major city thoroughfare

Toll highway, interchange   City street with median

Divided highway   One-way street

Major, minor route   Pedestrian Street

18 (21) Distance in miles (kilometers)   Tunnel

2149/655 Pass, elevation *(feet/meters)*   Steps – Gate

△6288(1917) Mtn. peak, elevation *(feet/meters)*   Drawbridge - Water tower

Airport – Airfield   Parking – Main post office

Ferry: Cars and passengers   University – Hospital

Ferry: Passengers only   Train station – Bus station

Waterfall – Lock – Dam   Subway station

International boundary   Digressions – Observatory

State boundary   Cemetery – Swamp

Recreation

Gondola, chairlift   Stadium – Golf course

Tourist or steam railway   Park, garden – Wooded area

Harbor, lake cruise – Marina   Wildlife reserve

Surfing – Windsurfing   Wildlife/Safari park, zoo

Diving – Kayaking   Walking path, trail

Ski area – Cross-country skiing   Hiking trail

Sight of special interest for children

Abbreviations and special symbols

NP	National Park	NMem	National Memorial	SP	State Park
NM	National Monument	NHS	National Historic Site	SF	State Forest
NWR	National Wildlife Refuge	NHP	National Historical Park	SR	State Reserve
NF	National Forest	NVM	National Volcanic Monument	SAP	State Archeological Park

National Park   State Park   National Forest   State Forest

All maps are oriented north, unless otherwise indicated by a directional arrow.

MAPS

MAPS AND PLANS

Michelin Travel and Lifestyle North America
A division of Michelin North America, Inc.
One Parkway South, Greenville, SC 29615, USA

ISBN 978-1-907099-80-9

Printed: February 2012
Printed and bound in Canada

Although the information in this guide was believed by the authors and publisher to be accurate and current at the time of publication, they cannot accept responsibility for any inconvenience, loss, or injury sustained by any person relying on information or advice contained in this guide. Things change over time and travelers should take steps to verify and confirm information, especially time-sensitive information related to prices, hours of operation, and availability.